Kayaking Coastal Maine
Deer Isle/Stonington
Volume 1

by

Richard Fleming

Seaworthy Publications, Inc.
Melbourne, Florida

Kayaking Coastal Maine
Deer Isle/Stonington
Volume 1
by
Richard Fleming
Copyright ©2018 by Richard Fleming

ISBN 978-1-948494-45-8 - (Print)
ISBN 978-1-948494-46-5 - (E-book)

Published in the USA by:
Seaworthy Publications, Inc.
6300 N Wickham Rd., #130-416
Melbourne, FL 32940
Phone 321-610-3634
Email - orders@seaworthy.com
Web site - www.seaworthy.com

All rights reserved. No part of this book may be reproduced, stored in a retrieval system, or transmitted in any form, or by any means, electronic, mechanical, photocopying, recording, or by any storage and retrieval system, without permission in writing from the publisher.

CAUTION: Sketch charts are not to scale and are not to be used for navigational purposes. They are intended as supplements for NOAA, DMA, or British Admiralty charts and no warranties are either expressed or implied as to the usability or the information contained herein. The author and publisher take no responsibility for their misuse.

Book design and layout by Nightflyer Enterprises, LLC, Stephen J. Pavlidis. Charts are Copyright ©2018 Joseph F. Janson

Library of Congress Cataloging-in-Publication Data

Names: Fleming, Richard, 1946- author.
Title: Kayaking coastal Maine / by Richard Fleming.
Description: Melbourne, Florida : Seaworthy Publications, Inc., 2021. | Includes bibliographical references and index. | Contents: v. 1. Deer Isle / Stonington -- v. 2. The Blue Hill Peninsula, Brooksville and Castine -- v. 3. Mount Desert Island / Acadia National Park. | Summary: "In the three-volume set of Kayaking Coastal Maine, the author uses kayaking trips to explore the history of the islands and coastline. Each volume in the set covers a different part of the historic Maine Coast, along with detailed trip recommendations, paddling instructions, and historical information. In addition, each volume contains maps and local knowledge relevant to paddlers such as camping and landing information, rules and regulations, tables, GPS coordinates, distances, and photos. For more than 40 years, author Richard Fleming has sailed, rowed, and kayaked along the Maine Coast. As a professional sea kayaking guide, he has shared his vast knowledge of some of the most beautiful parts of the Maine coastline. Frequently, during his work as a guide, clients wanted to know more about the history of the places visited and attempting to answer these queries, Richard developed a deep appreciation of Maine's rich maritime heritage. Let Kayaking Coastal Maine be your paddling guide to the beautiful coast of Maine"-- Provided by publisher.
Identifiers: LCCN 2020053603 (print) | LCCN 2020053604 (ebook) | ISBN 9781948494458 (v. 1 ; paperback) | ISBN 9781948494472 (v. 2 ; paperback) | ISBN 9781948494496 (v. 3 ; paperback) | ISBN 9781948494465 (v. 1 ; epub) | ISBN 9781948494489 (v. 2 ; epub) | ISBN 9781948494502 (v. 3 ; epub)
Subjects: LCSH: Kayaking--Maine--Atlantic Coast--Guidebooks. | Atlantic Coast (Me.)--History. | Atlantic Coast (Me.)--Guidebooks.
Classification: LCC GV776.M22 A754 2021 (print) | LCC GV776.M22 (ebook) | DDC 797.122/409741--dc23
LC record available at https://lccn.loc.gov/2020053603
LC ebook record available at https://lccn.loc.gov/2020053604

Dedication

I would like to dedicate this book to my friends on Little Deer Isle.

Ralph Duncan was the first person to read my manuscript and encourage me to publish it. A man of many talents, Ralph is a fisherman, gardener, local historian and true gentleman. As winter winds howled outside, we would sit in my old shed overlooking Eggemoggin Reach and pore over the maps and other historical material that Ralph had saved from years before.

I would be remiss, if I did not thank my neighbors Dan and Nancy Eaton, both of whom are descended from the earliest settlers on deer Isle. Dan and Nancy welcomed our family into their lives and taught us the values that have sustained generations of islanders. Dan was the rock of our neighborhood, always available to help others, always reluctant to accept help himself.

I would also like to mention my friends Pat and Burt Leach. I worked for a short time as a stern-man on Burt's lobster boat, the "Rock-an-Roll." As we fished among the islands we talked about everything from lobstering to politics and at the end of the day we had usually solved all the worlds' problems.

Acknowledgments

I would also like to thank Bruce Bourque for answering some of my questions about the Red Paint People, and the staff at the Maine State Museum for letting me photograph their exhibits. The wonderful people at the Deer Isle Historical Society let me examine the notebooks that Doctor Noyes had collected about the region. I would like to also acknowledge the work of Charles B. McLane, whose two-volume set "Islands of the Mid-Maine Coast" was an invaluable resource. During the summers he lived in the same coastal town as we did, but unfortunately we never met. I imagine he was off sailing on his wooden yawl *Suliko*.

Finally, I would like to thank Stephen J. Pavlidis for drawing the charts used in this book and the editors and staff at Seaworthy Publications for their support. Without their efforts these volumes would not have been possible.

Table of Contents

Dedication iii

Acknowledgments iii

Introduction 1

Disclaimer 2

The Organization of This Book 3
    Summary 3
    The Trips 3
    The Charts 4
    The Tables 5
    Directions and General Instructions 5
    Chart Legend 5

Public/Private Properties 6

Conservancy Organizations 7
    Leave No Trace 9

The Prehistoric Record 11
    The Retreat of the Glaciers 11
    Prehistoric Indian Periods 12
    Twelve Thousand Years of Human Habitation 12
    12,000 – 10,000 BP; The Paleo-Indian Period 13
    10,000 – 3,000 years ago; The Archaic Period 15
    10,000 – 8,000 years ago; The Early Archaic Period 15
    8,000 – 6,000 years ago; The Middle Archaic Period 16
    6,000 – 3,000 years ago; The Late Archaic Period 16
    5,500 – 4,500 years ago; The Laurentian Tradition 17
    5,000 – 4,000 years ago; Vergennes Phase 18
    5,000 – 4,500 years ago; The Small Stemmed Point Tradition 18

  5,000 – 3,800 years ago; The Maritime Archaic Tradition 18
  5,000 – 4,500 years ago; The Moorehead Phase..........................18
  3,700 – 2,600 years ago; The Susquehanna Tradition.....................20
  2,700 BP – 500 BP; The Ceramic Period 20

A Brief History of the Indian Tribes in the Penobscot Area 23
  The Wabanaki 23
  The Mi'kmaq 24
  The Maliseet 24
  The Penobscot Tribe 25
  The Passamaquoddy 25
  A Plethora of Names..27

A Brief History of European Explorations 28
  1524 – Giovanni da Verrazzano (France)................................28
  1525 – Esteban Gomez (Spain) 28
  1527 – John Rut (England)..29
  1555 – André Thevet (England) 30
  1567 – David Ingram (England)..30
  1580 – John Walker (England) 31
  1583 – Sir Humphrey Gilbert (England)..................................31
  1583 – Étienne Bellenger (France)...32
  1602 – Bartholomew Gosnold (England).................................32
  1603 – Martin Pring (England) 32
  1604 – Samuel de Champlain (France)...................................33
  1605 – George Weymouth and James Rosier (England)............33
  1609 – Henry Hudson (Holland) 33
  1614 – Captain John Smith (England) 34

Paddle 1: The Sand Beach/Stonington Paddle 35
  The Trip 35
  The Sand Beach/Stonington Paddle Chart 35
  Sand Beach/Stonington Camping and Landing Information 36
  The Launch Point: Sand Beach 37
  The Battle of Smalls Cove...37
  The Fort..37

Second Island 37
Andrews Island 37
The Sinking of the Royal Tar 38
The Mark Islands 40
Mark Island Light 40
The Wreck of the City of Richmond 41
Crotch Island 42
Sand Island 44
Mill Cove on Crotch Island 44
Rock Island 45
Green Island 45
Russ Island 47
Camp Island 48
Devil Island 49
Hells Half Acre 50
Shivers Island 51
Little Camp 51
Scott Island 52
Clam City 52
The Town of Stonington 53
Dr. Benjamin Lake Noyes 56
Colwell Boat Ramp 58
The R. T. Barter Fish Cannery 59
Two Bush Island 60
Peggy Island 61
Moose Island 61
The Billings Family and the Mercantile 61
The Take-out 62

Paddle 2: Webb Cove to the Upper Stonington Islands..63
The Trip 63
The Launch Point: Old Quarry 63
The Webb Cove Paddle Chart...64
Webb Cove Camping and Landing Information......................65
Webb Cove 66
Grog Island 66
Sheep Island 67

Eastern Mark Island 68
Bold Island 68
Saddleback Island 68
Millet Island 69
Spruce Island 70
McGlathery Island 70
Lindy's Cove 71
Gooseberry Island 72
Wreck of the Wawenock 72
Round Island 73
Wreck Island 74
Bare Island 74
Little Camp Island 75
The Take-out 75

Paddle 3: Circling Isle au Haut 76
The Trip 76
The Launching Point – Colwell Ramp, Stonington 77
The Isle au Haut Paddle Chart **78**
Isle au Haut Camping and Landing Information **79**
Rock Island 80
Merchant Island 80
Harbor Island 81
Bills Island 81
Wheat Island 81
Flake Island 82
Kimball Island 82
Captain John T. Crowell 83
Isle au Haut 85
Jefferson's Embargo and the War of 1812 85
Murder on Isle au Haut 87
Fishing 88
Lobstering 89
Isle au Haut Village 90
The Robinson Point Lighthouse 91
Decision Time 92
Seal Trap 92

Moore Harbor 93
Duck Harbor Campground 93
The Wreck of the USS Adams..94
Head Harbor 97
The Spoon Islands 98
Battery Island 99
York Island 99
Doliver Island 99
Burnt Island 100
Point Lookout 101
Nathan Island 103
Hardwood, Ewe, and Ram Island 103
Stonington Harbor 104
The Take-out..104

Paddle 4: Circling Little Deer Isle 105

The Trip 105
The Launch Site at Causeway Beach 105
The Circling Little Deer Isle Paddle Chart......................................**106**
Little Deer Isle Camping and Landing Information.....................**106**
Carney Island...107
Bowcat Cove 109
Clammers 110
Harbor Farm 110
Bar Island 112
Sheep Island 113
Blastow Cove 113
The Scott Islands 114
Swains Cove 115
Birch Island 116
Pumpkin Island Lighthouse and the "Wickies"...................................117
Eggemoggin 118
Pine Hill...120
Bridge Landing..120
The Deer Isle – Sedgwick Bridge..120
Stave Island 121
Eggemoggin – The Place of the Great Fish Weir 123

The Deer Isle Causeway 124
Scott's Landing 125
The Scott's Landing Ferry 126
Ellsworth Shist 127
The America's Cup 128
Richardson's Store 130
Sand Beach (on North Deer Isle) 130
The Take-out – Old Ferry Landing 131
Scott Island Preserve 132

Paddle 5: Little Deer Isle to Butter Island 133

The Trip 133
The Launch Point 133
TheLittle Deer Isle to Butter Island Paddle Chart 134
Butter Island Camping and Landing Information 134
Pickering Island 135
Crow Island 136
Bradbury Island 136
Butter Island 137
Samuel Waldo and the Great Proprietors 137
Dirigo 139
Montserrat Hill and the Cabots 140
The Barred Islands 142
Deer Isle Village 142
The Pilgrim's Inn and The Ark 143
The Chase Emerson Memorial Library 143
The Take-out 143

Paddle 6: Little Deer Isle to the Punch Bowl 144

The Trip 144
The Little Deer Isle to the Punch Bowl Paddle Chart 145
The Launch Point 146
Punch Bowl Camping Landing Information 146
The Deer Isle Sedgwick Bridge 147
Eggemoggin Reach 149
General Robert Sedgwick 149
The Eggemoggin Silver Mine 149

The Meniwokin and Deer Isle Canoe Trails 150
The Punch Bowl 151
The Billings Homestead 152
The Oakland House 155
Deadman Cove 155
Norumbega 156
Captain John Smith 158
The Sinking of the Isaac H. Evans 160
Bucks Harbor 160
Harbor Island 163
The Take-out 163

Appendix A: Float Plan 164

Appendix B: Contact Information 165
Conservation Organizations 165
Private Campgrounds 165

Appendix C: Suggested Reading 166
General Kayaking 166
Guidebooks 166
History 166

Appendix D: Prehistoric Timeline 168

Index 169

About the Author 176

Introduction

This book, and the other volumes in this series are about the people who lived on the Maine coast and the surrounding islands. In many ways they were very much like ourselves. They loved their children and did their best to take care of their families. They worked to better their lives and support their communities. Each generation built on what went before and each generation faced their military, economic and moral challenges.

For over forty years I have been sailing, rowing, and kayaking the coastal waters of Maine. As a professional sea kayaking guide, it has been my privilege to share with my clients some of the most beautiful parts of the Maine coastline. During these trips, I was often asked about the history of the places we visited. Attempting to answer these questions, I developed a deep appreciation of Maine's rich maritime heritage.

In these books, I use a series of kayaking trips to explore the history of the islands and coastline. I hope that my trips show how the future of Maine, and indeed America itself, was shaped by the struggles and sacrifices of the early settlers and the men and women who followed them.

I am not a professional historian and have relied on the work of scholars far more qualified than myself. What I have done is organize their information and place it into the locations where the events took place. As you follow each of my trips, whether on the water or from a cozy armchair, you will truly be *"Kayaking Coastal Maine."*

All of the trips in *"Kayaking Coastal Maine," Volume 1* take place in the waters surrounding Deer Isle. All of the trips are launched from either Deer Isle or Little Deer Isle. Deer Isle and Little Deer Isle are true islands, that are now connected to the mainland by the Deer Isle Sedgwick Bridge and the Deer Isle Causeway. Today, the picturesque lobstering village of Stonington on the southern tip of the Deer Isle is the focal point for commercial activity, but the entire region has a rich nautical history. The area is not large, but because of the number of beautiful islands accessible to the public for camping and day visits, and relatively protected seas, the waters around Deer Isle and Little Deer offer some of the best kayaking in the world.

Disclaimer

All of the paddles in this book assume that the kayakers using it are competent paddlers who are properly equipped. Sea kayaking can be a hazardous sport. In Maine, weather and sea conditions on the water can change rapidly. There are many excellent books available on the technical aspects of sea kayaking; some are listed in the Appendix, but books are no substitute for experience and professional training.

The charts and tables reproduced in this book **SHOULD NOT BE USED FOR NAVIGATIONAL PURPOSES**. They are presented simply to assist the reader in following the proposed routes. The navigational information presented in this book is not guaranteed and should always be verified by the paddler.

Neither the author or the publisher can be held responsible for any injury or other loss that might result directly or indirectly from the information presented in our books.

Helpful charts, tables and other information presented in this book are for orientation purposes only and should NOT be used for navigation. Refer to the NOAA and other approved charts for this purpose.

The author requests that any errors or omissions be brought to the publisher's attention.

The Organization of This Book

This book, and the other volumes in this series are about the people who lived on the Maine coast and the surrounding islands. In many ways they were very much like ourselves. They loved their children and did their best to take care of their families. They worked to better their lives and support their communities. Each generation built on what went before and each generation faced their military, economic and moral challenges.

For over forty years I have been sailing, rowing, and kayaking the coastal waters of Maine. As a professional sea kayaking guide, it has been my privilege to share with my clients some of the most beautiful parts of the Maine coastline. During these trips, I was often asked about the history of the places we visited. Attempting to answer these questions, I developed a deep appreciation of Maine's rich maritime heritage. In these books, I use a series of kayaking trips to explore the history of the islands and coastline. I hope that my trips show how the future of Maine, and indeed America itself, was shaped by the struggles and sacrifices of the early settlers and the men and women who followed them.

I am not a professional historian and have relied on the work of scholars far more qualified than myself. What I have done is organize their information and place it into the locations where the events took place. As you follow each of my trips, whether on the water or from a cozy armchair, you will truly be *"Kayaking Coastal Maine."*

"Kayaking Coastal Maine" is written in three volumes, each volume containing paddles around the islands and coastline surrounding their general areas.

Volume 1 – Maine Paddles: Deer Isle/Stonington

Volume 2 – The Blue Hill Peninsula, Cape Rosier, and Castine

Volume 3 – Mount Desert Island/Acadia National Park

Summary

Each trip begins with a few lines showing the name of the trip, the launch point, the approximate length of the trip in nautical miles, and which charts are needed. Unlike many kayaking guides I have not assigned a difficulty level because so much depends on weather conditions and the expertise of the paddler.

The Trips

Following the Summary is a brief description of each trip. The overall route for the paddle is shown and the historical events occurred at these locations are described.

All of the trips in *"Kayaking Coastal Maine" Volume 1* begin and end either on Deer Isle or Little Deer Isle. Many of the paddles leave from the town of Stonington on the southern tip of Deer Isle to explore the islands to the southeast of Stonington, an area commonly referred to as the Stonington Archipelago.

With the possible exception of the Isle au Haut paddle, all of the trips in the book can easily be completed in a single day, and the proposed routes offer numerous stopping points along the way. Where possible I have avoided long exposed crossings in favor of shorter, more protected hops. Many kayakers will wish to camp out on the islands or explore alternate routes. I would encourage you to do this. The islands offer so much that it would be a mistake to rush through the trips without taking the time to enjoy them.

The trip to Isle au Haut village can be done in a single day but kayakers considering circling the island will probably want to camp out on one of the nearby islands and take two or even three days to enjoy the trip.

The Charts

A chart of the proposed route is included at the beginning of each paddle. The charts show which islands are public and whether camping sites are available. The arrows on the path show possible landing sites. In their shallow draft boats kayakers may find other landing sites more to their liking. The legend attached to each chart shows the symbols used for campsites and the coloring used to designate the public from private lands as well as other information.

On most charts, I have indicated the approximate distances and general headings where the legs are long and the headings might be helpful. All distances are shown in nautical miles. One nautical mile is 6,067 feet. To convert standard miles to nautical miles multiply by 1.16, to go from nautical to standard divide by 1.16.

In the nautical world speeds are most often given in knots. A knot is one nautical mile per hour. Although some kayakers can travel four to five knots for brief periods I have found that most paddling groups average around two knots. At that speed it takes half an hour to travel one nautical mile.

The charts themselves are aligned to true north, (north is up), but if bearings are shown on the charts in the book they have already been converted to magnetic (compass) north. To convert the headings on a nautical chart from true degrees to the magnetic headings so that you can use your kayak's compass, you need to correct for magnetic variation. For the paddles in this book the magnetic variation is 17° 30' W. For general purposes in this book we will round this up to 18° W. To convert from True to Magnetic you would, therefore, add 18° to the true bearing as taken off your nautical chart. A simple mnemonic aid to help you remember is:

> EAST is LEAST (subtract), WEST is BEST (add)

The charts and tables in this book are for general guidance only and should not be used for navigational purposes (see the chapter entitled *Disclaimer*).

Chart Legend

The Tables

Following each chart is a table containing additional Camping and Landing Information. The tables show the names of islands and coastal landmarks, GPS coordinates and their Latitude and Longitude are given. The table also shows whether the island is public or private. If public the name of the conservation organization holding the easement or responsible for the land is shown. If camping is permitted the number of campsites and the total number of allowed campers, and other information is shown.

In some cases however, private owners have allowed public use. If an area is privately owned but at least some portion of it is available to the public I have marked it "Private-Accessible."

ISLAND NAME	GPS COORDINATES	LATITUDE/LONGITUDE
BOLD (Private, no landing)	44.155264, -68.615178	44° 09'18.9" N, 68°36'54.6" W
BUCKLE (MITA) Northeast beach & sandbar path-avoid Spruce, 2 sites, 4 campers	44.142191, -68.610239	46° 08'31.0" N, 68 36'39.0" W
CAMP (Private no landing)	44.149519, -68.631905	44° 08'58.3" N, 68° 37'54.9" W

For more information see the sections on "Property Status" and "Conservation Organizations" in the following pages.

Directions and General Instructions

Instructions for each leg of the trip are shown in bold, underlined italics and are centered on the page. For example, a typical instruction might read:

<u>Continue paddling south and cross the western entrance of Deer Island Thorofare</u>

Public/Private Properties

Where a kayaker can legally land or camp can often be confusing. Just because an island or piece of coastline is uninhabited does not make it available for public use. In Maine, it is not customary for an owner to post "No Trespassing" signs to ensure their privacy. If you are not sure whether a piece of land is public or private, assume the latter and do not land.

In many other states the area between high and low water, (the intertidal zone) is public property. In Maine however, under an old law dating back to the 1600s, the shore-front property owner owns the land out to the low tide mark. Since Maine has such high tides this means that in some shallow bays a person with a small seaside lot could end up owning acres of land when the tide goes out! The ordinance does exempt fishing, fowling, navigation, and of course emergencies. Under a recent legal ruling, paddlers are also able to "portage" their kayaks across inter-tidal flats when the tide recedes.

Kayakers need to carefully check the status of public lands. There are a large number of non-profit organizations that either own, administer or protect Maine the islands and coastline, but each of these organizations has its own rules and regulations. Take for example, the status of islands on the Maine Island Trail. Some have been donated or purchased by MITA, but in other cases the Trail Association has only been given restricted permissions. Kayakers can camp on Harbor Island just off Isle au Haut for example, but only on about thirty acres on the northeast corner of Harbor, the remainder of Harbor Island is private and off-limits. Russ Island is also on the MITA trail, but it is owed by the Cherwonki Foundation and their camping area is off-limits.

The extent of these restrictions and indeed the status of the lands themselves can and do change from year to year as new properties are added and old permissions are expanded or revoked. Some islands are off-limits during bird nesting season, typically February through August. The bottom line is this - before beginning your trip check the current status of the lands you are planning to visit by contacting the appropriate agency.

Conservancy Organizations

The following government or non-profit conservancy organizations own, or administer and protect the lands surrounding Deer Isle.

The Maine Island Trail Association

The Maine Island Trail Association (MITA) is America's first water trail. It is made up of two hundred islands and runs for three hundred and seventy-five miles from the New Hampshire border through Maine waters into Canada.

It is common for MITA islands to be owned or administered by other organizations and the islands and permissible uses of the MITA trail system change as owner preferences change. All visitors must read the printed Trail Guide or the new online Maine Island Trail Mobil app for the latest information. Both of these resources are available with a MITA membership. You can obtain the mobile app from iTunes or Google Place. Be aware however, that mobile phone service may not be available in all areas. Do not rely solely on the app for navigation.

The MITA app will give you access to all the information found in the paper Trail Guide plus Trail updates, interactive NOAA charts, and upcoming MITA events. It's quite a deal!

The MITA islands close to Deer Isle are Russ, Rock, Sheep (East of Webb Cove).

The following islands are also part of MITA but do not allow open fires: Burnt, Kimball, Sheep, and Sheep (off Sinsons's Neck).

Maine Coast Heritage Trust (MCHT)

The Maine Coast Heritage Trust (MCHT) owns or administers more than a hundred conservation preserves ranging from small public gardens to entire islands. MCHT provides statewide conservation leadership through its work with land trusts, coastal communities and other partners. At present time the MCHT owns or administers the following islands in the Deer Isle Archipelago: Gooseberry, Bills, Nathan, Sand, Green, Little Camp, Saddleback, The Fort, Green, Pond, Eastern Mark, and Bear.

Note: Permission is needed for groups greater than eight people, and for use by commercial outfitters or guides, call them at 207-244-5100. Green Island is owned by Cherwonki but stewarded by MCHT. Mark Island is a heron rookery. Before September 1st you are neither allowed to land on the island or ledges, nor venture into the interior.

Island Heritage Trust (IHT)

The Island Heritage Trust (IHT) was founded in 1987 by local citizens concerned about protecting Deer Isle from acute development pressure that threatened to cut off residents from the shore and traditional use of the land. As stated on their web site, islandheritagetrust.org, the mission of Island Heritage Trust is to: "Conserve significant open space, scenic areas, wildlife habitats, natural resources, historic and cultural features that offer public benefit and are essential to the character of the Deer Isle area."

The Island Heritage Trust owns or administers the following islands and coastal properties in or around the Deer Isle/Stonington area.

Islands:

Wreck, Millet, Round, Mark, McGlathery, Bradbury, Sheep, Carney (1/2), Polypod

Coastal Preserves:

Scott's Landing, Causeway Beach, Bowcat Cove, Settlement Quarry, Crystal Cove Oceanville, Shore Acres Preserve (Greenlaw Cove)

The Island Heritage Trust also manages Barred Island (north of The Fort) which is owned by The Nature Conservancy. Open fires are NOT permitted on IHT islands, but cook stoves are permitted.

State of Maine (Bureau of Public Lands)

Through the Department of Agriculture, and the Conservation and Forestry Bureau of Parks and Lands, the State of Maine owns and administers many of the islands and coastlines around Deer Isle.

Currently, the State of Maine owns the following islands in the Deer Isle area: Hardwood, Harbor, West Halibut Ledge, No Mans, Ram, Southern Mark, Sparrow, Hells Half Acre, Steve, Wheat, Weir, and Crow.

Overnight camping is usually allowed on state-owned islands, but there is a two-night limit. Fires are also usually permitted, but only with a state fire permit. You can request a fire permit by calling 207-827-1800. I suggest that when you ask for a permit you obtain permission for alternative campsites. That way if one island is filled you can still be permitted to light a fire on another.

National Parks (Acadia)

Most people think of Mount Desert Island when they hear the name Acadia National Park, but the park includes many other areas as well. A large part of Isle au Haut, Long Island in Blue Hill Bay and many other areas are also owned by Acadia.

The Nature Conservancy

Founded in 1951 in Arlington, Virginia, the mission of The Nature Conservancy (TNC) is to: "Conserve the lands and waters on which all life depends."

The Nature Conservancy is now a worldwide organization and the largest environmental nonprofit by assets and revenue in the Americas. In the Deer Isle area the Conservancy supports Barred Island.

Leave No Trace

The mantra for kayak camping should be "Leave No Trace" Following this set of seven commonsense rules (formerly known as No Trace Left Behind) will protect the lands we enjoy for ourselves and future generations.

1. **Plan Ahead and Prepare** – Know where you are going, campsites, bird nesting restrictions, fire rules, number of people allowed.

2. **Travel and Camp on Durable Surfaces** – Wherever possible walk on hard surfaces such as ledges. Keep to established trails and camp only in established sites. Be careful where you walk, stepping on plants can kill them and leave the thin island soil open for erosion.

3. **Dispose of Waste Properly** – Do not leave ANY waste behind. Police up your campsite, and leave it cleaner than you found it. Try to find a ledge below high tide zone for your cooking. Urinate below high tide zone. Do not dig "catholes." Pack out all solid human waste. Avoid using soap, use sand and water to clean your pots and utensils, rinsing them in the ocean.

4. **Leave What You Find** – Do not take anything away, shells, rocks, plants all have their purpose and should not be removed. Do not dig around shell middens looking for arrowheads or other artifacts.

5. **Kindle No Fires or Minimize Campfire Impact** – I have to admit that this rule is rather confusing. It begins by saying that you should not kindle an open fire, but then goes on to state that you should minimize your fire's impact.

For the island camper, the issue is even more confusing. Islands owned by The Island Heritage Trust do not permit any open fires, but state-owned islands allow fires (with a permit). Some islands have fire pits, but on others the administering organization is in the process of removing them. My personal preference is to simply avoid these myriad problems and use a portable cook stove.

If you still feel that you simply must have a campfire to make your wilderness experience complete, you need to follow the following fire safety rules:

- Make certain that fires are allowed on the island you are staying on. Island Heritage Trust islands prohibit open fires. Some owners have requested that no fires be permitted, others allow them. Please respect their wishes.

- Build your fire on the beach below the high tide line.

- Obtain a fire permit from the appropriate authority. In some cases, this is the local fire chief, in others the Maine Forest Service. You can reach the Forest Service at 888-900-FIRE.

• Use only driftwood from the shore. Do not cut down live branches. Do not gather dead wood from the interior of the islands as it is important for soil replenishment and bird habitat. Do not bring your wood because this might introduce diseases or pests into the island's fragile environment.

• Never leave a fire unattended.

• Do not build fires on granite ledges or large rocks. The soot and heat from the flames will leave marks that will last for decades.

• Fully extinguish your fire and clean up the fire site by scattering ash and unused wood below the high tide line and scattering any rocks.

• If a fire gets out of control immediately contact the Maine Forest Service or alert the Coast Guard by VHF radio on channel 16.

6. Respect Wildlife – When I would review the No Trace guidelines with a group of campers I would tell them that this rule meant that they should avoid the local lobster-men and keep clear of their boats. The paddlers would solemnly nod their heads and completely miss my joke.

What this rule means is that you should stay away and observe wildlife from a distance. I bring along a powerful waterproof monocular. Nesting birds are particularly sensitive and will neglect their eggs and chicks if you approach them too closely. The nesting season can run from February through the end of August. Most nesting islands have signs indicating that landings are forbidden during the nesting season, but birds will nest wherever there is a favorable habitat – keep away.

Seals also need to be left alone. During their breeding season seals tend to congregate on offshore ledges and the Maine Mammal Protection Act of 1952 made it a crime to disturb them in any way.

7. Be Considerate of Others – On many islands there are multiple campsites and you may need to share the island with others. Try to avoid intruding on their space and hope that they respect yours. Try to reduce your noise to a minimum, particularly at night. There is nothing worse to be woken up in the middle of the night by a raucous group partying next to you.

Give fishermen a wide berth, they are trying to make a living. They are not paying attention to kayakers and getting too close could be dangerous.

Stay away from anglers, surf-casting rods can throw a lure hundreds-of-feet. You don't want to get entangled in their lines or hit by one of their lures.

Boat ramps can get busy. Do your best to get set up and on the water as quickly as possible. I always let commercial fishermen go before me whenever possible. Many times it is possible to avoid the ramps completely, and launch from the nearby shore.

The Prehistoric Record

The Retreat of the Glaciers

Let us begin our story 20,000 years ago. At that time mile-high glaciers that were part of the vast Laurentide Ice Sheet covered all of Maine and extended out to the edge of the continental shelf. The glaciers took up so much water that the sea level itself was nearly a hundred meters lower than at present. Under the enormous weight of the glacial ice pack the land itself was pushed down.

About 18,000 years ago the earth began to warm temperatures rose nearly to that of the present day. The glaciers began to melt and began a long retreat. Sea levels rose and as they did so the ocean waters rushed in, submerging the land for nearly a hundred miles inland from the present coastline. A bed of blue-gray silt and clay containing the bones of walruses and other Arctic species provides evidence of this inundation.

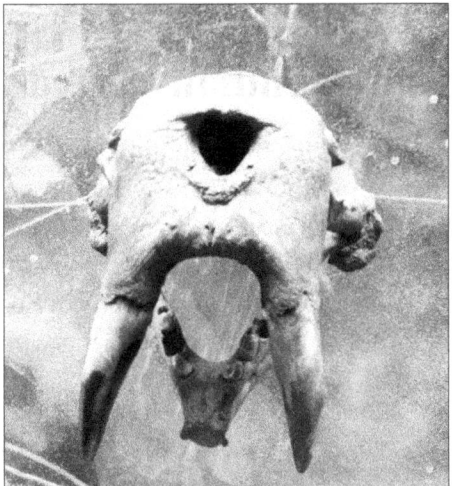

Walrus Skull

In geological periods, however, this arctic flooding was temporary; sediment from the seafloor created a clay deposit known as the Presumpscot Formation. Released from the enormous weight of the glaciers the land rebounded and the coastline of Maine extended far out into the ocean. It is hard to imagine, but thirteen thousand years ago mastodons roamed the drylands that we now know as the Georges Banks.

Most archaeologists believe that the first inhabitants of North America used the Bering Strait land bridge to cross over from Siberia to what is now Alaska more than thirteen thousand years ago, although some scholars believe that this could have occurred much earlier. The descendants of the roving bands of hunters who made the original crossing spread across the entire North American continent, with some groups reaching the Northeast Coast of North America at least twelve-thousand years ago. At that time the coast was twenty miles further out to sea than it is today and the climate had turned colder in what is known as the Younger Dryas cold period which lasted for nearly 1,200 years.

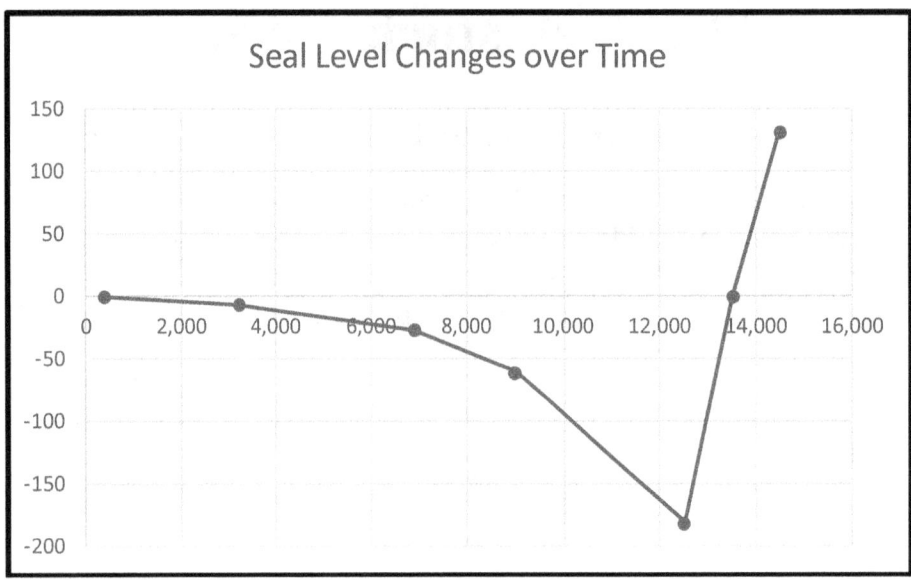

Prehistoric Indian Periods

Our knowledge of the prehistoric Indian tribes that inhabited the Penobscot Bay area of Maine is fragmentary at best. The Native American Tribes left no written records[1] and archaeologists have had to rely on the evidence they have found at scattered sites to build up a picture of people who lived on our coast thousands of years ago. Relying on radiocarbon dating, the design of stone tools and pottery, and the material of spearheads, archaeologists have divided these peoples into several Periods, Traditions, and Phases, based loosely on the periods during which they lived on the land, and an analysis of their overall cultures.

Twelve Thousand Years of Human Habitation

Archaeologists have classified the twelve-thousand-year history of human habitation in Maine into several Periods, Phases and Traditions, classifying the groups primarily on their analysis of the stone tools, hunting weapons and bone fragments that were discovered in archaeological digs.

Modern techniques of radiocarbon dating and Accelerator Mass Spectroscopy, have led to greater accuracy in dating the material, and by analyzing bone fragments using radioisotope mapping it is even possible for scientists to determine the primary food sources of ancient peoples. DNA analysis is another tool that modern scientists now have available to them. Despite these advances however, archaeologists still must place their finds into a cultural and regional framework, and it is to be expected that they have found that different groups inhabited different parts of Maine during similar periods. The various periods are shown in the following chart.

The work of the archaeologists in Maine has not been easy. Unlike other areas of our country, Maine's wet acidic soil destroys flesh, and hides, wood, and bones.

---

[1] Although the Mi'kmaq had a type of hieroglyphic written language only a few isolated samples exist.

Another problem is that many ancient peoples lived along the coast, but evidence of their occupation has now been lost due to rising sea levels.

The final problem is human vandalism. The islands and coastline of Maine are dotted with more than 2,000 shell middens, mounds of shells and other debris that the Indians used as their "garbage dumps." These middens range in size from a small half-buried layer of shells and sediment to extensive mounds. For archaeologists, middens are invaluable resources because they locate villages and campsites and intermixed with the shells and fragments of bone, shards of pottery, and stone implements such as arrowheads or other tools. Much of our knowledge of the ancient history of Maine has been gleaned by scientists carefully sifting through the various midden layers. The deeper they dig, the older the artifacts they unearth.

Ignorant of their importance to future generations, early settlers ravaged these middens for building material. When Fort William Henry in Bristol (Colonial Pemaquid) was constructed the lime used to mortar the stone together was made from clamshells taken from the Whaleback Shell Midden in Damariscotta. At one time, this was one of the largest of its time on the East Coast. In the late 1800s a Massachusetts company removed much of what was left to use the shells as an additive to the chicken feed they were selling! The middens also vandalized by trophy hunters digging around for arrowheads. Whenever such objects are taken out of their setting whatever archaeological they might have been able to provide to scientists is lost forever.

12,000 – 10,000 BP[2]; The Paleo-Indian Period

The Paleo-Indians were the first human beings to walk the land that we now call Maine. They roamed the tundra in small highly mobile hunting bands.

Paleo-Indian Diorama at the Maine State Museum

---

2 Before Present

Much of our information about the Paleo-Indians in Maine has come to us from archaeologists studying the Vail Sites, eight campsites along the Magalloway River in western Maine and that were occupied by a band of 30-60 Paleo-Indian people over 10,500 years ago. Archaeologists uncovered drills, scrapers, cutters and other beautifully made flaked stone tools. The scientists also uncovered a "kill area" nearby where a significant number of caribou were driven into a swampy area and slaughtered.

The large, beautifully worked spear points that archaeologists have uncovered from this early period are characteristically "fluted" or grooved, enabling the points to be strongly affixed to a stout wooden spear shaft. In some cases these spear points are nearly eight inches long! They are known as "Clovis spear points" for the Clovis New Mexico dig where they were first uncovered by Ridgely Whiteman in 1929.

Clovis spear points

Based on the large size of the spear points and other stone tools used for skinning game, archaeologists speculate that the early Paleo-Archaic Indians may have even hunted the huge mastodons and mammoths that roamed the region eleven thousand years ago. Some speculate that human hunting may have even led to the extinction of these animals. The massive tusks of these creatures have been uncovered at several locations in Maine. There is no information on how they died, however, descriptions of huge "stiff-legged bears" and other elephant-like creatures have been passed down in several Native American stories.

Throughout the Paleo-Indian period large herds of caribou migrated across the land and this was probably a more consistent and certainly less dangerous source of food. I suspect however, that human nature being what it is, that if mastodons and their ilk were around at the time, humans would have hunted them. The type of stone (chert[3]) used to construct many of the spearheads and stone tools at the Vail site is not found in Maine and must have come from Vermont or even more distant sources in New York or Pennsylvania. This implies the presence of either an extensive trading network or a highly nomadic population. Unfortunately, the entire area is occasionally flooded by the waters of the man-made Aziscohos Lake making further investigations difficult. Few other Early Paleo-Indian sites have been found in Maine, suggesting that at the time the region was sparsely inhabited.

---

3   Chert will produce a sharp edge when struck with another stone and fractured. The process is known as flaking.

Atlatl (note the stone weight midway down the shaft that gave the extra distance to the spear)

At the end of the Late Paleo Period the prehistoric Indians stopped making the fluted spear points and changed the design to a long, narrow point style known as a lanceolate. Their hunting equipment now included the atlatl, a spear-throwing device that gave the hunter greater accuracy and distance. The atlatl would have been particularly useful hunting swift herding animals such as caribou or powerful animals like the moose and the bear. Smaller animals, birds, fish and the variety of plants that the tribe would have gathered would have sustained them.

Archaeologists noticed that the spear points made by the Indians at the end of the Paleo Period were not made of the exotic cherts that their ancestors had used a thousand years earlier. This implied that the human population was becoming more sedentary. Ten thousand years ago the landscape was warming and the region was changing from tundra to forest and this change could have made long-distance travel and trading more difficult. The warming also affected the herds of caribou which had sustained the Late Paleo-hunters. As the climate warmed the caribou herds retreated further north and as the boreal forest replaced tundra, evidence of the Paleo-Indians and their distinctive culture disappeared about 10,000 years ago.

Some scientists believe that Maine became depopulated as the Paleo-hunters followed the caribou herds north, others believe that they moved in a completely different direction, to the south where the climate was more favorable and plant sources available longer in the year. A third proposed possibility is that scattered groups of early Paleo-Indians remained on the coast, but that evidence has been submerged by rising sea levels.

10,000 – 3,000 years ago; The Archaic Period

The period from 10,000-3000 years ago is called The Archaic Period and is divided into the Early (10,000-8,000 BP), Middle (8,000-6,000 BP), and Late (6,000-3,500 BP) Archaic Periods.

10,000 – 8,000 years ago; The Early Archaic Period

The few artifacts uncovered by fishermen in their nets and those found by archaeologists at inland sites indicate that the Early Archaic peoples continued to make tools out of flaking chert, rhyolite and quartz. They also, however, ground down other types of rocks to produce a variety of adzes and

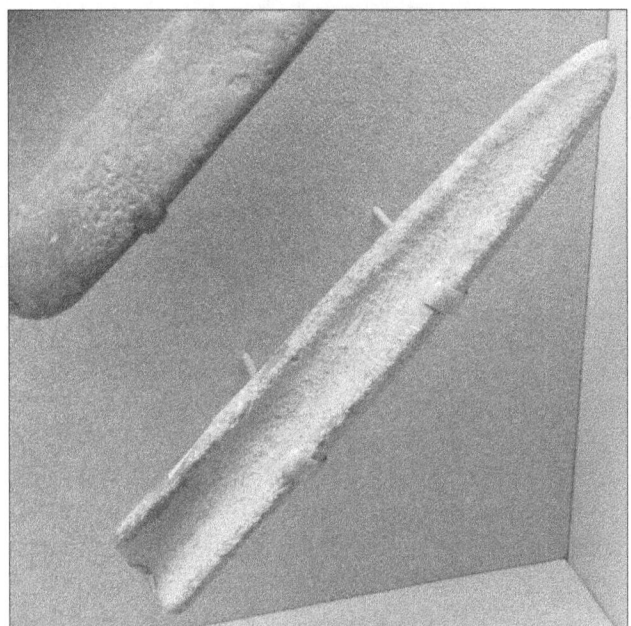
Stone adz from the Early Archaic Period

gouges. These types of specialized cutting tools indicate that the Indians of the Early Archaic Period were working wood, possibly even making dug-out canoes.

8,000 – 6,000 years ago; The Middle Archaic Period

There was a division of two cultures in Maine during the Middle Archaic Period 8,000-6,000 years ago. The tools to the south of the Kennebec River resemble those found in southern New England, while artifacts found in northeastern Maine such as slate spearheads, full-channeled gouges shaped by grinding, and stone rods used for whetstones are similar to artifacts found to the north in the upper Maritime Peninsula.

In Penobscot Bay, archaeological digs at islands such as North Haven, and Vinal Haven, as well as artifact finds at Lazy Gut Island where fishermen's nets pulled up proof that these and perhaps many other offshore islands were occupied during the Middle Archaic Period. Getting to the islands implies that the Indians of that time were capable of building reliable seagoing boats.

In a phone conversation, I once had with the archaeologist Bruce Bourque he speculated that the Archaic artifacts that scallop fishermen diving off the shoreline of Deer Isle recently brought to the surface had likely fallen out of a capsized boat - so perhaps their crafts were not as stable as the Indians might have wished!

6,000 – 3,000 years ago; The Late Archaic Period

The archaeological record picks up significantly approximately 6,000 years ago, the beginning of the Late Archaic Period. The number and size of the ancient sites indicate that the population of Maine was growing with some native people occupying the interior lands while others exploited coastal resources. Archaeologists have split the Late Archaic period into three broad "Traditions." The

Laurentian Tradition which applies to groups following a hunting lifestyle and living in the interior of Maine, the Maritime Archaic Tradition was followed by groups living along the coast and depending primarily on marine resources. The final Archaic Period classification was the Susquehanna Tradition which began about 3,500 years ago.

Archaeologists further divided the "Traditions" into "Phases" based primarily based on the stone tools they uncovered at a variety of sites. Based on this evidence scientists believe that about 5,000 years ago there were two groups of Indians living in Maine. Each of whom used different technologies and occupied different ecological niches. The group living in the northern interior of Maine was named the Vergennes Phase, while the other group living in the southern part of Maine produced a variety of different artifacts made in what archaeologists rather awkwardly named the Small Stemmed Tradition Phase.

Similarly the people living along the coast and also following the general Maritime Archaic Tradition have also been placed in their phase named the Moorehead Phase. This period was followed nearly a thousand years later by Indians who seemed to have moved up from the south and followed the Susquehanna Tradition.

5,500 – 4,500 years ago; The Laurentian Tradition

The hunting cultures of the interior lands were identified by archaeologists as belonging to the Laurentian Tradition which existed between 5,500 and 4,500 BP. This group can be identified by the large side-notched spear-head known as the Otter Creek Point named after the site where it was first uncovered.

Otter Creek spearhead of the Laurentian Tradition's Vergennes Phase

5,000 – 4,000 years ago; Vergennes Phase

In the uplands of northern Maine a group of Indians who relied on the hunting of large game animals such as moose, bear and deer developed. The distinctive "Otter Creek spearheads" made by these peoples have been found at locations ranging from Lake Ontario through northern New England and into western New Brunswick. The forests of Maine were transitioning into hardwoods at this time and this may have encouraged the migration of this group from the west, and took their distinctive spear-head design with them.

5,000 – 4,500 years ago; The Small Stemmed Point Tradition

In southern Maine a distinct group was living east of the Androscoggin River. Archaeologists studying their sites have found thousands of beautifully made small projectile points made of quartz, a very difficult material to work with. The archaeological evidence was so unique that these Indians were said to belong to the Small Stemmed Point Tradition. These points are small enough to be fitted onto arrows, but most archaeologists believe that the bow had not yet come into use. In Penobscot Bay in the midden refuse of the Turner Farm Site on North Haven were many small stemmed points, characteristic of the Small Stemmed Point tradition.

5,000 – 3,800 years ago; The Maritime Archaic Tradition

About 5,000 years ago the influence of the Gulf Stream brought warmer waters into the Gulf of Maine. As ocean levels continued to rise the biological diversity and productivity of the Gulf increased as well. The climate was also warming, a trend that increased forestation, and probably shifted the caribou herds even further to the north. As a result of these changes, some Indian people exploited the growing stocks of fish and marine mammals such as seals that were now abundant in the Gulf of Maine and Penobscot Bay. Archaeologists call this period the Maritime Archaic tradition[4], because evidence of spear points, and tools, and even isotropic analysis of skeletons all confirm that these groups' reliance on coastal resources.

5,000 – 4,500 years ago; The Moorehead Phase

In 1700, the governor of Three Rivers Quebec, Sigismond Hertel, donated a collection of prehistoric stone artifacts to the college of the convent of Ursuline. The governor's donation began what was probably the first archaeological collection in North America. Included in the collection were three long lance tips ground from slate. These long narrow "bayonets" were far too fragile to be used as spear tips and later archaeologists theorized that they might be ceremonial objects.

In 1881, Augustus Hamlin, a naturalist from Bangor found several more of these lance tips buried in a bright red power called ocher. In 1913, the archaeologist Warren K. Moorehead wrote that the people who produced these artifacts were a unique culture that he named "The Red Paint People." The period in which they flourished has been named the "Moorehead Phase" in recognition of his work.

---

[4] Named by James Tuck an archaeologist from Newfoundland

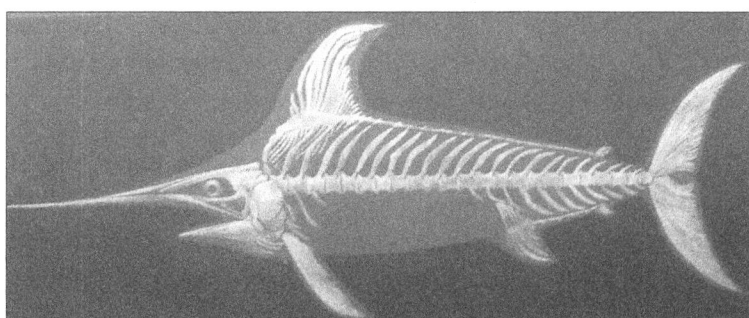

During the Moorehead Phase, the Red Paint People ranged far offshore to hunt swordfish

The story of the Red Paint People is particularly interesting because although evidence of their presence has been found as far north as New Brunswick, Penobscot Bay seems to be at the very center of their culture. Whether this culture evolved locally in Maine or was a single culture with its origins in regions far to the north and only a part of the Maritime Archaic Tradition is an argument best left to specialists, but projectile points and other artifacts found in many Moorehead Phase cemeteries suggest an extensive trading network.

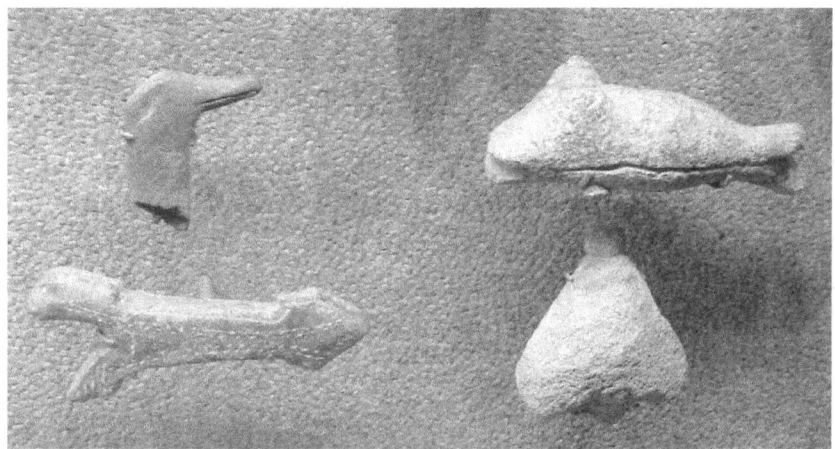

Figurines found in the burial mound of the Red Paint People

In 1971, the archaeologist Bruce Bourque excavated a shell midden on North Haven Island known as the Turner Farm site. The calcium carbonate of clam and oyster shells that covered the dig neutralized the acidic nature of the earth and allowed artifacts to be preserved for much longer periods. The Turner Farm site turned out to be one of the largest and best-preserved prehistoric sites on the Gulf of Maine. Archaeologists determined that it had been occupied more or less continuously from 5,000 years ago to the late 1500s. The group also uncovered bones from deer, beaver, the now-extinct great auk, and another extinct species the larger sea mink. They also found the bones of huge codfish nearly six feet long, and the swords (rostra) of swordfish that must have been ten feet or more in length.

Funeral artifacts such as projectile points, spear-thrower weights, adzes, gouges and other stone tools were also found in the burial grounds, as well as a unique long narrow "bayonet" that had been beautifully ground out of slate, but seemed fit only for ceremonial use.[5] Bourque suggests in his book "The Swordfish Hunters" that these objects might symbolize the bill of this powerful fish. Small figurines with engraved decorations often portraying animals or fish were also unearthed.

The Goddard Site in Brooklyn provided additional information about the emergence of The Red Paint People and more information on this fascinating site is discussed in Volume 2 of this series. As Bruce Bourque in his book the Swordfish Hunters wrote: "the culture of the Red Paint People arrived without warning, flourished for a few centuries and then disappeared without a trace."

3,700 – 2,600 years ago; The Susquehanna Tradition

Toward the end of the Archaic Period different cultural patterns first identified by archaeologists working on the Susquehanna River in Pennsylvania were seen for the first time in Maine. Further evidence of their distinctive culture has now been found throughout Maine and as far north as Nova Scotia. It now appears that this group extended their territories from the south, Unlike the members of the Marine Archaic Tradition these people paid little attention to fishing and focused their attention on hunting. Within a thousand years however, the linkages with southern groups seemed to have dissolved, and traditional local cultures reappeared and the Susquehanna Tradition became the last major tradition of the Archaic Period.

During this period the Indians of the Susquehanna Tradition produced the most skillfully worked stone artifacts ever found. Excavations at the Turner Farm site on North Haven Island produced a variety of previously unknown artifacts including stone "daggers," and beautifully crafted objects that seem to be ornamental or perhaps even for religious use. The bones of large land animals such as bear and moose were found at the dig, as well as the bones of seals. There was no evidence of swordfish taken during this period, and the isotopic signature of human remains shows little reliance on maritime resources. There is evidence however, that they did harvest acorns for roasting, and from the stone pestles that were uncovered these nuts must have been an important food source.

The people of the Susquehanna tradition like those of the Moorehead Phase also buried their dead in ways completely different from those of the Moorehead Tradition Indians. In the case of the Susquehanna Indians this involved what Bourque refers to as "ritualized manipulation of the dead."[6] After being interred for some time, the bones of the diseased were removed from the ground, cremated, and combined with the bones of other dead members of the tribe.

The question of whether the Susquehanna group migrated up from the south to Maine, or whether their culture was embraced by other groups that were living in the area is still under debate. What is known is that around 3,500 years ago their culture seems to have disappeared.

2,700 BP – 500 BP; The Ceramic Period

An emergence of clay pottery about 2,700 years ago marks the beginning of the Ceramic Period and ends with the historical accounts of the first European explorers. Because it is the most recent, it is

---

5 Ochre – a naturally occurring pigment containing iron oxide in various colors.
6 IBID Buerque pg. 66

no surprise that we have much more information on this period than on any of the others. The native population in Maine during this period is estimated at more than twenty thousand.

The naming of the period is obvious, the emergence of clay pots. Fired clay containers could be placed directly into a fire to boil water. These vessels must have lives so much easier! Before this innovation, the only way that water could be boiled would have been to place hot rocks in a wood or bark container. On the other hand, clay pots are fragile and must be handled with such care that they would not have been suitable for the highly mobile populations of prior epochs.

Shards of clay pots are found most often on coastal sites, leading archaeologists to believe that populations during the Ceramic Period led a more sedentary lifestyle. The pots were made by winding coils of clay together. The vessels were then ornamented either by a string pressed into the clay before it was fired or by patterns made by a grooved stick. The ornamentation changed over time and these changes enable archaeologists to date both the pottery and the encampments were they are found. Around 600 years ago the cylindrical pots with pointed bases were rather suddenly replaced by round bowls with a cylindrical collar which was decorated by complex incised decorations, to my mind a much more practical design. I imagine they must have lost quite a lot of soup when the pointed based pots fell over in the fire!

The Ceramic Period was a time filled with changes that affected the lives of the native people in many ways. By the time of the European contact the bow and arrow had completely replaced the spear and atlatl except for harpoons with detachable heads and the three-pronged fish spear. Arrows were tipped with both local stones as well as more exotic cherts which archaeologists believe must have come from regions outside of Maine. During the winter the hunters traversed their lands on snowshoes. For other seasons long-distance travel was made possible by the emergence of the birch-

A "pointed bottom" clay pot from the Early Ceramic Period

bark canoe sometime around a thousand years ago. These swift, lightweight crafts were perfectly designed for lakes and inland waterways of Maine.

Tribes in the area still lived in their small bark-covered wigwams, but they also built a more permanent structure known as the longhouse. Archaeologists have found post holes for buildings fifteen feet wide and nearly seventy-five feet long, capable of holding many families.

The first petroglyphs appeared during the Early Ceramic Period, strange symbols and drawings, scratched into rocks. Whether these petroglyphs were a form of writing, or simply a form of artistic expression is still unknown.

The writing of petroglyphs by Indian peoples continued into the early part of the 17th century. One of the drawings in the center of the petroglyph above looks like a European house. Images found on a petroglyph further north clearly shows an early European ship.

Archaeological records suggests that there was significant population growth indicated by the number and size of sites. It was also a time of wide-ranging changes in many areas.

About a thousand years ago, corn, in the form of maize was being cultivated and this new maize-bean-squash food supply must certainly have accounted for at least some of the population growth. Shortly before European contact the Indian tribes of Maine had established a thriving stable culture that provided for the sustenance, shelter, and religious needs of its members. With the arrival of European colonists around 1600 however, that structure was torn apart by wars and disease.

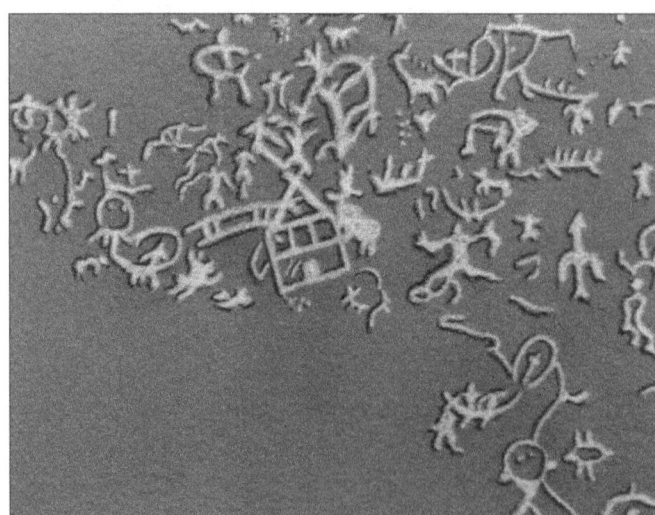

A Maine Petroglyph

A Brief History of the Indian Tribes in the Penobscot Area

At the time of first European contact the people who were living in what was to become Maine lived in relatively small family bands that often relocated on a seasonal basis. Each band was a part of a larger grouping or "clan." The members of each clan traced their origin to a common ancestor, a mystical bird or animal, descent being traced through the maternal line.

These family bands and associated clans would gather together on a seasonal basis to form villages. Each village loosely governed by a Sagamore or chief and a council of wise men known as sachems who determined critical questions such as war and peace. The authority of the chief depended to a large degree on persuasion rather than coercion. The Sagamore was chosen for life and was generally succeeded by a son or a near relative.

To the west near the Great Lakes lived the Huron, Mohawk, and Iroquois tribes who spoke the Iroquoian language and with whom the Wabanaki Indians of Maine were often in conflict.

The Wabanaki

The Wabanaki is a group of tribes living on the lands now known as Maine, New Hampshire, Vermont, Quebec and the Canadian Maritime Provinces. Although there were and are other tribes living in Maine the Wabanaki were particularly active in the Penobscot Bay area. The name Wabanaki can be traced to the Passamaquoddy word meaning "coming of the light," or "people of the dawn." Over time European settlers used the name as a generic term for all Maine Indians, and today it is often used by native American's when they refer to themselves. As I was once told by a tribal historian it is well to remember however, that although a Passamaquoddy may be a Wabanaki, not all Wabanaki are Passamaquoddy.

The four tribes currently making up the Wabanaki[7] are the Penobscot, the Maliseet, the Passamaquoddy, the and the Mi'kmaq. In times of conflict these tribes would put aside their differences and come together for diplomatic and military purposes as the Wabanaki Confederacy. Historically, there is evidence that this Confederacy was first formed before the coming of the Europeans to protect the Algonquin speaking tribes in Maine from attacks by the Mohawk Indians to their west, but it continued to be a strong military force in the region well into the 18th century. The Confederacy however, was never a unified block. Member tribes would have conflicting interests and often go to war with one another.

Historically, the Wabanaki allied themselves to the French. There are several reasons for this, the most important probably the fact that the tribes did not view the French as much of a threat to their lifestyle as the English. The early French were primarily traders whose presence benefited the Indians. The English were settlers and farmers who took over their hunting territories. French missionaries known as "Black Robes" by the Indians lived with them, studied the Abenaki language and often

---

7 Members of the Capuchin order

converted them to Catholicism. From a military standpoint the French considered the Wabanaki to be useful allies against both the Iroquois and the English.

The Mi'kmaq

The Mi'kmaq[8] is indigenous to northern Maine, the Maritime Provinces of Canada and the Gaspé Peninsula of Quebec. Like Viking raiders, the Mi'kmaq would swoop down by sea from their strongholds in the north to raid and pillage the southern tribes, taking slaves, food and whatever else they could steal

The Mi'kmaq were the first prominent tribe to make contact with European explorers who, following the shortest Atlantic crossing distance and aided by favorable wind patterns would sail north to Ireland, then traverse the Atlantic from Iceland to Greenland, to Labrador, and the Maritime Provinces of Canada. This had advantages and disadvantages. They were the first tribe to become exposed to European diseases, against which they had no protection, but they also were able to use European technology for their benefit. The Mi'kmaq quickly began to trade with the European intruders and soon established themselves as middlemen in the fur trade that was developing between the Europeans on the coast and the Indian tribes hunting and trapping in the interior lands. They learned to sail and began using wooden sailing vessels to raid their Indian tribes further south.

In 1605, Gosnold was approached by a European shallop[9] with sails and oars manned by eight braves. Gosnold later wrote that the Mi'kmaq captain wore, "A waistcoat of blackwork, a pair of breeches, cloth stockings, shoes, hat, and band."

When Champlain explored the Penobscot area he recorded that local tribes complained to him that they had even stopped raising corn, because the Mi'kmaq's would steal it from them as soon as it was ripe!

The Mi'kmaq Resource Guide says that the name means "the family," but other linguists believe the tribe's name derived from what they called themselves, the egumawaach "red on the earth," the name possibly referring to the red soil one often finds on the beaches of the Maritimes. I can't help but speculate whether the name might signify some affiliation with the Red Paint People who had supposedly died out thousands of years earlier.

In the winter the Mi'kmaq would remain in the interior forests hunting moose, their primary source of food and clothing. In the summer they would migrate to the coast to fish. In the centuries before European contact the Mi'kmaq had even developed a hieroglyphic based written language, but this has now unfortunately been lost.

The Maliseet

In the late seventeenth century the French began calling the Etchemins between the St. John and the Penobscot Rivers the Maliseet. This tribe's name for itself was Wolastoqiyik which meant "People of the Beautiful River," probably a reference to the St. John River. The Mi'kmaq, however, disparagingly

---

8   MicMac is also used (mainly by the English)..
9   Shallop – an early sailboat

called them the "Maliceet" which means "Bad Talkers," probably a reference to the fact that they spoke a different Algonquin dialect from their own. The French, who had met the Mi'kmaq before the more western tribe, did not realize that this was their real name for themselves. The English colonists anglicized it further to Maliseet.

A plaque at the Abbe Museum in Bar Harbor states that the word "Maliseet is the Mi'kmaq word for the Passamaquoddy people.

Members of the Maliseet tribe lived in large villages protected by stockades. The men hunted and fished, but unlike the Mi'kmaq the Maliseet society was agriculturally based with corn, squash and beans being the primary crops. Tobacco was raised for trading purposes.

The Penobscot Tribe

According to the linguist and historian Fannie Eckstrom, the name "Penobscot"[10] can be translated as "at the descending rock"[11] and which she believes refers to the series of ledges and falls between Bangor and Old Town. For the Indian tribes the rivers and streams of Maine were their highways and they would often give distinctive place names to anything that would affect a canoe such as rapids, falls or rocky areas. During the early 1600s, the tribe's hunting territories consisted of the entire Penobscot River Valley and perhaps beyond.[12]

The Penobscot people lived in eight to ten semi-permanent villages scattered along the river's bank. The people would travel down to the coast in the summer and move to their interior villages in the winter to hunt the forest. With their rich and varied diet the early explorers described the Penobscot people as physically attractive, healthy and unusually long-lived.[13]

The tribe well-known today for the beautiful sweetgrass, birch bark, and ash baskets that they decorated with bead-work and porcupine quills, but unfortunately perishable objects such as these have not survived from before European contact. What is known is that early white settlers often commented on the beauty of Penobscot workmanship. Archaeologists know that the tribe participated in a far-flung trade network and it is very likely that their basketry and beadwork was valued by the peoples with which they traded.

The Passamaquoddy

The name Passamaquoddy is an English variation on the name meaning "People who Spear the Pollock." The traditional homeland of the tribe was the area around Passamaquoddy Bay and Mount Desert Island. As their name indicates, the Passamaquoddy relied primarily on fishing for food although

---

10 The Penobscot Indians refer to themselves as Pa'nawampske'wiak
11 Indian Place Names of the Penobscot Valley and the Maine Coast, Fanny Hardy Eckstrom, University of Maine Studies, second series, Nov 1942, pg 1
12 The historian Fanny Eckstron believes that in earlier times the Penobscot (Etchemon) lands extended further west to beyond the Katahdin area.
13 IBID Nicolar, pg. 3

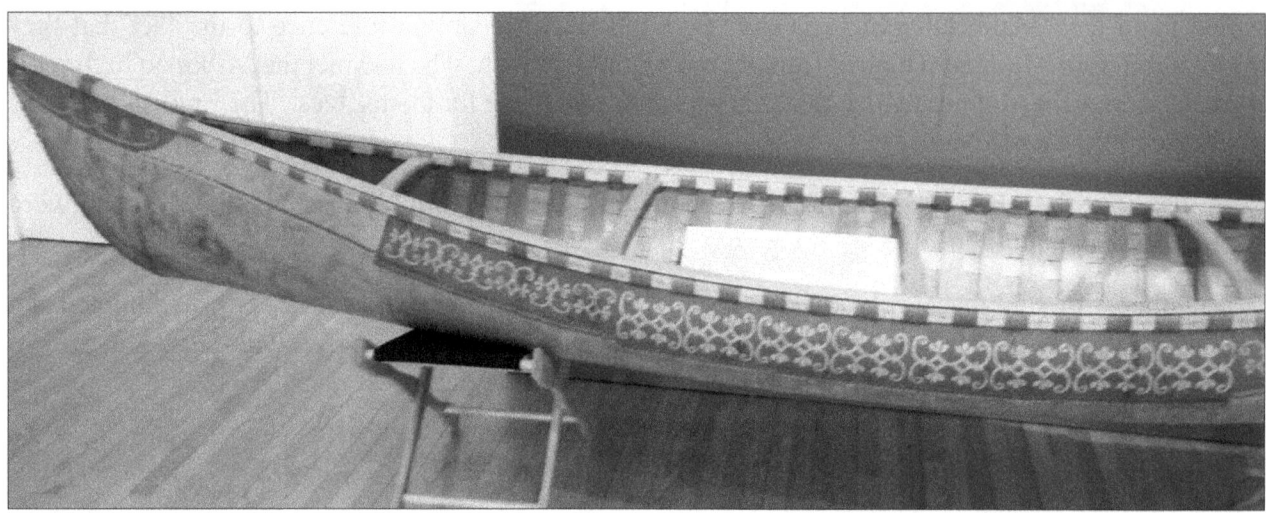
A replica of a Passamaquoddy Canoe built for the Abbe Museum by David Moses Bridges

they also hunted seals and porpoises. They created some of the most beautiful birch-bark canoes ever built out of birch bark, ash, and cedar. They were decorated by scraping away the inner bark.

During the winter months when the rivers and lakes were frozen the Passamaquoddy used sleds and snowshoes to through the forests. Dogs were used as pack animals because there were no horses in North America until they were brought over by European settlers.

In 1794, the United States signed a treaty with the tribe promising them the right to fish and hunt in their homeland forever. Since then however, the American government has imposed restrictions on their hunting and fishing rights. One controversy is over the Passamaquoddy's tradition of hunting porpoise, which is forbidden in the U.S. because porpoises are endangered. The tribe argues that commercial fishermen kill more than a thousand porpoises every year, while Passamaquoddy hunters only want to hunt a handful to feed their families and keep their traditions alive.

The Passamaquoddy were pushed off their original lands repeatedly by European settlers. After the Revolutionary War, tribal lands were limited to the current Indian Township Reservation and the smaller Passamaquoddy Pleasant Point Reservation, both in Washington Country, Maine.

Both the Passamaquoddy, along with the neighboring Penobscot Nation are given special political status in Maine. The two tribes are allowed to send representatives to the Maine House, and they can sponsor legislation regarding American Indian affairs, but their representatives cannot vote.

A Plethora of Names

In the early days of European colonization all Indians were simply referred to as the "savages,"[1] but even after the Europeans realized that they were dealing with many different cultural groups, the English in particular tended to group the Indians territorially rather than in broader cultural terms. Applying this kind of rigid paradigm to a semi-nomadic people who moved with the game and seasons was never an ideal solution, but lacking a deep understanding of the language at the time perhaps it was the best the early explorers could do.

The English tended to name groups by region, usually the closest river to the village. By doing this they often confused village with tribal names and often assigned more than one name to the same group. The rather rigid boundary lines, particularly those used by the English to demark Indian territories were never recognized by the tribes themselves. The English left a legacy of "tribal" names such as Wawenock, Norridgewock, and Sheepscot.[2] Perhaps at the time however, many more independent societies were living in the same region. Entire societies such as the Almouchiccogin in southern Maine, were obliterated by European diseases which, combined with warfare, killed off nearly 90 percent of New England's indigenous populations within the first one hundred years of contact. Before that time perhaps many more independent tribes living in the same region.

The French, on the other hand may have erred in the opposite direction grouping many tribal societies under umbrella names such as Abenaki or Etchemon.

Adding to the complexity is the fact that the English and the French often created their names for the same tribe. The Mi'kmaq's for example were called the MicMac by the English and the Souriquois by the French. Early English historians wrote about the Wawenok whereas French traders referred to the people in the same area at the same time as Etchemon.[3]

It seems to me that historians seem to like nothing better than revising the opinions of their predecessors. Records from early English colonists referred to all members of the Abenaki tribe as the Tarratine's and included the Mi'kmaq into this group as well. Later scholars included both the Etchemins and the Penobscots in their definition of Tarentine, and contemporary historians now seem to equate Tarentines only with the Mi'kmaq!

In the late 1600s, after King Philip's War the French stopped referring to Indians between the Kennebec and the St. John River as Etchemins and began calling them the Cannabis.[4] Native Americans to the north of the Penobscot and extending to the St. John, formerly called the Souriquois, were now called Micmac. In the 20th century the Cannabis Tribe were replaced by the more generic name Eastern Abenaki, a group consisting of the Kennebec, Penobscot, and Arosaguntacook tribes.

---

1 The English, when subjugating the Irish in 1565 and 1576 also called them savages.
2 Nicolar, Joseph "The Life and Traditions of the Red Man," Duke University Press, 2007, pg. 8
3 http://www.davistownmuseum.org/PDFs/TDMnativeAm.pdf
4 Possibly a Mi'kmaq name.

A Brief History of European Explorations

In this book we will confine ourselves to European explorers of Penobscot Bay, and do our best to keep to expeditions whose leaders kept some formal records of their discoveries. Given the crude navigational instruments of the period it was often difficult for the mariners to know their exact locations, and it is quite amazing that they were able to accomplish as much as they did.

1524 – Giovanni da Verrazzano (France)

Sailing for the king of France in 1524, Verrazzano's ship La Dauphine made landfall in what is now Cape Fear North Carolina. Verrazzano sailed north, rounding Cape Cod and trading with friendly Indian tribes as he mapped the coastline and finally entered Maine waters. Verrazzano was hoping to continue trading but complained that unlike the Indians further south who had traded furs and food for the baubles and trinkets, the Indians of Maine wanted only useful items such as steel knives and fishhooks. They were also very cautious, and would only trade by letting down a basket from a tall cliff. It is likely that they had either heard stories of kidnapping, theft, and disease or had experienced these things themselves from earlier Europeans. After completing the transactions with Verrazzano, the entire tribe mocked and abused the white men, turning round, slapping their bare buttocks hooting at them from the safety of their cliff[1]. It is no wonder that Verrazzano called Maine, "The Land of the Bad People."

Continuing north Verrazzano records passing thirty-two islands, "small and pleasant to the view." This certainly is a good description of the islands of the Deer Isle Archipelago. At the head of one of the inlets on his chart he wrote "Orambega," hopeful that this perhaps was the City of Gold that the Indians had told him existed somewhere in the area. When he later returned to France he also described the verdant land "Refugio,"[2] which added to the legend of the fabled city of Norumbega.

1525 – Esteban Gomez (Spain)

Esteban Gomez was a Portuguese sea captain sailing for the King of Spain. Gomez entered Penobscot Bay and sailed up the Penobscot River in 1525. The record of his exploration of Penobscot Bay is much more complete than those of Real or Verrazzano and for this reason he deserves more of our attention.

During the 1500s, Spain was the richest nation on earth. Following the voyage of Columbus in 1492, Spain explored and colonized the Caribbean islands and huge sections of Central and South America. Gold and silver from the Aztec empire filled Spain's treasure vaults. Having found vast riches in Central and South America the Spanish had every reason to believe that voyages to North American would prove to be equally lucrative.

In 1524, Gomez persuaded the King of Spain to finance a voyage of discovery to North America to search for cities of gold and the fabled Northwest Passage to the Indies. How Gomez even had access

---

1 Historians believe that the trading took place somewhere around Cape Elizabeth, or Cape Small.
2 Probably Narragansett Bay

to the king is a mystery. He had been accused of mutiny and had just been released from a Spanish prison!

Gomez had been captain of the San Antonio, one of five ships in Ferdinand Magellan's fleet. When his ship faced the fearsome storms at the Cape of Good Hope Gomez deserted Magellan and returned to Spain where he was promptly jailed[3]. Somehow the glib Portuguese pilot was not only able to talk his way out of prison but able to convince the king to sponsor an expedition to the New World.

In 1524, Gomez left Spain in a new fifty-ton caravel named La Anunciada which had been built specifically for his voyage. After spending a brutal winter in the Gulf of St. Lawrence, he sailed south trying to find a westward route across the continent. He explored and mapped the Bay of Fundy, Passamaquoddy Bay, Mount Desert Island, Somes Sound, Blue Hill, Jericho Bay, and Eggemoggin Reach.

When he entered the broad waters of Penobscot Bay he thought for sure that he had found the elusive Northwest Passage. He sailed up the Penobscot River as far inland as the mouth of the Kenduskeag Stream in present-day Bangor before being blocked by the falls. As he neared the location where Giovanni da Verrazzano had placed the golden city of Norumbega, all Gomez saw was a small Indian village and ruefully write on his map, "*No Gold Here.*"

Desperate to bring back at least something of value to defray the costs of his voyage, Gomez kidnapped fifty Indians, planning to sell them into slavery when he returned to Spain. When Gomez returned to Spain and presented the king with his wretched Indian captives. King Charles angrily set them free. One can only imagine how they must have fared being set loose in sixteenth-century Spain.

The records of the Gomez expedition were turned over to the king's cartographer Diogo Ribeiro for inclusion into his "Carta Universal" – a set of world maps which he published in 1529. Many consider the Carta Universal to be the first attempt at creating a truly scientific map. Although many details are of course missing, the coastline of North America is recognizable. Ribeiro labeled the Northeast coast "Tierra de Esteban Gomez" in the explorer's honor. Somewhat ironically, most of the other portions of the map are based on the around-the-world voyages of Magellan.

Following the unproductive voyage of Gomez the Spanish became convinced that there was no Northwest Passage to the Pacific and no golden cities either. They had their hands full plundering the riches of South America and paid no more attention to Maine.

1527 – John Rut (England)

Sailing for Henry VIII, John Rut set sail for the New World in 1527 on a small merchant ship named the Mary of Guildford. Henry was hoping that Rut would find the fabled "Northwest Passage" to the Orient, and he was also ordered to "*Seek strange regions.*" The expedition did not begin well, at the beginning of the voyage the expedition's Rut's sister ship, the "Sampson" was lost in a severe storm, but the Mary proceeded onward, made landfall in Labrador. Running into ice Rut turned south and

---

[3] Survivors of the Magellan expedition returned to Spain in 1522.

reached the harbor of St. John's where he was amazed to find ten fishing vessels, seven Norman, two Portuguese, and one Breton, busily pulling up tons of codfish from the rich waters.

Continuing south Rut ranged the coasts of Cape Breton and "Norumbega" (Nova Scotia and then New England). He landed often so that his men could "report on the state of these unknown regions," but these records, if they ever existed, have been lost. The *Mary* must have sailed through Penobscot Bay because Rut his ship sailed along the entire coast of North America! In November 1527, the Spanish authorities reported seeing the *Mary* at several locations in the West Indies!

No one knows what King Henry thought of Rut when he returned in the spring of 1528 with nothing more than a set of silver tableware that he had purchased in Puerto Rico. The voyage had turned out to be nothing more than a long sightseeing trip. Rut found nothing new and did not even bother to record his location with any degree of accuracy. Compared with the extensive knowledge gained by the French explorers, Rut's trip was a complete failure.

1555 – André Thevet (England)

Andre Thevet was an adventurous Franciscan priest who was a friend of Cartier. Cruising from Florida to Canada in 1555 he spent five days exploring the Penobscot region. Thevet spent five days in Penobscot Bay, exploring the area and trading with the Indians. He described Isleboro and many of the surrounding islands in quite a bit of detail. Upon his return to France he later wrote:

"Here we entered a river (Penobscot) which is one of the finest in the whole world. The natives call it Agoncy. Upon its banks the French constructed a fort about ten leagues from the mouth of the river. It was called the Fort of the Norumbega."

1567 – David Ingram (England)

In October of 1567, David Ingram sailed from England as part of a fleet of six ships bound for Guinea to pick up a cargo of slaves. The ships were under the command of the privateer John Hawkins and his cousin Francis Drake, a favorite of Queen Elizabeth. The fleet was returning when they put into a harbor near Vera Cruz Mexico and was attacked by a superior Spanish naval force that was there to escort a treasure ship carrying the annual shipment of silver from the New World to Spain. The Spanish probably thought that Hawkins was there to capture it, and perhaps he had been.

Hawkins escaped from the harbor with only two ships, both of which had been badly damaged. Drake immediately set sail for England leaving Hawkins with only one ship and inadequate supplies. Hawkins set Ingram ashore and a hundred other men ashore somewhere in the Gulf of Mexico. According to Ingram the group soon split up. Ingram and three other men started walking north. The Indian tribes they met on the way treated them as magical beings and passed them along from tribe to tribe, sometimes by foot, other times by canoe. In 1571, Ingram reached the coast of Maine and was eventually picked up by a French fishing vessel somewhere on the coast of Maine and taken to New Brunswick Canada.

When Ingram finally returned to England he told his incredible story to his old commander John Hawkins, and in 1559, a record of his journey was published.[4] The book describes Ingram seeing bison and a huge moose, animals that were unknown to Europeans. He also described the great Indian city of Norumbega with its wide streets, roofs of gold and an Indian king who sat on a throne of pearls. In 1583, Ingram returned to the New World as part of Sir Humphrey Gilbert's expedition to establish an English settlement.

1580 – John Walker (England)

The English captain John Walker sailed up the Penobscot to find Norumbega and determine the best site for the English colony that Gilbert had hoped to establish somewhere in Maine. Walker climbed the Camden Hills and reported finding the country *"excellent both for the soyle, diversity of sweete woode, and other trees."* As an added inducement, he claimed to have found several places where silver could be mined.

Walker sailed up the Penobscot village nearly as far as Bangor, where he raided a local Indian village and stole more than three hundred dried moose hides from a native hut. He was probably taking hides that the natives had intended to trade with other tribes for food.

1583 – Sir Humphrey Gilbert (England)

In 1583, Gilbert received a grant from Queen Elizabeth that permitted him to establish an English colony anywhere north of Spanish controlled Florida. The queen promised him that he would be her viceroy in control of whatever lands he settled. The colony would have been the first attempt by any nation to establish an independent British settlement on the coast of Maine. The objective of all previous voyages had been searching for the Northwest Passage or gold and silver. The colony that Gilbert envisioned would have been a self-sufficient English village.

In June of that year Gilbert set sail for the New World with a fleet of five vessels, intending to establish a self-sufficient colony somewhere near the lands that Walker had explored. It was late August however, by the time that Gilbert reached Newfoundland, when Gilbert and he realized that it was too late in the year to establish his settlement. He consoled himself by taking formal possession of Newfoundland in the name of the Queen and decided to return to England and try again the following year.

Gilbert was on his smallest ship, the *Squirrel* when he ran into a gale north of the Azores. The men on his larger vessel, the Golden Hind, pleaded with him to join them on the more seaworthy boat, but he refused, telling them that he could not "forsake my little company going homeward with whom I have passed so many storms and perils." As the two ships drifted apart in the mounting seas he called out *"We are as neere to haven by sea as by lande."* These words of encouragement turned out to his last words. Sir Humphrey Gilbert was lost at sea with all of his men.

---

4   In David Hakluyt's book about English Discoveries in the New World.

1583 – Étienne Bellenger (France)

Étienne Bellenger was a French merchant who sailed from Cape Breton and reached Penobscot Bay in 1583, hoping to establish a trading post in the region. On his return trip his small ship was attacked by a group of MicMac raiders who killed two of his crew and stole their boat. The records of Bellenger's journey quickly disseminated by the writer Richard Hakluyt, who included them in his books[5] promoting the English colonization of North America.

1602 – Bartholomew Gosnold (England)

In 1602, the merchants of Bristol England raised the funds necessary to establish a colony in New England and Bartholomew Gosnold was put in charge of the expedition. The colonists were expected to not only support themselves, but also earn money for their sponsors by fishing and fur trading. Gosnold reached the coast of Maine, landing somewhere between Penobscot Bay and Cape Elizabeth. He sailed south down the coast trading with the Indians for furs and sassafras roots which were used at the time to treat fevers and could be sold in London for enormous profits.

His ship, the Concord, also carried settlers for the permanent community that Gosnold hoped to establish in New England. Gosnold sailed south considering Cuttyhunk Island in Massachusetts as a good site for his colony, but after the Atlantic crossing, the settlers feared that they did not have enough provisions to survive the winter and refused to disembark.

In 1607, Gosnold returned to the New World, but this time made landfall further south. Despite great difficulties he succeeded in establishing the first English colony in the New World at Jamestown Virginia. Although the colony was funded by private subscriptions, the Jamestown settlers were instructed by the king to not only settle Virginia but to: *"find gold, and seek a water route to the Orient."* Most of the colonists died in the first year of starvation, disease and Indian attacks, but eventually under the leadership of Captain John Smith the Jamestown Colony managed to establish itself.

1603 – Martin Pring (England)

Martin Pring was only twenty-three years old when he was appointed as captain of a ship licensed by Sir Walter Raleigh to explore the northern parts of North America. He had two ships under his command: the Speedwell, and the Explorer. In June 1603, Pring reached Penobscot Bay. It is said that the Fox Islands in Penobscot Bay received their English name after Pring saw a pack of foxes cavorting on the shore. After sailing up the Penobscot River, Pring turned south, setting up a small palisade near Truro Massachusetts while his men searched for the sassafras or "ague tree."

Pring described how he would at first encourage the Indian's to come and trade with him, but "when we would be rid of the savages company, we would let loose the Mastiffs, and suddenly with outcries, they would flee away." I'm sure that Pring and his men thought that letting his dogs loose was very funny, but I doubt that the Indians felt the same way, and in August 1603 his ship was attacked by a

---

5 *The Principal Navigations, Voyages, Traffiques and Discoueries of the English Nation.*

large force of Wampanoag Indians. Pring set sail and fled. He returned to England in October with a load of sassafras and a stolen birch bark canoe.

1604 – Samuel de Champlain (France)

Samuel de Champlain, sailing for the king of France entered Penobscot Bay in 1604. He retraced Gomez's trip up the Penobscot River until his ship was also stopped by the Bangor falls. He met with the Abenaki Chief (Sagamore) Bassabez[6] at his village by Kenduskeag Stream in Bangor and exchanged gifts with him, laying the basis for more than two centuries of Franco-Indian friendship.

Champlain was an excellent navigator and cartographer, and his maps were the first to show the coast of Maine in any degree of detail. The chart that he gave to King Henry IV of France in 1612 showed coastline, islands, shoals and rivers. It also included the heights of land useful for navigation and the larger Native settlements. Indian guides had helped Champlain explore the area and also provided him with more information about the interior of the continent. Two of Champlain's place names have survived to the present day, Mount Desert and Isle au Haut.

1605 – George Weymouth and James Rosier (England)

The following year; in 1605, George Weymouth and James Rosier explored the Penobscot region under the sponsorship of Baron Thomas Arundell. Luring a group of curious Indians onto his ship The Archangel, Weymouth trapped them in the hold and took them back to England in chains. He delivered three of the Indians, including a young boy named Squanto, (also known as Squantum or Tisquantum), to Sir Fernando Gorges, who was interested in colonizing the area. Gorges taught the Indian boy English in the hope that he would act as a guide and interpreter on the voyages which he was planning.

Because of his unremitting efforts to establish a settlement in the New World Sir Ferdinando Gorges is known as "The Father of English colonization in North America" despite never having set foot on the continent. He eventually succeeded when the Pilgrims established the Plymouth Colony on November 11, 1620. The patent from Charles I gave Gorges and partner John Mason, the authority to colonize the land in "Ye Province of Maine." His patent was one of the first legal documents to reference the name, Maine.

1609 – Henry Hudson (Holland)

Henry Hudson was an English sea captain who made three voyages to the New World in search of the elusive passage to the Pacific. Hudson is known as a British explorer, but on his third voyage he sailed for the Dutch East India Company, and it is on this voyage that he sailed along the coastline of Maine. Hudson had not received encouragement from Captain John Smith who believed that the Northwest Passage could be found somewhere *North of Virginia.*

---

6 Also called Bashaba.

Much of what is known about the third voyage was from a journal kept by Robert Juet, the ship's treacherous first mate because Hudson's records returned with the Half Moon to Amsterdam and were eventually lost.

According to Juet the Half Moon made landfall in what is now Nova Scotia. Hudson turned southwest and on July 14, 1609 the ship entered Penobscot Bay. For three days Hudson sailed the bay and on the 4th day they encountered a group of Lenape Indians and traded with them, exchanging trinkets for food and furs. Juet wrote that the Indians *"showed them great friendship,"* but added, seemingly without a shred of evidence, *"but we could not trust them."*

Hudson put his crew to work repairing the Half Moon which had been dismasted during their Atlantic crossing. They marveled at the huge white pines that grew down to the shoreline and cut down several of them for spare masts. Juet also wrote that the crew held a lobster bake on the shore. It must have been quite a party because he recorded that the sixteen crewmen ate thirty-one lobsters! Hudson donated two large jugs of wine from his private store. The following day the men went fishing and returned with twenty great codfish and a huge halibut. Events however, soon took a darker turn.

On July 25,th Juet wrote that he and the other men, attacked the nearest Indian village, *"driving the savages from their homes and taking the spoil of them… as they would have done to us."* There is no mention of anything that the Indians had done to make them take such an action. After stealing food, pelts and anything else that they could find of value, Hudson and his crew left the Penobscot Bay and sailed south, eventually exploring what is now New York Harbor and the broad river which bears his name, the Hudson.

1614 – Captain John Smith (England)

Captain John Smith first sailed to the new world in 1607. Commanding and energetic he soon became the leader of the fledgling Jamestown Colony. He warned the gentlemen adventurers under his leadership that *"He who does not work will not eat."* In 1609, he was forced to return to England after being badly burned in a gunpowder explosion at Jamestown in what many believe was an assassination attempt. After recovering from his burns, Captain Smith was anxious to return to America and in 1614, he was put in charge of an English expedition that explored the coast of Maine.

Smith traveled up the Penobscot River in a small boat, carefully charting the coastline and named the entire area "New England." Smith had been instructed by his backers to search for a good location for a new English colony, but finding that the French had already established trading posts, fishing stations, and small farms throughout the Penobscot area he recommended that the colony be situated further south. The maps that Smith had made of the southern New England area were later used by the Pilgrims when they reached Plymouth on November 11, 1620, and established their colony on Cape Cod.

Paddle 1: The Sand Beach/Stonington Paddle

Distance: Approximately 10 nm
Launch: Sand Beach, Stonington, Lat/Long: 44° 09'14.3" N, 68° 41'20.9" W
Charts & Maps: Maptech Waterproof #75, NOAA #13315, Delorme Maine Atlas Map #15

The Trip

The Sand Beach trip is a wonderful paddle through the inner islands of the Stonington Archipelago. Because of the number of beautiful islands accessible to the public for camping and day visits, and the relatively protected seas, the waters around Deer Isle offer some of the best paddling in the world.

This trip begins at pretty Sand Beach on the southwestern side of Stonington. A short distance away is where the Battle of Smalls Cove took place during the War of 1812. After skirting the three small islands that can be seen from the beach (The Fort, Second Island and Andrews Island) the paddlers will cross Deer Island Thorofare and pass Mark Island Light. It was in these waters that the circus ship Royal Tar caught fire in 1887 and sank with the loss of nearly all the exotic animals on board, and many of the circus performers, passengers, and crew perishing as well in the cold waters.

The trip proceeds around historic Crotch Island, the site of one of the earliest island quarries in Maine, and the reason for the tiny fishing village of Greens Landing turning into a boomtown and changing its name to Stonington. Kayakers can see the remnants of the quarrying operation when they land on Sand Island or cautiously paddle into the Mill Cove on Crotch Island itself. Kayakers can also land on Green Island, Russ Island, Little Camp Island and the ominously named but benign Hells Half Acre. On the return paddle you will pass Clam Cove, notorious in past years for the drinking and carousing that went on at the cove. The trip concludes with the kayakers paddling along Stonington Harbor, passing Two Bush Island, Peggy Island and Moose Island, before ending with a take-out on Sand Beach.

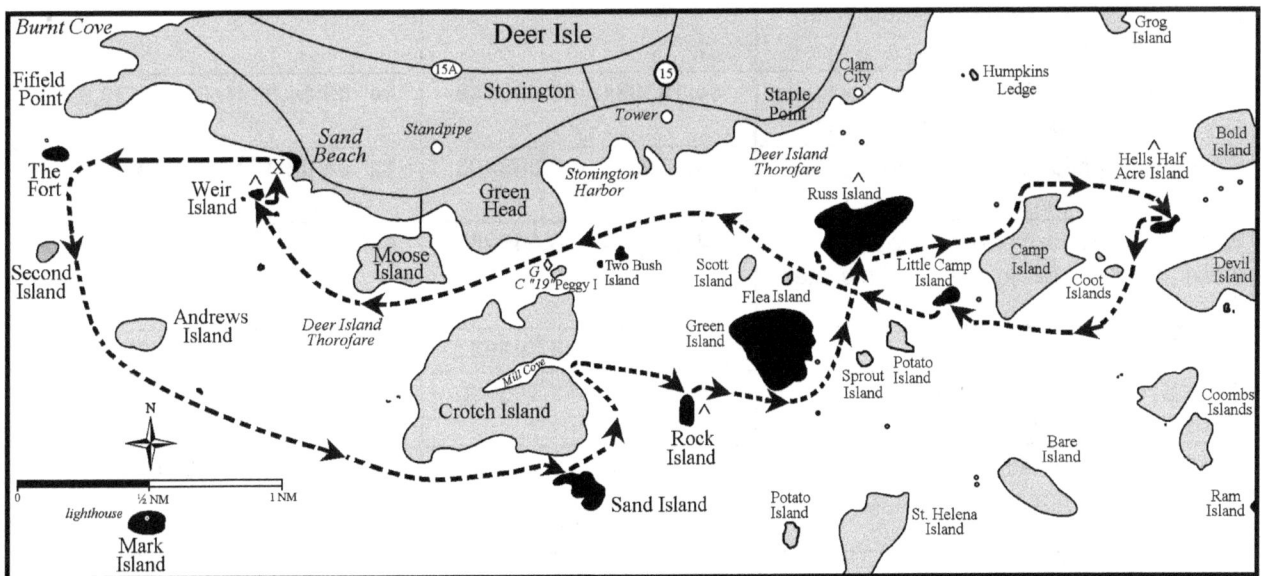

The Sand Beach/Stonington Paddle Chart

Sand Beach/Stonington Camping and Landing Information

ISLAND NAME	GPS COORDINATES	LATITUDE/LONGITUDE
BARRED (Owned by TNC-administered by IHT), day use	44.166713, -68.719511	44° 10'00.2" N, 68° 43'10.2" W
BOLD (Private - no landing)	44.155264, -68.615178	44° 09'18.9" N, 68° 36'54.6" W
BUCKLE (MITA) NE beach & sandbar path- avoid Spruce, 2 sites, 4 campers	44.142191, -68.610239	46° 08'31.0" N, 68° 36'39.0" W
CAMP (Private - no landing)	44.149519, -68.631905	44° 08'58.3" N, 68° 37'54.9" W
CROTCH (Private - no landing)	44.141809, -68.677555	44° 08'30.5" N, 68° 40'39.2" W
DEVIL (Private - no landing)	44.148148, -68.615312	44° 08'53.3" N, 68° 36'55.1" W
GEORGE HEAD (Private - restricted access) check calendar (mita.org/blackout dates) before visiting, 2 sites, 10 campers	44.128090, -68.654502	44° 07'41.1" N, 68° 39'16.2" W
GREEN (MCHT), day use, nice swim hole	44.144132, -68.652262	44° 08'38.9" N, 68° 39'08.1" W
LITTLE CAMP (MCHT), day use	44.146400, -68.638704	44° 08'47.0" N, 68° 38'19.3" W
LITTLE SHEEP, good beaches for landing, 4 campers	44.176400, -68.610056	44° 10'35.0" N, 68° 36'36.2" W
HELLS HALF ACRE (Maine), 2 site platforms, 14 campers	44.150598, -68.620157	44° 09'02.0" N, 68° 37'13.8" W
MARK (IHT - no landing)	44.134435, -68.702593	44° 08'04.0" N, 68° 42'09.3" W
MOOSE (Private - no landing)	44.149366, -68.682265	44° 08'57.7" N, 68° 40'56.1" W
ROCK (MITA), heavy use and high boat traffic, multiple sites, 8 campers	44.140435, -68.659215	44° 08'25.6" N, 68° 39'33.2" W
RUSS (CHERWONKI/admin by MCHT), after July 1st (Ospreys) camp east side, no pets, 8 campers	44.150798, -68.64339	44° 09'02.9" N, 68° 38'36.2" W
SAND BEACH (Stonington), launch site, day use, public beach, nice swimming	44.153961, -68.689148	44° 09'14.3" N, 68° 41'20.9" W
SAND ISLAND (IHT), day use, sandy beach on the west side	44.135953, -68.666693	44° 08'09.4" N, 68° 40'00.1" W
STEVE'S (Maine), several sites for individual tents, heavy use, multiple sites, 10 campers	44.126651, -68.645280	44° 07'36.0" N, 68° 38'42.0" W
THE FORT (MCHT), day use	44.155411, -68.709982	44° 09'19.5" N, 68° 42'35.9" W
THE SHIVERS, small island east of Hells Half Acre, 2 campers	44.152041, -68.608690	44° 09'07.3" N, 68° 36'31.3" W
WEIR (Maine), nesting island, seasonally closed, camp on the southeast corner, 5 campers	44.152797, -68.693610	44° 09'10.1" N, 68° 41'37.0" W

Note: For more information about public campsites in the Stonington area see the Webb Cove Paddle and the Isle au Haut Paddle.

The Launch Point: Sand Beach

Sand Beach is a beautiful little-known town beach in a small cove about halfway between Moose Island on the southwest side of Deer Isle between Stonington and Burnt Cove. Follow Route 15 to Deer Isle, then to Stonington, Maine. Follow West Main Street past Green Head and Moose Island. The parking area for Sand Beach is approximately a mile after the Moose Island causeway. There is parking for about a half dozen cars at the side of Sand Beach Road. A short trail leads down from the parking area to the beach itself.

Paddle west out of Sand Beach Cove

Paddling away from Sand Beach, you can see three small islands directly in front of you: Andrews Island, Second Island and The Fort. These islands were occasionally used by the early colonists to graze sheep but there is no record of anyone permanently living on them. A mile to the north is Smalls Cove, site of a naval battle during the War of 1812.

The Battle of Smalls Cove

In September of 1814, the *Bonaventure*, a small brig left British controlled Castine Harbor with a load of lumber. A fast American privateer, the *Paul Jones* spotted the lumbering ship as it was leaving Penobscot Bay and chased it into Smalls Cove on the west side of Deer Isle. Unable to maneuver in the shallow waters of the cove the *Bonaventure* ran aground in the mud of the cove where it was fired upon by local settlers as well as the *Paul Jones*. The British captain had no other option than surrender. The captain of the *Paul Jones* asked the settlers to unload the lumber from the British ship so that it could be re-floated. The locals obligingly stripped the *Bonaventure* of its cargo and the wood was said to be used to build the Olmstead House, "The Binnacle" on the shore of Smalls Cove.

The Fort

The Fort is the most northern island in the group directly off of Sand Beach. It supposedly received its peculiar name because for many years it was such a popular spot for duck hunting, that locals said it sounded as if a battle was taking place on the island. A weir on the north side of the island supplied bait herring for lobstermen until the late 1970s. The Fort was donated by the Crowell family of Deer Isle to the Maine Coast Heritage Trust. It is now protected and is available to the public during daylight hours.

Second Island

Second Island is nestled between The Fort and Andrews Island. It is therefore always the "second" island, no matter which direction you look at it. It is privately owned.

Andrews Island

Andrews Island is the southern-most island in the chain. It may have been named for Andrew Gray, the grandson of George Gray. George was a Scotsman who was one of a hundred and fifty soldiers captured by the British in 1650 in Scotland at the Battle of Dunbar. The Scottish prisoners captured during this battle were charged by the British with treason because they supported Charles II rather than Oliver Cromwell.

Following their conviction, the captured soldier's lives were saved, but they were transported to Berwick, Maine and forced to labor in the Berwick sawmills as indentured servants. At that time the town was known as Unity, after the ship that carried the men to servitude. In 1675, the *Andrew Gray* was one of the men who valiantly defended the town when it was attacked by Indians during one of the early raids of King Philip's War. George died in Berwick Maine in 1693, but his sons and grandsons migrated North and were one of the first settlers in the Deer Isle/Stonington area. Andrews Island is also privately owned.

Continue paddling south and cross the western entrance of Deer Island Thorofare

It was somewhere in these waters that in October 1887 the steamship *Royal Tar* sank with a loss of thirty-one lives.

The Sinking of the Royal Tar

The one-hundred and sixty-foot steamboat the *Royal Tar* was the first vessel to travel on a regular schedule between St. John New Brunswick and Portland Maine. The ship was named in honor of the English king William IV, who had served in the Royal Navy as a youth and was known thereafter as *"the Sailor King."*

When the steamboat left St. John in late October 1887, it carried ninety passengers, twenty crewmen, and "Fullers Caravan," a complete traveling circus. When it left port the *Royal Tar* was hauling a Bengal tiger, two camels, a zebra, six horses, two lions, a pair of giant pythons, an assortment of other wild beasts and an elephant named Mogul who was chained to the deck. Circus entertainers included a bearded lady, a group of acrobats and a family of jugglers. Onlookers watching the *Royal Tar* leave the St. John, New Brunswick harbor described the vessel as looking, *"a bit like Noah's Ark."*

About 2:00 p.m. on October 25, 1836, the *Royal Tar* had just passed Stonington Harbor and was entering East Penobscot Bay when a fire was reported in the engine room. It seems that for some reason the boilers ran out of water and destroyed themselves.

> *The Royal Tar, she went too far*
> *Her boiler got too hot*
> *She'll never see St. John again*
> *because she's gone to pot.*

The crew was ordered to cut the animals free and lower the lifeboats, but the owners of the *Royal Tar* had removed two of the ship's four lifeboats so that there would be enough room on deck for Mogul and the circus wagons.

Blinded by the smoke and burnt by the flames, Mogul the elephant burst his chains and jumped overboard. One of the passengers described the Mogul disappearing for a moment under the waves

A contemporary drawing of the sinking of the side-wheeler steamship the Royal Tar

and then, "*striking out lustily for shore, his trunk held high in the air.*" The camels and circus horses, confused by the smoke, swam in circles around the floundering ship.

Trapped by the rapidly spreading flames passengers were forced to jump into the frigid waters. The bearded lady was the first person to leap overboard. Another passenger jumped over the side with a money belt holding five hundred dollars in silver coin around his waist, only to sink like a stone beneath the waves. Men, women, and children struggled to stay afloat in the turbulent debris-filled waters. Sixteen members of the crew finally managed to launch one of the two remaining lifeboats, but once on the water they immediately started rowing for Isle au Haut, leaving the flaming ship, the passengers, and even their fellow crew-members behind to their fate.

Captain Reed gathered the remaining crew members together and managed to launch the last lifeboat. Keeping as close as possible to his sinking ship, he did his best to pull as many people out of the frigid water as possible. When his crew protested that their lifeboat was overloaded and in danger of swamping Captain Reed reportedly responded: "*I was captain of the big boat and dammed if I'll not be captain of this small one. If any man refuses to do as I say I'll throw him overboard!*"

Just when everything seemed hopeless, the U.S. Revenue cutter *Vero* appeared on the horizon. The *Vero* had been on a routine patrol out of Castine when the lookout spotted smoke from the burning vessel. The commander of the *Vero*, Captain Dyer brought his ship so close to the blazing ship that his boat caught fire.

Captain Dyer's men managed to save some of the passengers and crew but thirty-one people lost their lives when the *Royal Tar* sank. Poor Mogul the elephant never made it to shore, a few days after the disaster his body washed up on Brimstone Island. Two of the circus horses however, did manage to reach land, and it was rumored that other animals may have also survived. For years after the disaster, islanders reported seeing huge snakes slithering through the old quarries, and other strange beasts prowling the islands around Stonington. One sheep farmer swore that he had shot a tiger after it had eaten most of his livestock.

In 1962, two urchin divers spotted a piece of the charred rudder and a melted winch on the ocean floor between Deer Isle and Vinalhaven. Many believe that the wreckage they found was all that was left of the ill-fated circus ship the *Royal Tar*.

After crossing the Deer Island Thorofare head toward Mark Island

The Mark Islands

There are three "Mark" Islands in the Stonington area (Mark Island Light, Eastern Mark Island, and Southern Mark Island). Mark Island Light "marks" the western entrance to the Deer Island Thorofare connecting East Penobscot Bay to the west, with Jericho Bay to the east. Eastern Mark Island establishes the northeastern entrance to the thorofare. Southern Mark, which is located to the east off of McGlathery Island, marks the eastern side of the Merchant Row passageway. Together the three islands form a roughly equilateral triangle. Since Colonial times, these three islands have helped mariners find safe passage through the maze of islands and reefs surrounding the southern tip of Deer Isle.

Mark Island Light

In 1856, Congress approved the construction of a lighthouse to guide sailors into the southwestern entrance of the Deer Island Thorofare. Mark Island was chosen as the best location for the light and the government purchased the island for $175 from David Thurlow, who owned nearby Crotch Island.

Mark Island Light shortly after being built. Note the Square Tower

Congress appropriated an additional $5,000 to build a square twenty-five-foot brick light tower connected to a seven-room keeper's house. Placed into service in 1858 the light could be seen at sea more than twelve miles away. An automated bell was added to the lighthouse in 1884.

David Thurlow's cousin, Thomas Small, was appointed the first keeper of the light. Small had once been a sailor, but he had fallen from his ship's rigging and could no longer go to sea. When Small received his commission as keeper of the Mark Island light, it must have seemed like a godsend, giving him the ability to provide for his wife and fourteen children.

Continue to paddle past Mark Island Light

The Wreck of the City of Richmond

On August 30, 1881, the 200' passenger steamship *City of Richmond* was on her normal scheduled run from Rockland to Bar Harbor. The steamship was considered by many to be *"the most graceful of all the side-wheel steamers on Penobscot Bay."*

Her captain was experienced, and the ship had made the run scores of times before, but on this day, a thick fog covered the sea, reducing visibility to only a few yards. The captain reduced speed but mistook his position and the *City of Richmond* ran aground on Robinson Rock, just below Mark Island.

The side-wheeler City of Richmond at the steamboat wharf, Castine, Maine, 1883

Unlike the confusion and chaos that occurred when the *Royal Tar* sank, the captain and crew of the *City of Richmond* kept strict order. The passengers were taken safely ashore to Mark Island and the crew managed to salvage most of the freight. It was reported that the ship's steward even brought hot coffee to the wet and frightened passengers. The *City of Richmond* was eventually re-floated and towed to Rockland to be repaired. After many years of down-east service, she was sailed to Florida and renamed the *City of Key West*. During the Spanish-American War the old side-wheeler served as a troop transport.

The dedicated lighthouse keepers on Mark Island saved many lives. In 1917, keeper Allen Holt was commended for helping re-float the schooner *Sarah and Lucy* which had run ashore off Andrews Island; for towing the Maine Coast Mission's ship *Sunbeam* out of danger and for towing a disabled

Stonington motorboat to safety. Occasionally, however, events didn't go quite as well as lighthouse keeper Holt might have wished. When a sailing vessel went ashore on nearby Andrews Island, Holt hailed a passing tugboat, hoping to use it to pull the damaged ship off the rocks. When he boarded the tug however, he found the captain and the engineer falling-down drunk and fighting one another in the cabin!

In 1950, following a fire that destroyed the keeper's house, the Coast Guard automated the station. An electric horn replaced the old fog bell, and the station's outbuildings were torn down. Not everyone was pleased with the improvements; the new horn was so loud that Stonington residents called it the "Bull Moose Call." One irate resident complained that "When we get a good southwest breeze, the damned thing might just as well be in the living room." The Coast Guard eventually agreed to reduce the horn's power, yet it still can be heard blaring lustily from many miles away. Kayakers are warned to keep well clear of the island if there are foggy conditions, the horn can deafen.

In 1997, the Coast Guard transferred ownership of the Mark Island Light to the Island Heritage Trust. Due to the island's thin soil and fragile environment, landing on the island is not encouraged, and if there are fog or fog banks in the area it is wise to stay well away. The blast of the fog horn could damage your hearing if you venture too close.

Turn east toward Crotch Island - the center of Deer Isle's granite industry

Crotch Island

It is easy to see where Crotch Island got its name. The shape of the island resembles a giant pair of pant legs with Mill Cove nearly splitting the island in half, forming a "crotch." It was originally called Thurlow Island after its most famous resident, Captain David Thurlow, who moved to Crotch Island around 1800 with his wife Mercy. Unlike most of his maritime neighbors David was given the title "Captain," not because of his nautical experience, but because he served as an officer in the state militia during the war of 1812.

When Thurlow first arrived on his island the land was covered in a virgin hardwood forest. He built a small cabin at the end of Mill Cove and constructed a tide-powered sawmill at the entrance of the waterway. The mill operated until 1839 when it was destroyed in a storm.

Once he had his sawmill operating David started building boats using the island's virgin hardwood forest for lumber. Within a few years, he and his workers had constructed more than seventeen vessels. Most were small fishing boats, but a few were substantial ocean-going schooners. Thurlow used the larger vessels to transport dried fish to the sugar plantations in the West Indies where Maine fish was fed to African slaves laboring on the sugar cane plantations. For the return trip Thurlow filled the holds of his ships with casks of rum, molasses and sugar cane.

Even if he didn't participate in the actual buying and selling of slaves himself, Thurlow profited enormously by supporting those who did and using his profits he began purchasing many of the islands surrounding Deer Isle. (Mark, Sand, John, and Rock Islands), but many of these claims were later invalidated by the state. In addition to his business interests, Captain Thurlow was active in local

Tintype of Capt. David Thurlow of Crotch Island, 1774-1857: mill owner, shipbuilder, and merchant (Courtesy of Margaret Hundley)

politics and even served a term in the Maine State Legislature. He was active in community affairs until he did in 1857, at the age of eighty-three.

In 1870, a stonecutter from Massachusetts by the name of Job Gross opened a granite quarry on Crotch Island. In the late 1800s, American cities were experiencing a building boom. Granite was needed to build not only the stately bridges and elaborate city buildings that were constructed of stone during this period, but also to pave roads and walkways. The first island quarrying operation in Maine had begun around 1800 on the nearby island of Vinalhaven, but Deer Island granite was particularly prized because of its high quality and distinctive pink color.

At the peak of the granite boom, thirty-three quarries were operating in Maine, employing more than ten thousand workers. Job Gross employed nearly two hundred and fifty workers on Crotch Island. His company provided the granite used for the Holyoke Dam in Massachusetts and bridges in Providence and New York. His workers also cut and shipped hundreds of tons of granite cobblestones to eastern cities where they were used to pave roads.

The granite could be loaded directly onto ships that would transport it to the booming eastern port cities such as New York, Boston and Philadelphia. The combination of high-quality stone and inexpensive shipping gave island quarries a considerable advantage over their inland competitors who had to transport the huge blocks over poor roads to the trains that would take them into the cities.

Gross's quarry on Crotch Island was eventually acquired by larger companies that could afford to purchase sophisticated mining equipment, but by the time that happened demand for granite was slowing. Architects and builders had turned to steel framed buildings constructed of brick and concrete. As automobiles and trucks replaced horse-drawn transportation the old cobblestone streets were paved over with asphalt.

The high quality of Crotch Island granite however, kept the quarry running even when other local island quarries were forced to close. In 1933, the Rockefeller family ordered an immense granite bowl more than twenty-two feet in diameter for their estate in Tarrytown, New York. When President John F. Kennedy was assassinated in 1963, the family remembered that as a young man, Kennedy loved to sail the waters of Penobscot Bay. Pink granite from Crotch Island was selected for his grave in Arlington National Cemetery.

The Deer Island Granite Corporation on Crotch Island managed to survive until 1966 when it finally ceased operation, but the business reopened in 1979 when Tony Ramos, a former sculptor, purchased the island for his company, New England Stone Industries.

Today, Crotch Island granite is cut with high-temperature gas torches. The jet-like noise these cutters make when the quarry is operating can be heard for miles. The granite blocks are shipped by truck to the Ramos plant in Rhode Island for final finishing.

Paddle along the southeastern tip of Crotch Island and beach your boats on Sand Island

Sand Island

There is a narrow channel splitting Sand from Crotch Island, and a small picturesque beach on the western shore of ten-acre Sand Island where small boats can land. It overlooks an enormous pile of granite debris on Crotch left over from the years of granite mining. Sand Island was originally owned by Captain David Thurlow, who also laid claim to nearby John and Rock Island, but David's early 1834 claim was later found to be invalid, and in 1870 his daughter-in-law, Charlotte, was forced to repurchase Sand Island from Eben Small, a fisherman who was living there at the time. Sand Island is now owned by the Maine Coast Heritage Trust and is open to the public.

Push off from the Sand Island beach and follow the Crotch Island shoreline to the entrance of Mill Cove

Mill Cove on Crotch Island

Mill Cove forms the "crotch" of Crotch Island. It is named for the tide-powered dam that Thurlow had constructed there to power his sawmill. In Thurlow's day, the cove was known as "The Basin." When Job Gross began his quarrying operation the dam that controlled the flow of water in and out of the cove to power the sawmill was removed and the company built a granite dock at the entrance to the cove so that large ships could dock in deep water to be loaded.

Mill Cove is a shallow waterway but, at high tide there is more than enough water for kayakers to enter. Landing is forbidden - the blocks are dangerously unstable! The waterway is an eerie, unworldly place. Decades of mining have left huge blocks of granite rubble piled in hundred-foot mounds along the shoreline. It is easy to imagine the huge snakes and other creatures said to survive the sinking of the *Royal Tar* taking refuge among the debris. Rusted skeletons of massive cranes and other old mining equipment stand abandoned on the land where Captain Thurlow built his first cabin

The Crotch Island Basin

so many years ago. Crotch Island is private, and the quarry is still in operation. To repeat my warning, landing without permission is dangerous and strictly forbidden.

Paddle out of Mill Cove and head southeast toward Rock Island

Rock Island

Rock Island is part of the Maine Island Trail Association. You can land and pull your boats up on the lovely north beach. A trail leads to the campsites in the protected spruce. Hardy rugosa roses line the path and during the summer months fill the air with their fragrance. These roses are native to Asia but thrive on the island's sandy soil. How they originally came to grow here is a mystery.

Paddle eastward towards Green Island

Green Island

Early maps identify Green Island as "Island Poor." During the colonial period, settlers who found themselves in debt were often forced to work off their obligations on "poor farms," where they were treated as indentured servants. Perhaps the early name indicated that Green Island was the location of one of these farms. The island's name was subsequently (and rather ironically), changed to Worthy's Island, and then finally to Green Island after it was purchased by Sullivan Green in the mid-1800s.

Paddle into the deep water cove on the southern side of Green Island. An old granite wharf with a ladder leads up to a level area, but it is better to continue to paddle along to the end of the cove where it is easier to beach kayaks. The existing wharf is only a fraction of its original size. When the Green Island Quarry ceased operation many of the blocks were removed to build a coal dock for the Stonington Fuel and Lumber Company. The wharf is now used by local lobstermen who find

The old granite dock at Green Island

Green Island a convenient place to store their traps. During the summer months, you will often see Stonington teenagers jumping off the end of the twenty-foot dock and swimming over to the ladder to repeat the jump over and over again.

The cove is known locally as Charles Cove, presumably for Charles Gross, who lived with his family on the island in the 1830s. Early settlers included the Robbins family (whose descendants were still living in a homestead on the north end of the island in the 1870s) and members of the Harvey family.

Land your boats on the beach at the end of the Cove

There is a small sandy beach at the end of the cove. At high tide you can tie up to the rocks, or you can use the iron ring attached to the side of the large boulder on the north side of the cove. A well-used trail leads upward from the Beach to a Maine Coast Heritage Trust kiosk that displays a map of Green Island, describes its history and shows a map of the trails.

During the 1870s, Green and his son operated the Russ Stone Quarry on the southern end of their island. The company shipped granite to New York, Boston and Philadelphia. A few years later, the Gross and Small company, which ran operations on Crotch Island, opened up a second quarry on Green Island. In the heyday of the quarrying era, there were three derricks, two steam engines, a steam drill and a railway track leading down to the large granite wharf. By 1923, both of the Green Island quarries had closed and the abandoned quarry holes soon filled with water from underground springs. Today the old quarry above Charles Cove is a quiet swimming hole and a great place to enjoy lunch.

In 1934, Jeremiah McCarthy III, who had owned property on Green Island, bought the entire island as an investment. He later wrote; *"I paid the price quickly, feeling that I should own the entire island to prevent undesirable development and to have a complete entity to offer a prospective buyer."* For more than two decades, however, he struggled to find a buyer, ruefully joking that he had asked

The swimming hole on Green Island

everyone from "the President of the United States to Bing Crosby!" It was not until 1957, that he finally sold Green Island to the Clark family, who generously donated it to the Maine Coast Heritage Trust. Green Island became the first MCHT holding in Merchant Row.

Turn northeast and land on the eastern side of Russ Island

Russ Island

Originally, Russ Island was called Indian Island supposedly because every summer Native Americans camped there. Later it became known as Harvey Island after George Harvey, an early settler who moved his family to the island around 1840.[1] George's father John Harvey had been a soldier in the Revolutionary War, and George himself served in the War of 1812. There is no indication of anyone named "Russ" ever living on the island, but there is a Russ's Hill in Stonington and the Gross and Russ Quarry operated for many years on nearby Green Island and may have at one time had an interest in the island.

Like many islanders, George Harvey made his living as a fisherman-farmer. He built a home on the Island and supported his large family as best he could. When his first wife died, George married a local woman named Polly Morey. Stonington's amateur historian, Dr. Benjamin Noyes, described Polly in less than flattering terms:

> *"She was a strong, wiry character, who frequented the clam flats and was associated with boating during her early days - the same as the men of her time. Her career was one of widespread, romantic, sensational, notorious, and final of pathetic interest.[2] She had six or seven illegitimate children, the father of all or each being a matter of conjecture."*

---

1 Members of the Harvey clan also lived on Green Island.
2 Noyes, notebooks: Family Histories, Harvey, pg. 10.

Despite her marriage to George Harvey, Polly continued to lead a *"riotous and debauched"* life on Russ Island. It is said that Polly and her Morey kinfolk threatened and eventually drove George's children off the island and burned down their homestead to prevent them from ever returning. This set off a family feud between the Harveys and the Moreys that continued even after Polly's violent and mysterious death. Her battered body was discovered one morning on the northwest point of Russ Island. It was reported that she had taken part in an island brawl the previous night, but some islanders believed that she had been murdered by her son Charles, but nothing was ever proven. Polly was buried somewhere on Russ Island, but the location of her grave has now been lost. At the time of her death around 1880, Polly would have been in her seventies.

Russ Island was quarried for granite in the 1880s by Steven Morey. Huge stone blocks were shipped from the island to New York City and used to construct the towers of the Brooklyn Bridge. But the quarrying business on Russ Island was handicapped by the ongoing feud between the Harvey and the Morey clans. The Harvey family refused to give Steven Morey the right to quarry near any of the many Harvey gravesites that were scattered around the island. Their decision probably had more to do with revenge against Polly and the entire Morey clan, than respect for the dead.

There is a trail leading from the beach through a spruce forest and open fields to the western cliffs.[3] The path passes an old quarry (known locally as Eaton's quarry) at the southern end of the island and ends at a bronze plaque on the western cliffs. From the top of the hill you can see the town of Stonington nestled above the harbor. It is a beautiful place, to the east you can look out to the islands of Merchant Row, and the tall hills of Isle au Haut loom to the south.

Russ Island is now owned by the Chewonki Foundation and is under a conservation easement held by The Maine Coast Heritage Trust. It is also a stop on the Maine Island Trail. Eight campsites at the northeastern end of the island can be reached by following the Old Trail that branches off the island's Eastern Beach Trail.

Head east toward Camp Island

Camp Island

Nathaniel Merchant moved to Camp Island sometime around the 1830s and raised a family on the island. If Polly Morey was known for her scandalous behavior on Russ Island, Robert Merchant, Nathaniel's eldest son, Robert reportedly lived an equally drunken and violent life on Camp Island.

According to local legend, Robert was suspected of beating one of his sons to death and causing the intentional drowning of another. He supposedly ordered one of the boys to fetch cattle from nearby Little Camp Island knowing full well that the tide was coming in and it would trap his son. Fearing for her own life after the death of her sons, it is said that his wife hailed a passing schooner and begged the captain to take her off Camp Island and as far away from her violent husband as possible.

---

[3] Day use is permitted, but organized groups wishing to camp are asked to contact Greg Shutz at Cherwonki prior to their visit. gshute@chewonki.org, or 207-882-7323.

After his wife left him, Robert Merchant spent his days drinking and carousing at Clam City, a mudflat on the mainland just north of Stonington. There it is said he consorted with numerous women, and whom he had many illegitimate children. Robert eventually died a pauper on Swans Island.

In the 1880s, the Nelson and Shields Granite Company mined the island and the remnants of the granite pear they constructed can still be seen on the shoreline. There are many homes on this private island.

Circle the northern tip of Camp Island and you will see Bold Island to the north and Devil Island to the southeast

Devil Island

I had originally been told that this privately owned island got its name from the prison island in French Guinea where men convicted of crimes against France were sentenced to hard labor. Captain Dreyfus of the French Dreyfus Affair was sentenced to Devil's Island in 1894, and the escape artist Henri Charrière (Papillon) also served time on the French penal island. The island in Penobscot Bay however, had its name long before the French prison was built in 1852.

Charles McLane believes[4] that Devil Island may have received its name because of the actions of Robert Merchant who lived on Camp Island. Robert buried his two sons on Devil's Island, some say after causing their deaths, but others more generously suggest that his children simply died of diphtheria on Camp Island and that Robert buried them on Devil Island to limit the danger of spreading the contagious disease. Diphtheria was a terrible scourge during this period and children were particularly susceptible. Like so much of early history, the truth will never be known. Deer Isle's local historian, Dr. Benjamin Lake Noyes writes that the island got its ominous name because of its *"Satanic atmosphere."*[5]

The quarry on Devil Island wasn't as successful as others in the area. When the owner of the quarry shut it down and the workers sued for back pay, the island somehow became the property of the judge involved with the case, who then turned around and sold it for a handsome profit! The current owners refer to themselves as "the Devils" and over the years have built several small cottages along the southern shore. Landing on Devil's Island is discouraged.

Land on Hells Half Acre

Hells Half Acre is the small island between Devils, Camp, and Bold Islands. There are sandy beaches on both sides of the island. At low tide however, the smooth rocks on the upper part of the northern beach are covered in black algae which are as slippery as ice when it gets damp.

---

4 Charles McLane, *Islands of the Mid-Maine Coast, Vol. 1*, Tilbury House Publishers, 1997, page 257.
5 Benjamin Lake Noyes, *Devil Island*, page 4..

Hells Half Acre

The island's ominous name indicates that at one time it was the site of many a wild time, but there is little written material to support this conjecture. The island is now owned by the State of Maine and is maintained by the Maine Coast Heritage Trust. It is open to the public for overnight camping.

The tent platforms on Hells Half Acre

There are two campsites for up to fourteen people at a time. A trail leads from the beach on the northern side to the main campsite on the west end of the island. Hells Half Acre is one of the few islands on the Maine Island Trail to have wooden tent platforms. They were built to protect the island's fragile environment and should be used whenever you camp on Hells Half Acre.

Open fires are allowed on Hells Half Acre with a state permit, but it is strongly suggested that campers abide by the No Trace guidelines and use small cooking stoves instead. During the 1800s, nearly all of the islands around Stonington had been logged, some multiple times. Early settlers sold the lumber and then used the cleared land for grazing sheep and other animals. Unfortunately, these early practices not only weakened and eroded the thin island soils but resulted in an unfortunate ecological cycle that we are living with today. Following the lumbering of island hardwood trees, softwoods such as spruce quickly grew up to take their place.

During the 1800s, nearly all softwoods had a relatively short life span. Since they started growing at the same time, they weaken and die within a few years of one another, creating massive blow-downs on the islands. On Hells Half Acre and other MITA islands, volunteers have been removing the dead trees in the hope of stimulating new growth and one day breaking this cycle, but it is a long process.

Launch your boats and paddle towards the east

Shivers Island

Owned by the State of Maine the small group of islands to the east of Hells Half Acre is collectively known as "The Shivers." The largest island in the group, Shivers Island, hosts a MITA two-person campsite on its western shore. The islands were probably named, not as one would think, because they were a cold place in the winter, but because sailing vessels making for Stonington Harbor would need to beat[6] against prevailing southwesterly winds to reach the safety of the harbor. If sailboats are headed too close into the wind, their sails shake, or in nautical terminology "shiver."

Turn south and paddle between Camp Island, Devil Island and tiny Coot Island
Follow the southwestern shoreline of Camp Island towards Little Camp Island

Granite "dike" on Little Camp Island

Little Camp

The beach on the southern shore of Little Camp Island is a lovely place to stop. Kayakers can land at the large sandy beach on the southern shore or a smaller pocket beach at the northern tip of the island.

Evidence of ancient volcanic activity can be seen on the northeastern cliff face of Little Camp. On the rock bluff above the shoreline a line of lighter colored stone threading like a necklace for hundreds of yards along the granite rock face. At one time in the island's ancient past, hot magma from deep within the earth's crust was forced upward filling cracks in the overlaying stone and creating a feature known to geologists as an intrusive dike.

Land on the southern beach and follow the path leading to the top of Little Camp Island

---

6 Beat – Sail against the wind.

Although there is a spring of freshwater oozing out of the rock face above the beach there is no record of anyone living permanently on Little Camp. If you climb to the top of the hill, you will be rewarded with a beautiful open view of the nearby islands.[7] Little Camp Island is maintained by the Maine Coast Heritage Trust and is open to the public for day use, overnight camping is prohibited.

Turn west to pass between Russ Island's southeastern shore and head to Scott Island

Scott Island

Privately owned Scott Island[8] was originally owned by David Thurlow of Crotch Island. When David and his wife were getting on in years David deeded his entire estate to his son Paul. In return, Paul and his wife Charlotte promised to take care of the aging couple for the rest of their lives.

In the days before social security and other support programs this type of arrangement was common. In some cases men and women who were getting on in years and unable to fish or work the land would turn over their lands to the town, and obtain in return some support, but due to the large families of the time this was relatively rare.

Captain Thurlow probably believed that he was the rightful owner of Scott Island, but the State of Maine thought not, and put the island up for sale at a public auction. When no one else bid on the isolated island, Paul bought it from the state for $3.50. Almost immediately Paul leased out the island to a granite quarrying company, but demand for stone was slowing and the operation soon shut down. In the years that followed, Scott Island was occasionally leased to local farmers for sheep grazing, but no one settled there permanently.

Paddle towards the mainland and the gravel beachfront west of Russ Island to the area of shoreline known as Clam City

Clam City

Named locally for its once productive clam flats, the protected beach at Clam City just north of Stonington was used by generations of local fishermen to beach their boats during the winter months. Today, the area is quiet and serene, but at one time Clam City was quite a lively place. Deer Isle's local historian Dr. Noyes writes that Clam City and the islands immediately offshore were hangouts where: *"A large group of nomads[9] sought a lowly form of livelihood…they promiscuously mixed up with each other's wives and families…not half of these cohabitants were married and a few were the very limits of squalor."*[10]

Paddle along the shore past the Stonington Seafood Co-Op

---

7 The closest island, Potato Island, is privately owned and often confused with a public island of the same name but located several miles to the north near White Island.
8 Also shown on some charts as Round Island.
9 He explicitly identified the Harveys, Dunbars, Holbrooks, Bloack and Robbins.
10 Noyes, Devils Island, pg. 3-4.

The Seafood Co-Op is run by the Maine Lobstermen's Association. If you purchase lobsters at the Co-Op you support not only the local fishermen but also the many research projects conducted by the organization which is the oldest and largest fishing association on the east coast.

Paddle along the Stonington Shoreline

The Town of Stonington

The original settlers on Deer Isle were farmers who considered the granite covered southern half of Deer Isle worthless for farming, and built their homesteads in the northern section of the island. For a few years the virgin farmland may have yielded good crops, but the thin, rocky island soil was soon exhausted. To survive, the settlers turned toward the sea for their livelihood. A small fishing community was established in the protected waters of what was then known as Green's Landing, after an early settler. In the early days, fishermen in small open boats would fish the inshore waters, but by 1840, Penobscot fishermen were sailing as far as the Grand Banks to fish for codfish and mackerel. Deer Isle towns would specialize mostly in the mackerel fishery whereas Castine focused exclusively on cod. Large fishing schooners would even sail to the Bay of Chaleur in Labrador. These deep-sea fisheries employed many Deer Isle seamen and generated considerable wealth for the small community. In 1850, Deer Isle fishermen caught more than a hundred thousand dollars worth of fish. By comparison the value of Castine's catch was only a little over half that amount. Most of the profits went to the owners of the boats and the fish merchants who supported the industry. The average fisherman received enough to live on but not much more.

In 1853, the cod schooner *Martha Burgess* fished for six months and brought back a catch of codfish worth $3,500. The owner/captain of the vessel received $1,000, the three-man crew split $619. In 2014 dollars,[11] the owner would have received $30,000 (30% profit after expenses), but each crewman would have received only a little over $6,000. Not much for six months of work, but more than what a skilled quarryman would make ten years later, and far more than a farmhand of the day could ever expect to bring home.

On the other hand, a farmer would be able to be at home with his family and wouldn't have to worry about being drowned at sea. In the days before weather forecasting this happened all too frequently. The "Yankee Gale" of October 3-5, 1841 drove thirty Maine vessels onto the lee shore of Prince Edward Island, and seventy-seven fishermen lost their lives.

From the 1840s-1860s the fishermen of Deer Isle had enjoyed significant advantages over their competitors. They were closer to the rich Nova Scotia and Newfoundland fishing banks than their rivals in towns further south. Maine boat-builders could also take advantage of the largely untouched pine forests on the islands and coastlines. Federal fishing subsidies also encouraged the growth of the Maine deep-sea fishing fleet.[12]

After the Civil War ended, competition from the Canadian fishing industry based in Lunenburg, Nova Scotia, the growth of the Gloucester fishing fleet, and the loss of Federal subsidies had taken their toll.

---

11 According to the Federal Reserve Bank of Minnesota, $1 in 1850 would be worth $28.60 in 2014.
12 Hornsby, S. J. ed. & Judd, R. W. ed. (2015). *Historical Atlas of Maine*. pg. 32. Orono, ME: University of Maine Press.

By the mid-1860s Maine fishing dominance had essentially ended. Many of the fishermen from Deer Isle adapted by switching to the growing lobstering industry while others were employed by the granite quarries.

In 1860, Job Gross established a granite quarry on nearby Crotch Island and the quiet fishing village of Green's Landing changed completely. At the height of the granite boom, money seemed to pour into the town. The quarry owners made the most profit, but local businesses providing food, lodging and entertainment to the granite workers also prospered. Two music halls: the Eureka and the Olympic provided cultural amusement, while gambling dens, whorehouses and speakeasies catered to coarser natures. Special boats ran out to Crotch and other islands to bring the workers into town for their Saturday night fling. Steamship service to Rockland and other coastal towns was soon established, carrying freight and passengers from as far away as Boston.

An island stonemason cutting granite blocks for the growing northeastern cities

In 1897, the citizens of Greens Landing separated from the town of Deer Isle, and the citizens renamed the town Stonington in honor of the beautiful hard stone upon which their new prosperity was founded.

To meet the demand for experienced stonecutters, the granite companies imported skilled workers from the British Isles, Scandinavia and Italy. Experienced stonecutters were paid around twenty dollars a week, a good wage at the time.[13] Less skilled workers were usually paid on a piece basis, toiled away cutting cobblestones for a few cents a block. Unmarried men were housed in two large bunkhouses on Crotch Island or found lodging in one of the town's rooming houses. Workers with families rented small houses in town or found rooms with local families. The company supported a school on Crotch Island and ran a store. Every day the workers staying in the town would board barges that would tow them out to their job sites.[14]

---

13 Bill Caldwell, *Maine Coast,* pg. 348.
14 The Granite Museum in Stonington features a working model of the granite quarry on Crotch Island as it existed in 1900.

The Tug Minnihaha towing quarry workers to and from Stonington

The small fishing town of Stonington began to resemble a western boomtown more than a staid New England village. With the gambling dens, speakeasies and houses of ill-repute doing a thriving business, the town soon earned a notorious reputation. As one old stonecutter related:

*I still remember the amount of rum we drank...
the gambling and the fights in the rooming houses were wild!"*

Their money spent, it must have been a sorry, hung-over crew that boarded the company barges and reported back to work on Monday morning.

The Stonecutters Monument (Stonecutter making granite blocks) overlooking Stonington Harbor

Maine had an active temperance movement, and in 1851 became the nation's first "dry state," the teetotalers, or "cold-water men" promising to stay away from the booze as the women threatened that "lips that touch liquor will never touch ours." The state's prohibition laws however, did little to stop the flow of illegal liquor into speakeasies of Stonington. The police had more important problems than enforcing the prohibition ordinances, when robberies, assaults and other violent crimes were commonplace in the town. At the turn of the century several murders were still under investigation.

Aside from the rabble-rousers, most of the workmen were simply trying to make an honest living and build new lives for themselves in America. The granite cutters established an early form of a labor union, the Knights of Labor. The union supported their members during hard times, campaigned for

Dr. Benjamin Lake Noyes

In my research into the history of the area I am always surprised to find that nearly every town in Maine has at least one person who stands out and characterizes the spirit of the age. For Deer Isle, Stonington's physician Dr. Benjamin Lake Noyes deserves that distinction.

Dr, Noyes was born in Lisbon Falls, Maine, but grew up in Grand Manan in New Brunswick. He learned the printing trade from his father who also owned a drug store and acted as the local doctor. Benjamin attended Bowdoin Medical College and in 1883, at the age of 25 established his medical practice on Deer Isle. As Stonington prospered due to the granite trade Dr. Noye's practice prospered, and he built himself a large mansion[1] overlooking the harbor.[2]

Dr. Benjamin Lake Noyes

In the days before telephones, Dr. Noyes would sit on his high porch overlooking the islands and watch for puffs of smoke coming from signal fires set to indicate that his skills were needed. He would grab his black doctor's bag and row out in all kinds of weather to offer assistance. For house calls on the mainland Dr. Noyes would use his automobile, but he was said to be so preoccupied with his thoughts that everyone knew to get out of the road when they saw his car coming!

Dr. Noyes however, was far more than the town's medical doctor, he was a true renaissance man adept in a variety of fields. After learning the printing trade he became an accomplished painter, and later took up photography. Like many of his generation he was fascinated by the occult, and with an open mind, spent many hours seeking answers from beyond the grave. He was a talented musician proficient in numerous instruments including the violin, piano, flute, and banjo. He was

---

1 Dr. Noyes' home was built on a huge granite foundation high on a steep cliff overlooking the harbor and cost nearly $20,000 to build - a fortune at the time.

2 The huge granite foundations, and the stone room where Dr. Noyes stored his archives still exists, but the original house burned to the ground in 1981. A new home of similar size and style was rebuilt on the site of the old.

familiar with ornithology and zoology and served as the first officer of the Davenport Expedition to tropical America in 1890-91. A biographical review published in Boston in 1898 described him as a person who, *"Spent all of his waking hours in self-improvement and never lost time in idleness or dissipation."*[3]

It is largely due to the diligence and industry of Dr. Noyes that we know so much about the Deer Isle area. He became interested in determining the cause of a peculiar lameness that showed up in several generations of the local Haskell family. Dr. Noyes suspected that the lameness might be genetic[4] and began to collect genealogical and historical data on Haskell's relatives. Eventually his research led him to compile information on the other families in the area. It is said that every time he went out on a house call he would ask to see their family-tree, usually kept in the family bible. He collected photographs, news-clippings, business transactions and a vast trove of other information to supplement his investigations. By the time of his death in 1945, he had over 37 volumes of material stored in a granite building below his home that he named the *"Penobscot Bay Archives."*

Dr. Noyes on his way to see a patient, with his beloved Penobscot Bay Archives building shown behind him

In 1945, Dr. Noyes died of radiation poisoning. While still in medical school he had become interested in the possibility of using X-rays to treat cancer. In the early days, the dangers of X-ray poisoning were not known and Dr. Noyes would often unintentionally irradiate himself. Searching for a cure for his patients he became one himself. Working through increasing pain he struggled to perform his medical duties and at the same time continued to work on his historical research.

---

[3] http://workingwaterfrontarchives.org/2007/05/01/Passionate-collector-preserved-deer-isles-genealogy-history.
[4] Dr. Noyes' suspicion was correct subsequent investigation determined the problem to be a particular gene that was transferred down the family line.

> When Dr. Noyes died, his second wife Estelle sold the entire collection to the Mormon Church[1]. The Mormons had been active in the Stonington Area since the Eaton's had embarked on their ill-fated mission to Palestine (See the Sand Beach Paddle). Estelle had rented rooms to Mormon missionaries and had become acquainted with their teachings.
>
> Members of The Church of Jesus Christ of Latter-Day Saints believe that to save their souls, even the dead can be baptized into the Mormon faith. To accomplish this goal, they have accumulated the largest database of genealogical information in the world.
>
> When the missionaries saw Dr. Noyes' extensive records, they immediately offered to purchase the material and Estelle agreed. The volumes containing Dr. Noyes' life work were carefully boxed up and sent to the Mormon Church in Utah to be cataloged.[2] In 1983, the Mormon's archiving group completed their work of transferring the material to microfilm and the original collection was generously returned to the Deer Isle Historical Society for safekeeping.
>
> ---
> 1 Mormons – The Church of Jesus Christ of Latter-Day Saints.
> 2 The Mormon Church now has billions of records in their database, making it the largest collection of genealogical data in the world.

higher wages and negotiated with the quarry owners for better working conditions. It was the Knights of Labor who provided the funds to build the Stonington town library. A monument honoring the memory of these men stands on the town dock, overlooking the islands where they worked so many years ago.

The statue romanticizes what was in reality hard dangerous work. Working with explosives, huge blocks of stone and little to no safety equipment injuries and deaths were common. There was only one doctor in town, Dr. Benjamin Lake Noyes, who set up his medical practice in Stonington in 1895.

Paddle past the Isle au Haut ferry terminal and land at the Colwell boat ramp

Colwell Boat Ramp

The Colwell boat ramp is owned jointly by the towns of Stonington and Isle au Haut. The boat ramp is located at the end of Seabreeze Avenue behind the Isle au Haut ferry terminal. During the early years of the town, this dock was the town's steamboat landing. The substantial granite pilings can still be seen.

Colwell boat ramp is one of the few places within the town of Stonington itself for the general public to land or launch a kayak. During the summer, it is difficult to find free parking along the side streets close to the ramp because of the ferry traffic. One possibility is to drop off your boats at the Colwell ramp and then drive up the hill to a private parking lot where you can park all day for a small fee.

There is a public town dock behind the Harbor View Store, the local supermarket in the center of town, but an ordinance prohibits launching a boat from the dock itself. This landing is mainly used by either commercial fishermen or by the small launches ferrying people to and from the yachts that fill the harbor during the summer months.

The Fishermen's Wharf at the south end of town is used exclusively by commercial fishermen and out of bounds for kayakers. Lobster boats are constantly loading and unloading their boats at this wharf, and paddlers should stay far away.

<u>Paddle away from the Colwell launch and head W toward the old R. T. Barter Fish Cannery</u>

The R. T. Barter Fish Cannery

Boys as young as 7-years-old often worked in the canning houses

When early explorers first sailed the waters of North America, they were astounded by the abundance of fish. In 1497, John Cabot wrote that there were so many fish on the Grand Banks that his crew didn't need hooks or nets to catch them, but could use baskets to scoop them up.

In the days before refrigeration however, it was difficult for fishermen to keep their catch from spoiling before they could get back to port. Native Americans preserved fish and other seafood by smoking it. Portuguese fishermen working North American waters as early as the 1500s salted the fish for the long voyage home. European colonists dried their catch in the sun on wooden racks, (a process known as flaking or pickled it in casks of brine.

In 1809, a French chef by the name of Nicolas Appert invented a process of preserving food by boiling it and then storing it in airtight tin containers. Food processed by Appert's method could be kept for many years. French soldiers in Napoleon's army were the first to eat food preserved by Appert's process, but it wasn't long before canned goods became extremely popular with the general public. The canning process broke the seasonal food cycle that had governed what people ate for thousands of years. Appert's method enabled anyone with a can opener to enjoy a wide variety of food whenever they wished. It wasn't long before American's were buying canned goods of all kinds, and canneries were soon being constructed all along the Maine coast to meet the demand for processed seafood.

In the early 1900s, Maine's herring canneries were the most valuable part of the United States fishing industry. These fish factories provided jobs to hundreds of men, women, and children, and helped families make it through the long winter months when fishing and farming could not be done.

In Stonington, a young man named Ralph Barter formed the local canning company. Ralph had been a young lobsterman when World War II broke out and he enlisted in the Army. He was sent to France, losing an arm in the battle of the Argonne Forest. When he returned from the war and told his family that he couldn't wait to get back to fishing, his father objected, telling him: *"A seagull can't soar with one wing, and a man can't handle a pitching boat with one hand."*[15] Ralph took his father's advice and formed the cannery, a coal company, and the Barter Lumber Company, which is still run by the family.

The cannery would blow a whistle when a boat filled with fish arrived, and the "cutters," usually small children, would run to their work-stations. Women packed the fish in tin cans and sent them down the line to the men who soldered on the lids. The cans were then labeled as sardines, and the processed fish shipped around the world.

In the early years of the 20th century, the schools of herring seemed to be a limitless resource, yet as the demand for sardines grew, the stocks were slowly declining. In efforts to increase their catch, fishermen turned to new fishing methods. Instead of waiting for the fish to enter coves and weirs where they could be netted, Maine fishermen began seeking the schools of fish in the open ocean. Specially equipped boats, called purse seiners, hauled huge nets that closed up "like a woman's purse" trapping the entire school of fish. Electronic fish finders using the sonar technology developed during World War II enabled fishermen to locate their prey deep underwater. Some of the larger operations even used planes to spot the herring schools from the air. Stretched to the breaking point, the sardine industry collapsed suddenly in the 1950s and has never recovered.

Somewhat ironically, the Barter building is now home to the Penobscot East Resource Center, a non-profit organization that works to secure a fishing future for coastal communities. Penobscot East was co-founded in 2003 by a local fisherman, Ted Ames, who pioneered the idea that fishermen's deep knowledge of their environment could play an important role in resource management decisions. In 2005, Ames was awarded the MacArthur "Genius" award, for his work in mapping fish spawning grounds over time.

Paddle across the harbor and land on Two Bush Island

Two Bush Island

Two Bush Island[16] is two small islands connected by a sandbar at low tide. The island was probably named because of the low shrubbery growing on both islands. The island occasionally boasts a flagpole proudly flying the Stars and Stripes. Two Bush is a nice place to stop if you would like to take photographs of Stonington Harbor.

Continue paddling west toward Peggy Island

---

15 *Images of America, Deer Isle and Stonington*, The Deer Isle Historical Society, Arcadia, 2004, pg. 87.
16 There is another Two Bush Island on the northwestern side of Deer Isle.

Peggy Island

Peggy Island is a small private island attached at low tide to a sandbar to the northwest side of Crotch Island. It is a private island on which the owners have built a replica of an old wooden lighthouse. The Crotch Island dock and the massive cranes used to load the granite blocks onto barges can be seen as you pass Peggy Island and paddle along the western side of Crotch Island.

<u>Paddle between Crotch Island and Moose Island</u>

Moose Island

Moose is a small island that sits just off the Stonington mainland and is connected to the town by a causeway. It has kept the same name at least since at least the 1780s. The island's original owner was the Reverend Samuel Allen, the first Baptist minister on Deer Isle. Reverend Allen purchased the island in 1819 for $25. His descendants lived on the eastern side of Moose Island and at the height of the granite boom opened up a quarry. On nearby Russ Island the owners had forbidden the miners from disturbing gravesites, but the descendants of Reverend Allen had no such scruples. When they expanded their operation into the old graveyard, they simply dug up the bodies and reburied the bones somewhere in Stonington!

Eventually, Moose Island was sold to Hiram and Clementine Robbins, who had moved there from Wreck Island around 1884. The brothers eventually sold Moose Island to the owners of the Benvenue Granite Company, which continued mining operations until the 1920s. The island is now nearly entirely owned by Billings Diesel and Marine Company which uses it as a base for their large boat building and repair business. When the *Mayflower II* needed to be repaired after re-enacting the journey of the Pilgrims crossing the Atlantic in 1620, it was towed from Plymouth to the Billings Yard to have the work done by Maine craftsmen who knew wooden boats.

The Billings Family and the Mercantile

Billings Boatyard began in 1909 The first of five schooners[17] were built by Pearl Billings, his father John and brothers Walter and Arthur at their shop on Little Deer Isle.[18] The men usually worked on the boats only during the winter months, when other employment was scarce. One of their ships, the schooner *Mercantile,* which was built in 1916, is still afloat.

The *Mercantile* spent many years as a commercial vessel, carrying cargoes of salt fish, barrel staves and firewood to towns and cities throughout New England. In 1942, nearing the end of its useful life as a transporter, the ship was purchased by Frank Swift, the founders of the Maine windjammer[19] fleet. Swift completely rebuilt the vessel and it is considered by many to be the prettiest coaster on the bay. Today the *Mercantile* takes up to twenty-nine guests on voyages along the Maine coast.

---

17 *The Enterprise*, *Mercantile*, *Progress*, *Billings Brothers* and *The Philosopher.*
18 Probably a small crew of other boat builders were employed as well.
19 The term windjammer comes from an English word "to jam" because the sales were so large that they seem to 'jam' the wind. The *Mercantile* is really a schooner, rather than a true windjammer.

It is said that Pearl Billings chose the name *Mercantile* because he saw the word lettered on a bank window. He liked the fact that the name had an even number of letters. He believed that odd numbers were unlucky. Pearl must have known what he was doing, because the old boat is still going strong, and Pearls descendants are still running their Moose Island business. Today, Billings Diesel and Marine Company are one of the largest marine facilities on the East Coast.

The Take-out

<u>Follow the Deer Isle Coastline back to Sand Beach</u>

Paddle 2: Webb Cove to the Upper Stonington Islands

Distance: Approximately 11 nm
Launch: Old Quarry Adventures, Settlement Road, Stonington, Lat/Long: 44° 10'20.4" N, 68° 38'22.8" W
Charts & Maps: Maptech Waterproof #75, NOAA #13315, Delorme Maine Atlas Map #15

The Trip

The Webb Cove Trip is a nice paddle around the islands northeast of Stonington. The trip begins at Captain Bill Baker's Old Quarry Ocean Adventures, a kayaking mecca and campground located directly on scenic Webb Cove. Some kayakers will want to stay at Captain Bill's Campground, but many of the islands along the proposed route are open to the public and allow camping.

From the launch area the paddlers will visit Hells Half Acre, a lovely little island set among Camp, Bold and Devil Islands. After stopping off at Hells Half Acre, the kayakers will pass the Shivers Islands as they head eastward to land on Saddleback Island. Turning to the south the paddlers will pass Millet and Spruce Island and paddle into the cove on the northern shore of McGlathery.

In the mid-1800s, McGlathery supported a small community of fishermen farmers who were converted to The Church of Jesus Christ of Latter-Day Saints by a wandering Mormon elder. Caught in the grip of religious fervor, many of the islanders sold all of their possessions and followed their new leader to the Holy Land to establish a Mormon colony in Palestine. Nearly half of the colonists died within a year and only a few ever made it back to their island homes in Maine.

In 1928, the three-masted schooner *Wawenock* ran ashore in dense fog on the southeast corner of McGlathery. The ship was destroyed on the rocks, but the crew and cargo were saved.

In a more pleasant event in 1929, the aviator Charles Lindberg and his bride Anne Morrow spent their honeymoon on McGlathery, safe from the prying eyes of the reporters and paparazzi of the day.

Returning to Webb Cove, paddlers can visit Round Island and then turn northwest to stop at the beach on Little Camp Island. This is a small, but beautiful little island that offers spectacular views of the Deer Isle Archipelago from its summit.

It is only a short hop from Little Camp to the protected waters of Webb Cove and the final take-out at Old Quarry.

The Launch Point: Old Quarry

Captain Bill Baker's Old Quarry Ocean Adventures Campground on Buckmaster Neck in Stonington has everything a kayaking group could desire. The campground is located directly on scenic Webb Cove. Most campsites overlook the water and there is also a three-bedroom bunkhouse available for rent. Old Quarry rents kayaks and the shop sells kayaking gear, charts, and snacks. Guide services and

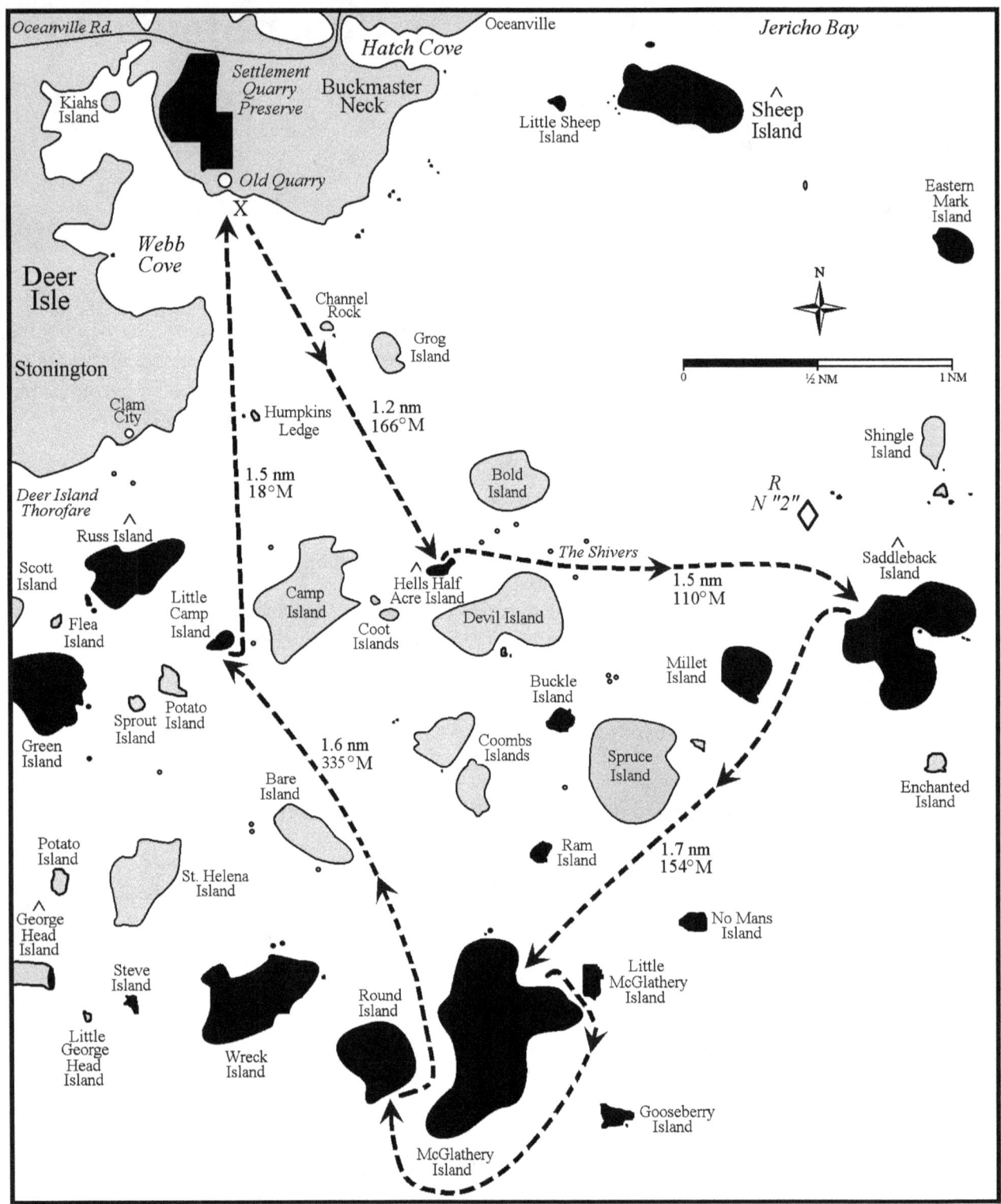

The Webb Cove Paddle Chart

Webb Cove Camping and Landing Information

ISLAND NAME	GPS COORDINATES	LATITUDE/LONGITUDE
BUCKLE (Private - owner allows access -MITA), 2 sites (northeast beach & sandbar path), avoid Spruce, 2 sites, 4 campers	44.142191, -68.610239	46° 08'31.0" N, 68° 36'39.0" W
COOMBS ISLANDS (Private), no landing	44.140679, -68.620927	44° 08'26.4" N, 68° 37'15.3" W
GEORGE HEAD (Private - restricted access), beautiful beach campsite in trees on the western shore	44.128090, -68.654502	44° 07'41.1" N, 68° 39'16.2" W
GOOSEBERRY, day use, landing south side	44.120142, -68.607473	44° 07'12.5" N, 68° 36'26.9" W
GROG (Private), no landing	44.162240, -68.625063	44° 09'44.1" N, 68° 37'30.2" W
HARBOR (Maine), 3 campsites, 18 campers. Southwest meadow 8 campers, northeast woods 8 campers, southeast point 2 campers	44.111599, -68.645046	44° 06'41.8" N, 68° 38'42.2" W
HELLS HALF ACRE (Maine), 2 site platforms, 14 campers	44.150598, -68.620157	44° 09'02.0" N, 68° 37'13.8" W
LITTLE CAMP (MCHT), day use	44.146400, -68.638704	44° 08'47.0" N, 68° 38'19.3" W
LITTLE SHEEP Good beaches for landing, 1 site, 4 campers	44.176400, -68.610056	44° 10'35.0" N, 68° 36'36.2" W
MCGLATHERY (IHT), day use, sandy beach on the east and north sides, trails	44.124520, -68.617678	44° 07'28.3" N, 68° 37'03.6" W
MILLET (IHT), beach on northwest side	44.144802, -68.596544	44° 08'41.0" N, 68° 35'47.0" W
ROUND (IHT), day use, southeast beach	44.123691, -68.625876	44° 07'25.3" N, 68° 37'33.1" W
SADDLEBACK (MCHT), campsite on the north side in the cove, avoid cabin west side	44.147875, -68.582310	44° 08'52.9" N, 68° 34'56.2" W
SHEEP (Private - access), 2 sites & 8 campers, southwest corner 6 campers northwest end 2 campers	44.176384, -68.610593	44° 10'37.0" N, 68° 36'18.0" W
SPRUCE (Private), no landing	44.140226, -68.606218	44° 08'24.8" N, 68°36'22.4" W
STEVE'S (Maine), heavy use, 10 campers		
WEBB COVE/ OLD QUARRY (private launch site), private campsite, tent sites, showers, cabins	44.172346, -68.63965	44° 10'20.4" N, 68° 38'22.8" W
WRECK (IHT), day use only, sandy beach on east side	44.126879, -68.636179	44° 04'.47" N, 68° 38'37.0" W

Note: For more information about public campsites see the Sand Beach Paddle, and the Isle au Haut Paddle.

kayak instructions are available. There is even a freshwater "practice pond" where you can practice your roll before heading out of the harbor. Non-paddlers can book a trip on Bill's excursion boat the "Nigh Duck" and go for a puffin cruise or book his boat to deliver you and your kayak to Duck Harbor Campground on Isle au Haut. Non-paddlers can hike the walking trails that wind through the Nature Conservancy park at nearby Settlement Quarry. If you are planning on camping out on the islands, for a small daily fee you can park your vehicle at Old Quarry and launch from their ramp.

To get to Old Quarry go over the Deer Isle Bridge and continue on Route 15 for approximately ten miles. Turn left by Ron's Auto onto Oceanville Road. After approximately a mile you will come to Settlement Road (Fire Road 22) on your right. Follow this dirt road to the end, past the lobster pond and straight through the granite pillars marking the beginning of the campground. Check-in at the store to pay the small launching fee.

Webb Cove

Webb Cove is a large cove on the eastern shore of Deer Isle. The village of Deer Isle borders the south shore and the Buckmaster Neck peninsula that runs along the northern shore. A good number of lobster boats are docked in the well-protected western end of the harbor where a granite wharf provides deep water access. The wharf was built to service the granite schooners when the Settlement Quarry, located on the hill above the cove, was in operation.

Webb Cove is named for Seth Webb who settled on the point of land almost directly opposite where the lobster boats are docked today. A creek flowing down from Burntland Pond would have provided him with fresh water. Despite having been captured by the Indians as a young man, Webb remained on good terms with them after he was ransomed in 1752. Although some captives were savagely mistreated, others were adopted into the tribe and this occurred in Webb's case. He eventually gave up his land on Webb Cove and moved to Kimball Island on Isle au Haut.

Paddle out of Web Cove towards the south side of Grog Island

Grog Island

It is said that Grog Island got its name for the enormous quantities of rum said to have been consumed on the island by the early settlers. During colonial days rum was used instead of cash to purchase everything from food to Indian lands. Grog, a mixture of rum, lemon or lime juice and water has had a rich nautical heritage. For more than 300 years sailors of Great Britain's Royal Navy looked forward to their daily ration of a pint of Pusser's[1] Rum to "live' en em up." The rum was said to make the foul water the ships carried more palatable, and the Navy found that lemon juice reduced scurvy.[2]

---

1 A corruption of the word "purser" who was the ships officer in charge of stores and whose duties included issuing the grog..
2 The lemons and limes added vitamin "C" to the sailor's diet, thus preventing scurvy

Colonial New England was awash in rum. The settlers had an abundance of good oak lumber and skilled coopers[3] to make barrels and pack their fish in brine, or dry their catch and like David Thurlow, sell it in the West Indies to feed the slaves laboring on the sugar cane plantations. Their ships returned to Maine with their holds full of molasses and sugar cane which they turned into rum. During the early 1800s Portland Maine imported more than three times as much sugar cane as Boston.

Some Mainers were staunch abolitionists and detested slavery, but others profited handsomely from the lucrative rum/slave trade. As Maine's state historian Earle G. Shettleworth Jr. wrote:

"Mainers were caught in a dilemma between whether they wanted to support the Union and the abolition of slavery during the Civil War, versus their own incomes."[4]

Trafficking in slaves was declared an act of piracy in 1820 and carried the death punishment, but there was little enforcement until the election of President Abraham Lincoln. When Captain Nathaniel Gordon, from Portland Maine, was captured after trading casks of rum for nine-hundred slaves, President Lincoln pressed for his execution and Gordon became the only American ever hanged for slave trading.

Paddle across the Deer Isle Thorofare heading for the north side of Bold Island

Take care when crossing the Deer Isle Thorofare. It is heavily used by Stonington lobstermen who in the past referred to kayakers as "speed bumps." Having worked as a stern-man on a lobster boat I know how hard it for a fisherman to see directly ahead once the boat gets up on a plane. Lobstermen returning to Stonington harbor are busy sorting their catch and getting their boat ready to land. They are not expecting to see kayakers in their path. Although nearly all of the lobster boats now have radar, it won't pick up a kayak floating only a few inches above the water. If it is foggy and visibility is poor it is best to issue a "Security"[5] warning call on VHF channel 16 before starting across.

As you make the crossing on a clear day you will see Sheep Island to the northeast, and Clam Island and Eastern Mark a little further to the east.

Sheep Island

Sheep Island was the first private island to be made available to members of the Maine Island Trail Association (MITA). The Maine Island Trail is a 375-mile waterway that extends from the Isle of Shoals in southern Maine, east to Machias Bay and even extending to several islands along the New Brunswick coast in Canada. The trail consists of nearly two hundred island and mainland sites available for day visits or overnight camping. If not for this association and others like it, these beautiful places would have been developed long ago and restricted to the wealthy, instead of being available for the enjoyment of the general public. There are two campsites available on Sheep Island that can accommodate up to eight campers.

---

3 Barrel makers.
4 Portland Press Herald, *Portland's torn past on slavery re-emerges* Oct 21, 2013.
5 Pronounced 'C cure ah tay."

Eastern Mark Island

Eastern Mark Island is known locally as the "Dumpling" for its irregular rounded shape. The shoals to the east of the ten-acre island are dangerous to deep-draft vessels and many vessels have run aground there. The island is heavily forested around the perimeter with some birch and fern meadows in the interior. It was purchased by the Maine Coast Heritage Trust in 2003 and is open to public access except between March 1st and September 1st. It is restricted during these dates because the island is home to the only known offshore great blue heron rookery in Penobscot Bay, and the birds need to be left undisturbed during these months.

Paddle between Camp and Bold Island and land on Hells Half Acre

There are nice beaches on both the north and south side of Hells Half Acre, and it is a good place to stop as you travel on to Saddleback.

Bold Island

The freshwater springs on Bold Island were used by mariners throughout the 1700s to refill their water kegs. The small house on the island was built by a group of musicians, who still summer there. The deep-water channel between Grog and Bold Islands is strewn with ledges, and before the Deer Isle Thorofare was clearly-marked, many vessels came to grief on these hidden rocks.

Launch your boats from Hells Half Acre and paddle past the Shivers and land on Saddleback beach

Saddleback Island

Saddleback is a 76-acre island at the far eastern end of Merchant Row. It may have had year-round settlers as early as the 1760s. James Cooper from North Haven purchased it from Anthony Merchant[6] for $200 in 1837. Cooper and his family farmed and grazed sheep on their farm, and supplemented their income by fishing. At least three family members are known to have died there. Two cellar holes and a dug well in the island's "saddle" date from this era.

According to historian Charles McLane, Saddleback Island was a popular site for plume hunting. During the late 1800s hunters, many of whom were funded by gun-manufacturing companies, hunted waterfowl solely for their feathers that were gathered and turned into fashionable hats. There is no record of year-round residents after the mid-1800s, but there may have been seasonal use by those coming to fish, graze sheep or cut timber.

An 1899 newspaper clipping refers to "highly civilized and cultivated" Indians from Pleasant Point (near Eastport) returning annually in the 1890s to make rustic furniture from the island's ash trees and sell these and other curios to summer visitors in Stonington. There are only a few ash trees on

---

[6] The son of Nathaniel Merchant

Saddleback today, but these trees may have been common at an earlier time as the island was named "Ash Island" on older charts.

In 1925, Saddleback Island was purchased by Cressy Morrison, a chemist who was president of the New York Academy of Sciences and who wrote a series of books attempting to reconcile his scientific beliefs with his strong religious views.[7]

The next recorded owner, Frederick Way, was a pilot with Eastern Airlines. He sold Saddleback in 1956 for the cost of back taxes to John Blum. Blum and his wife had passed Saddleback while cruising and picnicked on what was then the open saddle between the two coves. Blum and his large family subsequently enjoyed decades of summer adventures on the island, camping initially and eventually staying in a modest cabin they built during the 1960s. A wharf constructed in the 1980s of steel girders and granite blocks washed out twice in major storms and was not rebuilt the second time.

After enjoying the island as a family campground for many years the family donated an easement to Acadia National Park which prevented development on two-thirds of the island. When the Blum family decided to sell the island in 2004, they listed it on the open market and offers came in from across the country. Fortunately, the family valued the unspoiled character of Saddleback and wanted to see that preserved. John Blum had known the founders of MCHT for decades and the family ultimately selected MCHT over competing bidders, thus preserving the island for future generations. MCHT has improved the trail system on Saddleback and offers the old Blum cabin to its members for a modest rental fee.

In October 2014, a group of kayakers was paddling the six miles from Isle au Haut to Marshall Island. The wind was gusting over twenty knots, the seas were high, and a Canadian man got separated from his companions and landed on Saddleback. He spent a cozy night in the cabin as the Coast Guard searched the surrounding waters for him in vain and his fellow paddlers battled the elements on Marshall.

Launch your boats and paddle southwest towards Millet Island

Millet Island

How Millet Island received its name is open to question. The outline of the Island does resemble a millet seed, but perhaps it was named because some form of millet grass was growing there in past years. You can take-out at one of the two small sand beaches on the northwestern side of the island.

The local ornithologist Margaret Hundley donated Millet Island to the Nature Conservancy, and in 1997, it was transferred to the Island Heritage Trust to be forever maintained as a nature preserve.

Continue southwest, paddling along the eastern shore of Spruce Island

---

7 *Man Does Not Stand Alone* and *Seven Reasons Why a Scientist Believes in God*

Spruce Island

Spruce Island is privately owned. There seems to be little historical information available about Spruce Island. This is rather surprising considering its relatively large size. The island was briefly quarried during the late 1800s, and McLane writes about finding steel eye-bolts and a flywheel from the operation.[8]

Paddle into the cove on the northern shore of McGlathery Island and land

Although a granite shelf surrounds much of the island there are several sandy beaches on the east and west sides of McGlathery where kayakers can land.

McGlathery Island

McGlathery Island is located approximately midway between Stonington and Isle au Haut. According to McLane it may have been named after William McGlathery who traded in Penobscot island properties as early as the late 1700s.

In the 1830s the island became the home of Peter Hardy Eaton and his large family. The Eaton's farmed, fished and raised sheep on McGlathery. The Eaton's were a large family, and by the standards of the day relatively prosperous. Over the years, other families had moved to the island, and in 1840, the islanders built a schoolhouse for their numerous children.

In the mid-1800s, George and Samuel Eaton were inducted into The Church of Jesus Christ of Latter-day Saints by a wandering Mormon elder, a former British actor by the name of George Washington Adams. The Eaton's brought Adams back with them to McGlathery on their schooner *Lavinia,* where he continued his proselytizing.

Mainers have a reputation for being shrewd, practical people, but Adams must have been a truly charismatic individual. Under the spell of the former actor's words, the islanders seemed to lose their common sense. Adams convinced them to sell their possessions, and follow him to the Holy Land to establish a Mormon colony. Adams told his followers, many of whom had never been more than a few hundred miles from their homes, that they were the *"chosen ones"* selected by God to colonize Palestine and free Jerusalem from the heathens.

Adams called his movement the Palestine Emigration Association and proclaimed himself the leader of the Church of the Messiah. Joining him on the expedition would be S. L. Wass, Bishop of the Mormon church in Addison and Jonesport, and by Captain Norton of Addison, who would guide the schooner *Nellie Chapin* on their voyage from Maine to the Holy Land. In August 1866, Adams, and a hundred-fifty-six of his followers set sail for the Near East in the schooner *Nellie Chapin*.

The ship arrived safely and the small group of Maine farmers, fishermen, and tradesmen set about establishing themselves near Jaffa. Adams chose an uninhabited valley for their colony, a bleak location that the Arabs referred to as: "The place where the sword melts in the scabbard." The sandy

---
8 Mclane, pg. 242.

desert landscape that the colonists attempted to farm couldn't have been more different from the homes they had left in Maine. Unable to speak the language, unwilling to adapt to the customs of the native population, battling disease and even starvation, the small colony began to fail. At the end of the first year only seventy-six of their original party were left, the remainder having either died or returned to America.

The desperate survivors struggled on for a few months, but eventually they were forced to appeal to the American consul for aid. A New York Sun reporter, fortunately, happened to be visiting the Holy Land at the time and being told of their plight, he raised enough money to bring the destitute group back to New York City. George Washington Adams reportedly traveled across the country to California where he turned his persuasive talents to obtaining a trusted position for himself at a local bank. He then disappeared from history, but not before making off with the bank's money!

George Eaton was one of the few colonists to make it back to Maine, moving to Stonington where he established a Mormon church on the mainland. George and one of his sons drowned when their schooner floundered just off Wreck Island in a fierce December storm. They were probably less than a mile from their home on McGlathery when their ship went down.

Not everyone on McGlathery had followed George in his quixotic trip to the Holy Land, but life on the offshore islands was always precarious. A dreadful diphtheria[9] epidemic struck the Deer Isle archipelago in the late 1800s. Hitting children particularly hard, diphtheria earned the macabre name "The Strangling Angel." In 1873. Sam Judkins, the schoolmaster on McGlathery Island reported that fifteen of his eighteen pupils had died during that dreadful winter. The loss of so many of their children resulted in many early settlers leaving the island.

Lindy's Cove

In 1929, Charles Lindberg (Lucky Lindy) and his bride Anne Morrow, were on their honeymoon. Desperately trying to avoid the reporters and "paparazzi" of the day, they found a secluded cove on the northeast shore of McGlathery and anchored. Cutting down some spruce branches from the

A photograph of Charles Lindbergh and his wife

---

9 Hitting children particularly hard, diphtheria earned the macabre name "The Strangling Angel."

surrounding trees they camouflaged their boat and spent the remainder of their honeymoon safe from prying eyes. The cove is still known locally as Lindy's Cove and is often used as an anchorage by ships of the schooner fleet out of Camden.

<u>Launch your kayaks and paddle south around the eastern shore of McGlathery Island</u>

Gooseberry Island

The gooseberry (Ribes grossularia) is a green or red edible berry that can be eaten raw or baked into pies and other dishes. It is not native to America but was brought over from Europe as cuttings during colonial times. Gooseberry Island could have been named for its resemblance to the shape of the gooseberry, or perhaps the plant was found growing wild on the island.

Stan and Peg Myers, the former owners of the five-acre island originally protected it with a "forever wild" conservation easement that they granted to the Acadia National Park. Eventually they offered the island to the Maine Coast Heritage Trust at a steeply discounted price to ensure that Americans could continue to enjoy its varied shoreline, swimming cove, and the beautiful view of Isle au Haut.

To the east you will see the Southern Mark Island, the southernmost point of the triangle made by the three Mark islands. Even today, it makes a good reference point for mariners sailing between Jericho Bay and the Merchant Row passage.

Marshall Island can be seen three and a half miles away to the east and a trip to Marshall would make a nice day-trip from Web Cove.

Gooseberry is a Maine Coast Heritage Trust Preserve and offers beautiful beaches, two campsites and dock.

<u>Paddle around the southern tip of McGlathery Island</u>

Wreck of the Wawenock

In December of 1928, the three-masted schooner *Wawenock* ran ashore on the southwest corner of McGlathery Island. The ship was sailing from Sullivan Maine to New York with a cargo of granite blocks when it ran aground on aptly named Fog Island a few miles to the southeast of McGlathery. The captain, Anders Anderson, believed that the vessel would float free once the tide rose, but the crew panicked. Ignoring the captain's orders they lowered lifeboats. As one frightened sailor later wrote, *"When these granite ships go, they go fast!"*

Abandoned by his crew, Captain Anderson was forced to also leave his vessel. The abandoned ship lifted off the rocks as the tide rose but drifted onto the southeast shore of McGlathery. Pushed by the wind and waves against the shore, the *Wawenock* began to sink. Captain Anderson's grandson wrote: *"My grandfather was not a swearing man, but he told his kids that; "if he were…he would have [swore] that night!"*

The *Wawenock's* cargo of granite blocks was salvaged by a Rockland salvage boat the *Sophia*,[10] but the ship itself was declared a total loss. Local islanders quickly stripped the ship of anything of value. At low tides the keel of the *Wawenock* can still be seen lying at the bottom of the cove. Captain Anderson took command of another granite carrier and remained at sea until he was 67.

The Wreck of the Wawenock (Courtesy of the Maine Maritime Museum)

There is an extensive shell midden on the bank of McGlathery overlooking Round Island to the west. A short distance away a spring trickles down from the bank. An archaeologist once told me that the Indians would always try to camp where there were two things; water and a beautiful view. The location of this ancient Indian campsite meets both of these requirements.

In 1954, Martin Hasse, then a summer resident of South Brooksville, organized The Friends of Nature to buy McGlathery and preserve it for future generations. Its trails are now open for hiking and the beaches available to day-trippers, but there are no overnight campsites on the island

Follow the shoreline between McGlathery and Round Islands

Round Island

Forty acre Round Island was known by that name since at least Revolutionary times. At least two families lived year-round on Round Island during the 1800s, but the original settlers left-over time. The absentee owner rented the fields for livestock pasturage to farmers living on nearby McGlathery Island, and the animals stripped the island of its trees. In 1874, Round Island was sold for $3.50 to

---

10 http://blogs.mainemaritimemuseum.org/mainbrace/2012/03/a-wreck-on-mcglathery-island.

Charlotte Thurlow, the daughter-in-law of David Thurlow. It was a bargain even in those days and Charlotte immediately recouped her investment when she leased out her new property for quarrying.

Round is now owned by the Maine Heritage Trust and is part of the Maine Island Trail. Kayakers will find the best place to land is on the southeast side of Round Island facing McGlathery where there is a sandy beach. Day use is allowed, but no overnight camping, fires or pets are permitted. You will see Wreck Island to the west.

Launch your kayaks and paddle northwest

Wreck Island

One would assume that this island got its name from the sinking of some ship, but if so, the name of the boat has been lost to history. It is interesting however, to hear local fishermen pronouncing the name as "Wrack Island," possibly the island's name today is a corruption of "*wrack*," which either refers to seaweed dried onshore, or violent wreckage (in early English).

Shortly after the American Revolution the island was owned by Joseph Colby, Jr. who remembered as a child being rowed by his mother to Castine when she presented the first news of Cornwallis's surrender at Yorktown to a British officer. After reading the notice that she showed him the young Lieutenant sadly replied: "*Alas I fear the news is all too true.*" When he grew up Joseph became a sea captain and boat builder, working with his brother-in-law David Thurlow building boats on nearby Crotch Island.

Today Wreck Island is owned by the Nature Conservancy. Kayakers can land on the beach at the southeast tip. There is a trail leading to the top of the hill which offers a wonderful view of the surrounding area. Wreck Island is available for day use only.

Paddle along the northeastern shore of Bare Island

Bare Island

Bare Island is another one of the islands that David Thurlow owned at one time, and there are a few cellar holes and a well remaining on the island, It is reputed to be the final resting place of three Italian sailors who drowned in the early 1900s when their ship struck Black Horse Ledge off the eastern shore of Isle au Haut near Spoon Island. Bare Island is a private island used by the owners as a seasonal residence.

Land on Little Camp Island

The view from the top of Little Camp Island looking towards Potato Island

Little Camp Island

Little Camp Island lies a short distance off the western tip of Camp Island. There is a small sand beach on the southeastern side where kayakers can find a protected place to land. Little Camp is nearly bare of trees and the granite outcrop has been smoothed by the erosive power of wind, ice water and waves.

There is a small freshwater spring seeping from the rocks on the southern side of the island. Not a lot, but enough to support some animal life because I have seen deer and fox scat near the spring. The animals must have gotten there by swimming from one of the larger islands.

Paddling around to the north side of the island you can see a string of darker rock winding through the granite and encircling the shoreline like a necklace. Clumps of larger stones can be seen encased in the rocks. Eons ago, hot magma from deep within the earth had forced its way upward, cracking and filling the gaps in the harder granite and encasing the stones. Several large erratic boulders can also be seen from the water, dropped there by the last glacier. Little Camp Island is available for day use only and despite its name, no camping is allowed.

The Take-out

Paddle back to Webb Cove and take-out

Paddle 3: Circling Isle au Haut

Distance: 10 nm day trip to the lighthouse and return, 23 nm for full circle route
Launch: The Colwell Ramp, Stonington, Lat/Long: 44° 09'15.3" N, 68° 39'38.8" W
Charts & Maps: Maptech Waterproof #75, NOAA #13313, Delorme Maine Atlas Map #15

The Trip

Isle au Haut is one of the most spectacular islands on the Maine Coast. Paddlers will cross waters where smugglers murdered a Revenue agent, were captured, and then broken out of jail by a group of citizens disguised as women. You will visit the site where the Navy's first warship was nearly lost, and have to opportunity to taste some great chocolate candy!

Much of the island is owned by Acadia National Park and is available to the public. The camping facilities on Isle au Haut itself, however, are limited to the Duck Harbor campground. Kayakers can however, take advantage of the numerous camping opportunities available on the islands surrounding Isle au Haut, but careful planning is necessary to ensure a safe and pleasant trip.

For the Isle au Haut paddle I have proposed two routes. The first trip is a day trip from Stonington to Isle au Haut village, returning to Stonington the same day. This trip is only about 10-12 nautical miles and there are plenty of public islands along the route to break up the trip. The second route is a full twenty-five-mile circumnavigation of the island and will probably require more than a single day even for the most enthusiastic paddler.

Both routes begin at the Colwell Ramp in the town of Stonington. Paddling south out of the harbor you will pass between Green Island and Crotch Island. Continuing on a southerly heading you will paddle past the islands of the Stonington Archipelago, perhaps stopping at Harbor Island before heading for Merchant Island. From Merchant it is only a short paddle to Isle au Haut Village. To break up the paddle even more day kayakers can also stop at Nathan Island or Kimball Island as they head for the village.

Paddlers wishing to circle Isle au Haut (see The Isle au Haut Paddle Chart) will probably want to plan for a multi-day trip, and it would be a shame not to stop along the way to enjoy the spectacular views. My advice for even the most avid paddler would be to plan on camping overnight before setting out, and camp overnight for the return trip as well. Setting out in the morning will also allow you to make sure that the weather and sea conditions are favorable for your trip.

Fortunately, there are several camping options available. If you have the time to plan well ahead you may be able to stay at Duck Harbor. Doing this will cut about five miles from your trip around the island. Another option would be to contact Old Quarry and arrange to be picked up and dropped off at Duck Harbor by their boat the Neigh Duck. Another excellent option is to camp on one of the public islands around Isle au Haut such as Kimball or Burnt.

Before setting out on the circumnavigation you will need to take into consideration the tides and sea conditions. For long paddles, you will want to have the tides working in your favor. If possible, try to schedule your paddle so that you reach the exposed southern point of Isle au Haut shortly before low tide, Kayaking around the bold cliffs of Western Head and Eastern Head is best done when the tide is slack, or nearly so. In the summer months, the prevailing afternoon winds are usually from the southwest. If you time your paddle correctly, you will have the wind pushing you along on your return trip.

No matter which option you choose, once again check out the weather and the sea conditions and do not proceed if they are not in your favor. As I always told my clients:

"It's better to be on the land wishing you were on the water than to be on the water wishing you were on the land!"

One nice thing about the trip to Isle au Haut is that it is not easy to get lost. Unless there is fog the high hills of Isle au Haut can be seen from Stonington Harbor.

The Hills of Isle au Haut seen in the distance from Stonington

On the return trip, the town's blue-green water tank sitting atop the highest point in Stonington will give you an easy visual landmark to help guide you into the harbor, and the take-out at Colwell Landing.

The Launching Point – Colwell Ramp, Stonington

The Colwell Ramp is located within the town of Stonington but is a little hard to find. Travel on Route 15 to Deer Isle and continue to Stonington. As you enter the town of Stonington you will see the Methodist church on Seabreeze Avenue. Turn south on Seabreeze Avenue. From the top of the hill you can see a really special Maine scene, lobster boats bobbing at their moorings, classic sailing vessels of all kinds, and further out the hundreds of islands which dot the waters around Stonington. The hills of Isle au Haut loom in the distance to the south. Mount Chamberlain, rises 540 feet above sea level, Rocky Mountain is 511 feet, and Sawyer Mountain's summit is 486 feet above sea level.

The Stonington public launching area is located behind the Isle au Haut Boat Services building, where the *"Mattie Belle"* takes passengers and freight between Isle au Haut and Stonington several

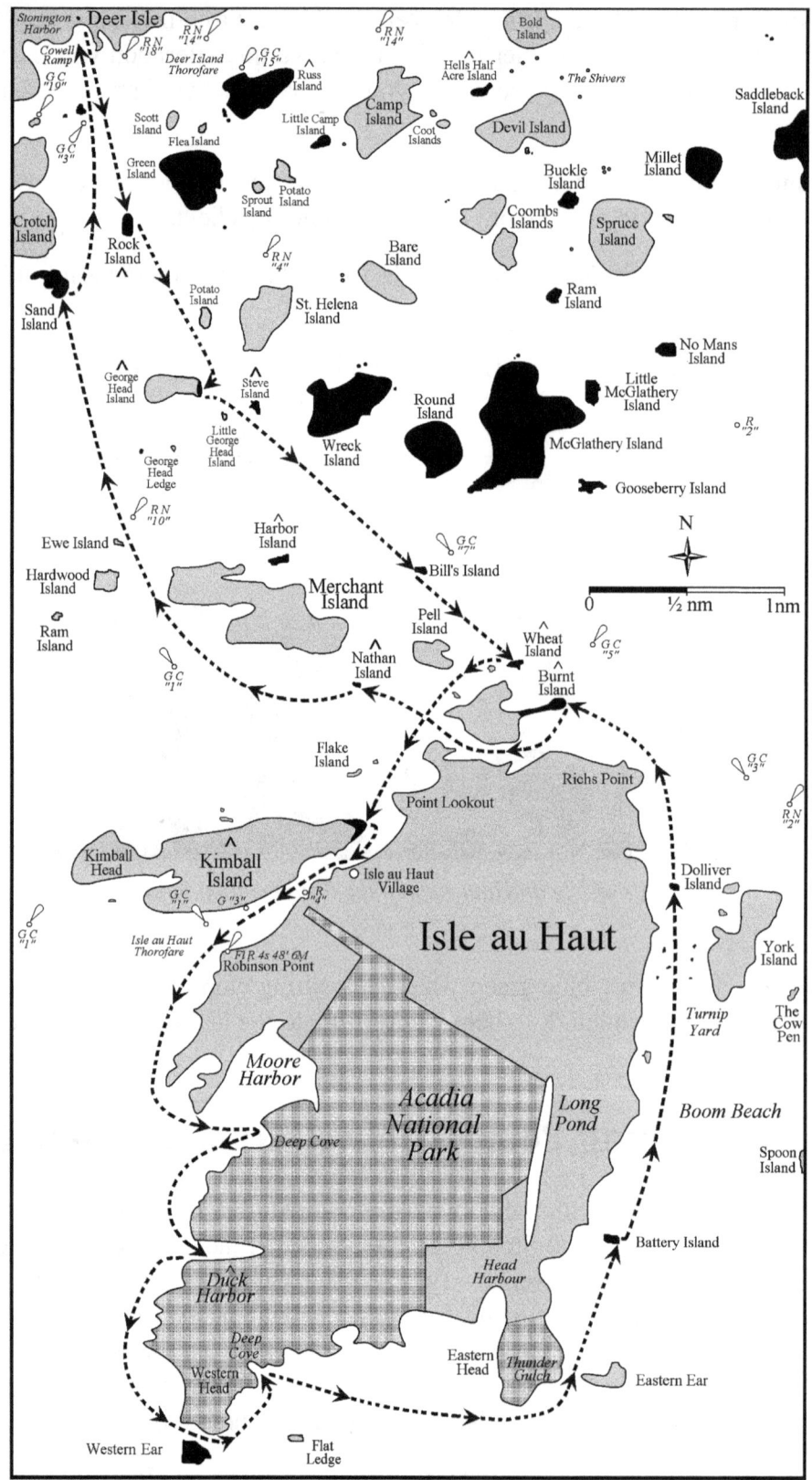

The Isle au Haut Paddle Chart

Isle au Haut Camping and Landing Information

ISLAND NAME	GPS COORDINATES	LATITUDE/LONGITUDE
BATTERY (Maine), camping, a beach on the northwest side	44.051842, -68.600098	44° 03'06.6" N, 68° 36'00.3" W
BURNT (Private but limited access), camping restricted to east arm, 2 sites, 4 campers	44.094054, -68.610766	44° 05'38.6" N, 68° 36'38.8" W
BILLS (MCHT), day use	44.107211, -68.628456	44° 06'26.0" N, 68° 37'42.4" W
DEEP COVE (Acadia), landing in the cove north of Western Head	44.014480, -68.649112	44° 00'52.1" N, 68° 38'56.8" W
DOLIVER (Maine), poor camping site, land on the southwest beach, 1 site, 4 campers	44.051742, -68.600152	44° 03'06.3" N, 68° 36'00.6" W
DUCK HARBOR (Acadia), camping (with reservations only), 5 lean-tos	44.028536, -68.652986	44° 01'42.7" N, 68° 39'10.8" W
EASTERN EAR (Private), no landing	44.013556, -68.607522	44° 00'48.8" N, 68° 36'27.1" W
HARBOR (Maine), southwest meadow, northwest woods, southeast point, 3 sites, 18 campers	44.110715, -68.645993	44° 06'38.6" N, 68° 38'45.6" W
HARDWOOD (MCHT), eagle nesting, no landing February-August	44.107849, -68.665688	44° 06'28.3" N, 68° 39'56.5" W
ISLE AU HAUT VILLAGE, day use only, landing by the town dock	44.074562, -68.636647	44° 04'28.4" N, 68° 38'11.9" W
KIMBALL (Private) limited access, camping restricted to northeast end, 2 sites, 6 campers	44.080282, -68.634350	44° 04'49.0" N, 68° 38'03.7" W
MERCHANT (Private), no landing	44.103499, -68.645593	44° 06'12.6" N, 68° 38'44.1" W
NATHAN (MCHT), pocket beach on the east side, 1 site, 4 campers	44.096459, -68.634553	44° 05'47.3" N, 68° 38'04.4" W
ROCK (MITA), heavy use and high boat traffic, multiple sites, 8 campers	44.140435, -68.659215	44° 08'25.6" N, 68° 39'33.2" W
SAND BEACH (Stonington), launch site, day use, public beach, nice swimming	44.153961, -68.689148	44° 09'14.3" N, 68° 41'20.9" W
STONINGTON TOWN DOCK (launch), Colwell Ramp (behind Isle au Haut Ferry)	44.154626, -68.660374	44° 09'15.3" N, 68°39'38.8" W
WESTERN EAR (Acadia), no passage at low tide	44.006184, -68.655079	44° 00'22.3" N, 68° 39'18.3" W
WHEAT (Maine), 2 sites & 10 campers. northwest facing Deer Isle 8 campers, southeast 2 campers,	44.098858, -68.616263	44° 05'55.9" N, 68° 36'58.5" W
YORK (Private), no landing	44.061186, -68.591336	44° 03'40.3" N, 68°35'28.8" W

Note: For more information about public campsites around Stonington see the Sand Beach Paddle and the Webb Cove Paddle.

times a day during the summer season and on a less frequent basis year-round. Residents call her the "*mail boat,*" while people from other places talk about the "*ferry.*"

You will need to unload your kayaks and park your cars either on Seabreeze or on Bayview Avenue. You can also park for a small fee behind the Greenlaw building on Indian Point Road. Public restrooms are available at the fire station next to the Hagen Dock.

Paddle south to Rock Island and land

Rock Island

The waters around the white sand beaches of Rock Island are so clear and green/blue that it reminds me of the Caribbean. I only wish the water was as warm. You can land your kayaks on the western shore of the four-acre island and follow the trail back into the woods to the campsites. During the summer months the air on the island is filled with the scent of wild rugosa roses which love the soil and line the trails. Although privately owned, Rock Island is a MITA protected island and camping is allowed for up to 8 people.[1] Unfortunately for overnight campers, it can be noisy. There can be a lot of lobster boat traffic passing the island and the scream of the granite cutters on nearby Crotch Island can also be heard across the water.

Continue paddling south passing between Rock and Crotch Islands towards Merchant Island

Use caution when traversing Merchant's Row, particularly in foggy conditions. The channel is heavily used by vessels of all sizes. The lobster boats often travel through this area wide-open. The Green "9" navigational buoy warning seamen away from Harbor Island Ledge marks the watery property boundary separating Stonington from Isle au Haut.

Merchant Island

Merchant Island is named after Anthony Merchant Sr., a master mariner who originally came from Cape Cod around 1770. Anthony was the first permanent settler in the area between Stonington and Isle au Haut. He lived on the island with his wife Abigail and their family. Other settlers soon joined them on the island and the families intermarried. Life on an island at the beginning of the 19th century may have been hard, but the islanders had their share of fun, as a bawdy song from the period attests:

Oh, the wind blew up 'bout nor'nor'east,
Blew right up on Monty's beach;
The men got drunk and the women too –
'Round the shack the pisspot flew!
Now, Sammy was a good old man,

---

[1] Campfires are allowed with a state permit, call 207-827-1880.

But he could not make his rhubarb stand;
So he took it in his hand –
Down on Merchant's Island...[2]

Merchant Island is private, but if you are planning on circumventing Isle au Haut you will pass several good island campsites, on Harbor, Wheat and Burnt Islands.

Land on Harbor Island slightly to the north of Merchant Island

Harbor Island

Harbor Island is less than two miles from Isle au Haute and would make a good camping spot if you plan on circling Isle au Haut. It is state-owned and offers three camping spots, each with their shore access points, the popular southwest meadow, the southeast point which has a small area suitable for one or two people, and a wooded eight-person site on the northeast side of the island. There is no record of anyone ever living permanently on Harbor Island, but it was used for many years by settlers on Merchant Island to graze sheep.

Continue Paddling past Bills Island

Bills Island

You will pass tiny Bills Island which was named for William Barter, an early settler. The island is now owned by the State of Maine and administered by the Maine Coast Heritage Trust. Bills Island is available for day use.

Paddle past Pell Island to Wheat Island and land

Wheat Island

Wheat is a small wooded island slightly to the north of Burnt. It is also owned by the State of Maine. The north-facing campsite has a beautiful view of the Stonington islands. The other sites are further back from the shore but are better protected.

Launch your boats and paddle southwest towards Flake Island

---

[2] www.charlieipcar.com/lyrics/merchant.htm#notes; This song is based on a fragment of the same title collected by Jennifer Puleston from fishermen in the Stonington, Maine, area in the early 1960s.

Flake Island

Flake Island is two small open islands connected at low tide. The island was probably named because it was used for drying or "flaking" fish during colonial times. The fish would be laid out on long wooden racks, dusted with salt and exposed to the sun. The strong breezes blowing across the open waters west of Flake Island would have kept down flies and made this a good spot for the drying.

Head for the north shore of Kimball Island and land

Kimball is a MITA island and the public has permission to use about 30 acres on the northeast corner. Up to six people can camp overnight, but no open fires are allowed. Campers are asked to not camp in the view of Isle au Haut and to respect the privacy of the owners who have cottages on the western portion of the island.

Paddle along the northern point of Kimball Island and turn southwest

If a swell is coming in from the open ocean to the west, you can paddle around the northeast point into the more protected waters of the Isle au Haut Thorofare. You can land at a small beach a few hundred yards from the point. A path designated by a cairn with a buoy leads across the point and through the woods to the campsite. The trail is marked by blue blazes and rock cairns.

Kimball Island

The large clam middens scattered around Kimball island shows that it was visited at least seasonally, by local Indian tribes for hundreds if not thousands of years.

Kimball Island was originally called "Little Isle au Haut" by Europeans, but the name was changed after it was bought in 1791 by Solomon Kimball. Like many islanders living in the region at the time Solomon converted to the Mormon religion and when an old man moved to California in the 1850s.[3] Kimball's descendants however, lived on the island until the late 1930s.

As mentioned earlier in the previous chapter, Paddle 2: Webb Cove to the Upper Stonington Islands, Kimball Island was originally settled by Samuel Webb, who lived there with his wife and family as early as the middle 1700s. Webb had been captured by Indians, probably sometime towards the end of King George's War, but was not ransomed until 1752. A true frontiersman, Webb lived by his skills as a hunter. It was said that Chief Joseph Orono, leader of the Penobscot tribes, would frequently visit the Webb family on their island homestead.

Unfortunately, when Samuel died of a gunshot accident, his wife was unable to provide the title of the land she and her husband had settled. Some say she was cheated out of her inheritance by the man she had entrusted to represent her. In any case, Solomon Kimball, then a well-to-do merchant farmer from near Boston was able to purchase the island in 1791 from the Commonwealth of Massachusetts

---

3 Van Doren, Harold, *An Island Sense of Home*, Penobscot Bay Press, 2012, pg. 240.

for $60. When Solomon died, his son George inherited the Kimball Island farm as well as more than 1,300 acres that his father had purchased on the southern half of Isle au Haut. With the threat of Indian attacks now long past, additional settlers moved to Kimball Island and a small community of fishermen and farmers began to establish it.

The fortunes of the Kimball Islanders waxed and waned over the next hundred and fifty years. In the 1880s Ben A. Smith established a summer boarding house for visitors and the census of 1910 shows eight people living on the island, but the last permanent resident of Kimball Island died in 1954.

Launch your boats and paddle across the Thorofare to land at Isle au Haut Village landing

Use the tall white spire of the 1857 Congregational Church as a navigational aid to guide you into the town of Isle au Haut. You can land on the beach by the town store, or proceed a little further to the south and take-out by the town dock.

Captain John T. Crowell

Kimball Island's most colorful resident was the noted Arctic explorer Captain John T. Crowell, known to his friends and shipmates as "Captain Jack," who moved with his wife Alice (Cain) from Burnt Island to Kimball after World War II. Captain Jack Crowell's adventurous maritime life as a seaman and explorer spanned for nearly fifty years. As a young man he sailed "before the mast" on one of the last square-rigged sailing vessels. During World War I, his ship was torpedoed and he spent several days on the open ocean in a lifeboat. In the 1930s Jack was aboard the schooner *Bowdoin*, exploring the area around Frobisher Bay. He had joined Donald MacMillan's ship as a mate in 1930, and eventually captained the vessel on a voyage of discovery to the Arctic.

In 1937, on one of his arctic exploration voyages his classic schooner, *The Gertrude L. Theband*[1] struck a reef in remote Frobisher Bay, and Crowell and his crew were stranded on Baffin Island. In a testament to Captain Jack's leadership skills, the men managed to repair their stove in the boat and save themselves from certain death.

In 1940, Jack and Alice were living on Burnt Island where Alice had grown up, but in 1942 they purchased land on Kimball Island where they planned to make their home. World War II began however, and Jack served as a captain in the Air Force, setting up weather stations in the Arctic.

When the war ended, the couple was finally able to complete their modest home on Kimball. They cultivated a garden and even raised a small herd of sheep. To make ends meet, Jack did a little lobstering and even built a fish weir hoping to replicate the successes of weir's that were built in

---
1 The native Inuit called the ship " The Great White-Winged Flyer."

the past. Captain Jack ruefully recalled that the *"fish were in no danger from him,"* and Alice later wrote: *"We were in the red and our bank balance was declining as rapidly as were the herring."*[2]

In 1951, Jack returned to the Arctic, taking a job as manager of one of the weather stations in Thule Greenland, and this time Alice went with him, the only white woman for hundreds of miles. In the 1960s he captained or accompanied the research vessels *Eltanin* and *Hero*, both ships that he had helped design, on several scientific voyages to the Antarctic.

Alice Crowell, his companion for so many years, died at Christmastime in 1984. Captain Jack passed away two years later, working away to the very end cutting bush and firewood on his beloved Kimball Island Farm. He was eight-eight years old at the time. An island in Frobisher Bay, a harbor in northern Labrador, and a mountain in Antarctica are named after him.

When asked by his friend Captain Jim Sharp, how he could even think about sailing into the treacherous waters of the arctic with no charts and no experience in those waters, Captain Jack replied: *"What's to stop ya?"*[3]

Jack Crowell at the wheel of the schooner Sachem, 1926[4]

---

2 Appolonio, S. (Ed.). (2010). *I Loved This Work...I have been Delightfully Busy*. pg. 137. Searsport, ME: Penobscot Books.
3 Spear, C, & Crowell, J. Penobscot Bay Press, Web exclusive, December 2010.
4 Appolonio, S. (Ed.). (2010). *I Loved This Work...I have been Delightfully Busy*. Searsport, ME: Penobscot Books.

Isle au Haut

Native American tribes visited Isle au Haut during the summer months to fish, hunt and escape the black flies of the interior woodlands. They would also collect sweet grass[4] which they used for basket making and other purposes. The Abanaki's called the island So-i-Kuk for "Shell Place."

In 1524, when Giovanni da Verrazzano first saw the lovely high hills of Isle au Haut rising above the ocean he named the island Isabeau, after one of the three young princesses then residing at the French court. They were all between fifteen and eighteen years old, celebrated for their beauty and grace. Verrazzano was the first explorer to begin naming the places he discovered after personalities and beloved spots in France. Previous explorers had generally used descriptive names such as grapes, or flatlands, much as the Indians had done.[5]

On his 1604 voyage to the Penobscot region the French explorer Samuel de Champlain however, ignored Verrazzano's name and changed it to the much less romantic "Isle au Haut," obviously because "the high island" towered above any of the others in Penobscot Bay. The distinctive outline of the Isle au Haut hills can be seen by mariners twenty miles out to sea. The name is pronounced in many different ways. Off-islanders pronounce it either "Isle-a-ho' or 'Eel-oh-ho' but island residents pronounce more like "Ile-a-holt."

In 1614, when Captain John Smith explored the area he used the Abanaki Indian name Sorico for Isle au Haut writing in his journal: *"The highest Ille is Sorico in the Bay of Punnobscot."*[6]

The first European settler on Isle au Haut was Peletiah Barter,[7] who arrived in 1792, three years after Isle au Haut had been incorporated as part of the Deer Isle Plantation. Over two centuries later, members spanning four generations of the Barter family continue to live and work on Isle au Haut.

Scottish and English settlers and fishermen continued to move onto the island and by 1800 the island supported about fifty people who survived by fishing and farming. In the early 1800s however, the prosperity of Kimball Island, and indeed the entire Northeast, was affected by President Thomas Jefferson's shipping embargo and the War of 1812.

Jefferson's Embargo and the War of 1812

In 1801, Thomas Jefferson was elected the third President of the United States of America. Two political parties dominated American politics during this period. The Republican Party, headed by Jefferson thought that America should be a self-sufficient agrarian nation. This is not surprising considering that Jefferson himself was a Virginia farmer. The Federalist Party favored manufacturing and commercial interests such as seaboard trade. Not surprisingly the Federalists were strong in the New England commercial states which relied on coastal trade. During his first term Jefferson

---

4. Explorer and Captain Jack Crowell.
5. Eckstorm, pg. 90.
6. Rich, L. (1970). *The Coast of Maine, Thomas Crowell Company*. Pg. 32.
7. McLane questions this, relying on the survey of Rufus Putnam in 1785 which lists John "Banter" to be Barter's predecessors.

supported New England shipping by having the American Navy take military action against the Barberry Pirates, but in his second term he found his administration embroiled in a long-simmering dispute with Great Britain. The Napoleonic Wars were raging throughout the European continent, and all of the belligerent nations were seizing American goods on the high seas. Desperate for experienced sailors to main their fleet, Great Britain impressed thousands of American men into the Royal Navy.

At six miles long and three miles wide, and with cliffs rising more than five hundred feet above the surging ocean, Isle au Haut is surely one of the most impressive islands on the Maine coast. For many early New England settlers Isle au Haut must have been their first sight of Penobscot Bay. What a relief it must have been for them to know that their voyage was nearing an end and that they would soon be in protected waters.

In an attempt to avoid open war with Great Britain Jefferson in 1807, Jefferson recommended that Congress impose commercial sanctions and forbid all maritime trade. He hoped that by denying the warring nations supplies that they would agree to stop seizing American goods and impressing seamen on the high seas. As a southern farmer, Jefferson's knowledge of the maritime-based trade of New Englander's was limited. Congress however, supported his decision and to discourage smuggling set up the Revenue Service to enforce the embargo and collect taxes.

The colonists struggling to establish themselves on the coast of Maine[8] were incensed. They had just overthrown their British overlords and thought that they had finally freed themselves from the harassment and tariffs that the English had imposed on them. One of the reasons for New Englanders supporting the revolution was the British Navigation Act and the Molasses Act of 1733, which granted customs officers the right to inspect any ship or any building at any time.[9] Now the islanders felt that their government was doing the same thing!

Jefferson's hope that his embargo would force the warring nations to give in to American demands was never achieved. Loopholes in the legislation greatly reduced the impact of the embargo on the warring nations and because New England merchants and shipowners did their best to evade the unpopular restrictions.

To the merchants, shipbuilders, and seamen of New England, Jefferson's embargo was nothing less than a disaster for New England. Maine was particularly hard hit because it relied on the unrestricted maritime trade of fish and timber for food. Unlike their fellow countrymen in the southern regions, the short growing season of the New England farmer made it impossible for them to grow the grains they needed to make flour. The poor were put most at risk. As the embargo took hold thousands of sailors found themselves without the hard cash they needed to purchase the items they needed to survive. Many of the islanders found themselves in real danger of starvation.

The local communities of Castin, Bucksport,[10] and Bangor first tried to convince the Federal government to change its policies. When this failed, the islanders revived the smuggling networks that they had set up to support the American cause during the revolution. The northern Maine town of

---

8 Maine was then still part of Massachusetts.
9 Duncan, R. *Coastal Maine, a Maritime History*. pg. 199.
10 Then known as Buckstown.

Eastport which abutted the Canadian border became a focal point of smuggling activity. The Federal Government brought in two warships, the *Chesapeake* and the *Wasp*, in an attempt to stop the trade but it continued unabated.

The Revenue Agents responsible for enforcing Jefferson's laws were particularly despised. Few local men took up the task of oppressing their neighbors and therefore most of the revenue agents were "from away." Particularly galling was the fact that the agents were given half the value of any cargo that they confiscated. Can you imagine the outcry today if state troopers were given half the value of any drugs they collected?

In the early 1800s, the Federal Government established a Revenue Station at Kimball Harbor,[11] and in 1808 a Revenue Agent was murdered by a group of smugglers. It is quite a story.

Murder on Isle au Haut

Sunday November 6, 1808 was a particularly dark and stormy night. Around 7:00 p.m. a group of armed men in the schooner *Peggy* sailed from Eastport into Kimball Harbor determined to take back a hundred and fifty barrels of flour that the Revenue Service had confiscated from them several weeks earlier. They knew the flour had been taken to the Revenue Station's warehouse on Isle au Haut, and they were determined to retrieve it.

The men from the *Peggy* anchored off the government dock and forced their way into the warehouse. In the ensuing fight a customs agent with the foreign-sounding name of Lazaro Bogodomovitch was fatally shot and his body unceremoniously tossed off the dock and into the sea. There was a great deal of animosity at the time against "foreigners" who took the unpopular job when "locals" wouldn't. However, two other agents managed to escape. They commandeered a small boat and immediately sailed for their headquarters in Castine to report the attack. The commander of the revenue station Josiah Hook was a faithful Republican who had been selected for political reasons. Hook had previously been involved with the construction of Fort Madison in Castine which the residents believed was built not to protect the town, but to enforce Jefferson's embargo. They were probably right.

Despite a now raging gale, Hook immediately gathered fourteen of his men and set off for Isle au Haut in the fast revenue cutter. A smaller boat with four more agents aboard followed shortly after, but the smaller craft sank in the turbulent seas and all of the Customs agents were drowned.

The smugglers had loaded up the *Peggy* with their barrels of flour and had set sail for Eastport, but before they could disappear into the night Captain Hook and his men caught up with them. After a brief fight, the men of the *Peggy* were forced to surrender and they were taken back to Castine where Hook charged them with murder. Local sentiment however, was overwhelmingly on the side of the smugglers! There seemed to be few tears shed for the unfortunate Bagodomovitch, who, the local papers wrote, *"was nothing more than a deserter from Napoleon's army."*[12]

---

11 Kimball Harbor is now known as the Isle au Haut Thorofare. I suspect that the Revenue Depot was located somewhere near Isle au Haut village.

12 Smith, J. M. *Maine History,* Maine Historical Society, Portland Maine, Volume 29, Number 1, Spring 2000, Isle au Haut Violence,

When mobs began to gather outside the Fort Madison jail where the smugglers were being held, the guards feared for their lives and Hook requested more support. The U.S. Navy dispatched the *USS Argus* to Castine, but it arrived too late.

In the early morning of December 13, 1808, a mob of local men wearing dresses and disguised as women took control of the jail and unlocked the cells. Four of the eight prisoners escaped, but Hook and a party of armed guards arrived before the remaining four smugglers could be freed. The four remaining men were put on trial, but charges against them had to be dropped when no witnesses could be found to testify against them. The government however, refused to give up. The men were retried, this time in federal court, and found guilty.

The court auctioned off the schooner *Peggy* and its cargo, splitting the proceeds between the federal government and Captain Hook! Huge fines were assessed. Andrew Webster, a Castine physician, and deputy sheriff was fined $2,500. Knowing he could never pay such a fine, and unwilling to spend the rest of his life in debtor's prison Webster somehow broke a hole in the ceiling of his cell. Using a bed cord to reach the ground he fled to Nova Scotia. The other three men were not as fortunate and died in prison.

Violence continued to grow against the despised revenue agents. In April 1809, Deer Isle's first selectman assaulted a customs officer. Newspapers predicted a Civil War if Jefferson's embargo was not repealed. Jefferson realized that his embargo had not only failed to achieve any of its objectives but was tearing the country apart and a few days before leaving office he signed the repeal order ending his ill-considered law. Tensions with Britain however, continued to grow, and eventually led to the War of 1812.

Fishing

The original setters on Isle au Haut were nearly all fishermen. In these early days the waters around the island simply teemed with fish, particularly Atlantic cod. Small fishing settlements were established on nearly every sheltered cove on the island. Head Harbor, Moore's Harbor, Duck Harbor, Rich's Cove, and Turner's Cove were used by local fishermen and occasionally by boats sailing up from Castine, or over from Deer Isle.

As David Thurlow had done in the 1820s, the men of Isle au Haut sailed as far as the West Indies with their holds full of dried fish. Their catch fed the slaves who worked in the fields of sugar cane. The New Englanders returned with their hold full of rum and molasses.

When internal combustion engines began to replace sailing vessels it became much easier for fishermen to reach the fishing grounds from ever-greater distances and the small communities scattered around Isle au Haut began to die. In the early 1800s for example Rich's Cove had three wharves and nearly a dozen boats at anchor in the harbor. Today only the homes of a few summer people remain from what was once a thriving town.

Lobstering

Before the 1850s, lobsters were caught by dipnets and relatively few fishermen bothered with them. In the 1850s however, Joe Eaton built himself a few dozen lobster traps and quickly caught enough lobsters to fill a dory![13]

In 1860, two brothers set up the W. K. Lewis Bros. Fish Factory on the thorofare. It was known locally as the "Whiz-Bang." The cannery employed more than twenty-four local men, women and children.

Canned lobsters were shipped as far away as London, but unlike fish, lobster meat spoils very easily, and even today is difficult to can reliably. Given the unsanitary canning practices of the 1860s it was a wonder that any of the lobster meat was edible when the cans were finally opened!

The factory building also served as a social center for the community. The building was the largest structure in town and the open second story of the cannery doubled as a dance hall on Saturday nights. Isle au Haut was said to have "one of the best floors in the State of Maine"

Working at the lobster cannery

By the early 1870s however, the Lewis cannery began to experience financial problems. The Wizbang was competing with many other canneries[14] in the area and there were conflicts with the local lobsterman over the prices they received for their catch. Perhaps the largest problem however, was the fact that uncontrolled fishing had severely decimated the lobster stocks. To protect the resource the State of Maine had established size limits on the lobsters and stopped the canning of lobsters during the shedder season. The Isle au Haut factory closed in 1873, the last lobster cannery in Maine closed in 1895.

---

[13] http://www.cfr.washington.edu/research.cesu/reports/J8W07080015_Final_Report.pd pg. 37.
[14] There were at least thirty in the state.

The fishermen adapted by selling live lobsters. They constructed a fleet of "wet smacks," which could carry tanks filled with more than 1,500 lobsters as far as New York City and Boston. Water could circulate freely through the compartment and keep the lobsters alive, but the boat's hull remained watertight. With a "wet smack" a lobsterman could keep his catch alive for many days, long enough to sell it in Gloucester or even Boston.

Joe Harmon was one of the first fishermen in the area to convert his boat. According to a story, Joe was hailed by a Coast Guard vessel who approached for an inspection. Fearing that his vessel wouldn't pass, Joe pulled off the fish compartment's hatch cover and yelled back: *"Are we glad to see you! We've just sprung a bad leak!"*

The captain of the Coast Guard vessel took one look at Joe's water-filled boat and in a horrified voice cried out: *"Good God man get that boat ashore as fast as you can!"* Under his breath Joe muttered: *"Just what I thought – hay shakers."*[15]

Moving the catch long distances to sell them took a lot from lobstering or fishing and profit margins were always thin. The Isle au Haut fishermen were also plagued by "off-islanders," particular men from Stonington, who fished in areas that Isle au Haut lobstermen had always considered to be their territory. The settlers felt like they were being squeezed from all sides. In 1891, a local Isle au Haut resident wrote: *"The population is small, poor and decreasing... and' the inhabitants eke out a poor living by raising a few sheep, fishing a little, farming a little, and gathering blueberries."*

Isle au Haut Village

Isle au Haut had been originally part of the Deer Isle municipality but when the island's population grew rapidly to more than eight-hundred residents in 1874, it was incorporated as an independent town. At that time the island had two schools, the "Winsome School," above the town landing, and the "East Side School" near Turners Cove. Today only about forty people live on Isle au Haut year-round with perhaps another two-hundred staying during the summer months. Most houses still don't have electricity, and Isle au Haut was the nation's last community to stop using crank-style telephones.

The village on Isle au Haut is accessible by mail boat three times a day from Stonington during the summer months, and less often during the winter. The village contains a grocery, tiny post office, one-room schoolhouse, town hall/library, a church, softball field, wharf and fire station, and Black Dinah Chocolatiers, whose candy shop is located about ½ a mile up from the town landing.

A few years ago, Kate and Steve, the owners of Black Dinah wrote a book[16] about starting a business on an isolated island. Over the years, their business had grown and they had a second store in Blue Hill. They also have a small café and serve breakfast during the summer months. My favorite of all their rich concoctions are "hedgehogs," dark chocolate covered dates with almond filling.

Paddle down the Isle au Haut Thorofare past the Lighthouse on Robinson Point

---

[15] http://dis-historicalsociety.org/blog---montys-memories-of-joe-harmon-and-the-wet-well.html.
[16] http://blackdinahchocolatiers.com.

The Robinson Point Lighthouse

Robinson Point is named for James Robinson, who came to America around 1800 from Scotland. After living in Camden for several years he moved to Isle au Haut where he owned the point and surrounding land.

The lighthouse on Robinson Point is thought by many to be the most "picture-perfect" light on the coast. The tower itself is owned by the town although the Coast Guard maintains the light. The adjacent lighthouse keepers house is operated once again as a B&B named "The Keepers House."

The forty-foot lighthouse and attached house for the lighthouse keeper were constructed in 1907 for $14,000. It was the next-to-last traditional style lighthouse built in Maine. The first keeper was Frank Holbrook, who had previously been stationed at remote Matinicus Rock. Charles Robinson had sold the land to the federal government back in 1906. When the lighthouse was automated Robinson in 1937, Charles purchased the keeper's house and for the next fifty years three generations of his family used it as a summer home.

Robinson Point Lighthouse

Linda Greenlaw known to millions of readers of "The Perfect Storm" as the captain of the fishing boat *Hannah Boden*, sister ship to the doomed vessel *Andrea Gail,* summered there as a child. Following the success of her first book, Linda continued to write about her experiences in a series of lively books,[17] one of which, *The Lobster Chronicles*, focuses on her life on Isle au Haut. Linda now owns a home overlooking the lighthouse.

In 1986, the Robinson property was purchased by Jeff and Judi Burke who converted the keeper's house into bed and breakfast inn and wrote a book[18] about their first ten years running a business on the island. Jeff wrote about the lure that Isle au Haut held over him: *"We all need an island somewhere."*

In 2012, the Burke's sold the Keeper's House Inn to Dr. Marshall Chapman who planned to continue to run the Bed & Breakfast.

The property surrounding the lighthouse is public, but the solar-powered lighthouse itself is run by the Coast Guard and off-limits to the public. Robinson's Point is steep and rocky and even in calm seas landing can be tricky. If you wish to visit, consider leaving your boats in the village, and follow the winding trail through the woods to the lighthouse which is only about a mile away.

Decision Time

You will now need to decide whether you wish to continue around the island or retrace your route and return to Stonington. Base your decision on a frank assessment of your abilities and the sea and weather conditions. The southern half of Isle au Haut is truly spectacular, but it is exposed to ocean swells and strong currents. In many places, such as Western Head, the steep cliffs and rugged coastline offer few places to take-out and ocean swells can make a landing on even the few open beaches challenging. It is also a long paddle, at least 25 nautical miles to circle the island.

Another major consideration is whether or not you have reservations at Duck Harbor Campground, the only overnight camping area on Isle au Haute. You will need an Acadia National Park pass and reservations if you wish to stay overnight at Duck Harbor. Reservations are opened up by the Park Service on January 1st, and the Duck Harbor campsites are usually quickly reserved.

If conditions are favorable and you decide to continue...

Paddle south along the western shore of Isle au Haut

Slightly over a mile past the lighthouse there is a charming little inlet between Trial Point and Moose Head named the Seal Trap.

Seal Trap

The Seal Trap is a protected spot to tuck into if you find that conditions are worsening. The water in the shallow cove is usually much warmer than the open ocean and makes it a delightful swimming hole. Some believe that the name of this narrow cove has nothing to do with seals at all, but is a

---

17 *The Lobster Chronicles, All Fisherman are Liars, Slipknot,* and *The Hungry Ocean.*
18 Burke, J. (1997). *Island Lighthouse Inn: A Chronicle.* Pilgrim Press.

corruption of the French word *ceil,* which means sky or heaven.[19] The land around the Seal Trap is privately owned but the owners generously allow limited public access.

Paddle across Moore Harbor

Moore Harbor

Moore Harbor was once a busy fishing port, and there is still a weir across the head of the harbor. If you wish to land, there is a nice beach and a road which leads north to the thorofare or south to Duck Harbor, Duck Harbor Mountain. You can also kayak east into Deep Cove where you will find protection on a rocky beach surrounded by low granite cliffs.

Continue to follow the coastline south into Duck Harbor and land

The Duck Harbor public landing for the campground is on the south side of the cove.

Duck Harbor Campground

The narrow Duck Harbor inlet was used for thousands of years by the Wabanaki Indians to trap ducks during their molting season. The Indians would wait until the eider ducks began to molt. Without their feathers the birds could not fly for several weeks. The braves would then use their canoes to drive the swimming birds into Duck Harbor where they would be either killed by women and children on the beach or snared with nets stretched across the narrow head of the harbor. The ducks would be killed by the hundreds. Most of the ducks would be smoked so they could be kept and eaten during the winter months when food was scarce.

The colonists would either shoot the ducks using special birding shotguns or suspend large nets across the surface of the water with floats. When the birds came up after diving for mussels and other crustaceans, they would become entangled in the nets and drown. The settlers hunted the ducks for food and used the feathers to make them into bedding and other purposes that could be sold.

The first permanent European settler reported living in Duck Harbor was Ebeneezer Leland who arrived not long after the Barter family in the late 1700s. Leland had originally come from Bar Harbor (then known as Eden) and had been a lieutenant during the Revolutionary War. After being discharged from the army Ebenezer was living in Brooksville near Castine,[20] but when he traveled to British controlled Castine for supplies the redcoats accused him of being a spy for the American's and had him arrested. They were all set to hang him when at the last minute his wife arrived with his discharge papers and the British were forced to let him go. Fearing for his life, he fled, to the safety of remote Isle au Haut.

---

19 Duncan, pg. 557.
20 American's would often enlist for a short time, sometimes no longer than a few months.

By 1803, he was married and had set up a modest homestead in Duck Harbor with a house, a wharf and a fish house on the south side of the Cove. He was soon joined by other families and the small community of Duck Harbor was established. The small hooked peninsula on the north side of the Ducks Harbor entrance is known locally as Eben's Head. Acadia National Park maintains a small campsite at Duck Harbor with five rustic lean-to shelters. Each site has a picnic table, and a fire ring. A water tap is also available. Day visitors are welcome.

From the campground, paths lead north to the thorofare, or south to Head Harbor. Another trail marked by orange disks leads to the top of Duck Harbor Mountain where you can look out over the entire expanse of lower Penobscot Bay.

Paddle along Western Head

As you paddle towards the western tip of Isle au Haut be sure to check the conditions before proceeding. There are several cobblestone beaches on the west shore of Isle au Haut before you reach the point where you can land if you feel challenged or need a rest. During calm conditions, it is even possible to land on Western Ear Island, which is part of Acadia National Park. As you proceed around Western Head the coastline becomes increasingly rugged with the cliffs rising more than a hundred feet above the ocean.

Paddle between Western Ear and Western Head

You will paddle past Flat Ledge where the *USS Adams* ran aground during the War of 1812.

The Wreck of the USS Adams

The *USS Adams* was the first warship constructed by the newly formed U.S. Navy. Although the ship was designed to be fast and maneuverable, the twenty-eight-foot corvette but not particularly seaworthy. Built in Brooklyn, New York, in 1798, Naval Inspectors nearly refused to take possession of the ship because they found that it was a foot shorter on one side than the other![21] Despite these shortcomings however, the *USS Adams* was pressed into service when the War of 1812 began and the British tried to blockade the New England Coast.

The captain of the *USS Adams* was Captain Charles Morris who had gained fame fighting the Barberry Pirates in North Africa. Many were like the pirates of present-day Somali, but on a far larger scale, these pirates captured thousands of ships and raided coastal towns in Italy, France Spain and Portugal, occasionally venturing as far as the British Isles, the Netherlands, and even Iceland. Men and women captured in the raids were sold in Ottoman slave markets throughout North Africa and the Middle East. Women captured in these raids were mourned by their relatives at home as if they were dead. In their swift ships powered by both sails and oars the pirates or "corsairs" as they were also known captured thousands of ships and sold over a million people into slavery.

---

21 A corvette is a fast, lightly armed warship. During the War of 1812 corvettes were smaller than frigates and larger than sloops of war.

Before the American Revolution, American shipping was protected by the treaties that the British government had negotiated with the North African states. Throughout the American Revolution however, the pirates were free to attack American shipping. When the war ended Morocco became the first nation to recognize the newly formed United States. In 1787, Morocco's Sultan Mohammed III declared that American ships would be under his protection. The Moroccan-American Treaty of Friendship is the oldest non-broken friendship treaty in our nation's history, but unfortunately not all of the pirates came from Morocco. The attacks continued until the American government agreed to pay an annual tribute to Algiers to guarantee that American shipping in the Mediterranean would not be attacked.[22]

In 1803, President Thomas Jefferson refused to continue to pay the tribute which amounted to more than 1/6th of all the U.S. Treasury income. Thus the American Navy which had been established in 1794 went to war.[23] Unfortunately, the action did not begin well for America. The *USS Philadelphia*, one of America's largest warships was captured by the Barberry Pirates when it ran aground in Tripoli Harbor.

Captain Charles Morris, a twenty-year-old midshipman was chosen by his captain, Stephen Decatur, to lead a raiding party. Morris and his men successfully boarded and destroyed the captured American warship before it could be used by the enemy. Morris was said to be the first man to storm the ship. No less a man than the British naval hero, Admiral Nelson, reportedly called the action of Morris and the sailors and marines under his command as *"the most bold and daring act of the age."* This raid and the Marine attack of Tripoli shortly after is immortalized in the third stanza in the Marine Corps Hymn which reads: *"From the Halls of Montezuma to the shores of Tripoli; we fight our country's battles on the land as on the sea."*

Following the *USS Philadelphia's* engagement, Morris was assigned to the *USS Constitution*. He was seriously wounded in sea battle when the *USS Constitution* destroyed the British frigate *Guerriere* during the War of 1812. The *USS Constitution* was often referred to as "Old Ironside" because the way that the British cannonballs seemed to bounce off her oak hull. After recovering from his wounds from this engagement Morris was promoted to Captain and was given command of the *USS Adams* as his first command.

On August 17, 1814, the *USS Adams* was on patrol off Isle au Haut when suddenly it was in a dense fog. At 6:30 a.m. the forward lookout yelled, "*Breakers*" just before the ship plowed at full speed into Flat Ledge, just off Western Head on Isle au Haut. Morris put over boats and the crew found a small cove where they could land on the eastern shore of Western Head. The British prisoners that Captain Morris had taken in a previous engagement were put ashore. Under Morris's command his crew removed guns and supplies in a desperate attempt to lighten the ship, and when the tide came in they managed to re-float her. Unfortunately for the young Captain, the ledge where the Adams struck was often called, even on fairly recent charts, "Captain Morris's Mistake."

Morris sailed his ship up the Penobscot towards Castine, hoping to find refuge under the guns of what we now call Fort Madison,[24] but the British spotted the vessel and the *HMS Rifleman* a heavily

---

22 *Milestones of American Diplomacy, Interesting Historical Notes, and Department of State History*. U.S. Department of State.
23 The First Barbary War (1801-1805).
24 It was originally named the "4 Gun Penobscot Battery," then renamed Fort Castine by the British.

armed sloop set off in pursuit with an entire British squadron of nearly 3,000 men not far behind. When the *USS Adams* finally limped into Castine Harbor and Captain Morris saw the small ill-equipped fort and the ragged group of 28 soldiers manning it, he realized that the small battery could never resist the British forces pursuing him. The commander of Fort Madison, Lt. Andrew Lewis reached the same conclusion. When the British appeared at the head of Castine Harbor Lt. Lewis fired a salvo at the enemy, but then spiked his guns blew up the powder magazine, and abandoned the fort to the British.

Morris had retreated up the Penobscot River but soon realized that his stricken vessel could not escape the British warships blocking his only escape route. He gave the order for his force of 150 sailors to transfer the ship's cannons to the shore. He was aided by Lt. Lewis and his small force of men from Fort Madison as well as a motley group of five hundred militiamen hastily assembled from Brewer. The American's managed to drag the ship's cannons up a steep hill to where Morris hoped to make a stand but to prevent the *USS Adams* from falling into enemy hands, Captain Morris was forced to blow up his ship. The *USS Adams*, already only half afloat, quickly sank to the bottom of the Penobscot River.

The Battle of Hampden was fought on September 2, 1814. Instead of sailing up the Penobscot as Lewis had probably expected, the British landed ground troops below him in Winterport and attacked by land before Captain Morris and his men could finish constructing their defenses. After a few exchanges of cannon fire, the redcoats advanced with fixed bayonets. The inexperienced citizen-soldiers of the Brewer militia broke ranks and ran for their lives. Nearly surrounded, Captain Morris was forced to spike[25] his cannons and retreat before he was overrun.

Several weeks later Captain Morris and his men finally made it back to their base in Portsmouth, New Hampshire. To the end of his days Captain Morris was enormously proud of the fact that every sailor under his command was still with him when they finally reached safety.

After lying in the mud of the Penobscot River for nearly fifty years the *USS Adams* was eventually raised. To everyone's surprise it was found that the 30" oak hull of the *USS Adams* was in remarkably good condition. The vessel was rebuilt as a steam-driven sloop and used until 1921 as a U.S. Navy training ship. The *USS Adams* made several voyages to locations as far away as Alaska and Hawaii. Quite an accomplishment for a vessel that the Navy inspectors had disparaged as having been constructed of "substandard" material with one side of the ship a foot longer than the other!"

Paddle into Deep Cove and land

Deep Cove is located just to the north of Flat Ledge. There is a cobble beach in Deep Cove where you can pull up your boats and land. A road from the beach joins the Cliff Trail and Goat Trail at this point and there are spectacular views from the Cliff Trail. Deep Cove is part of Acadia National Park.

Launch your boats and paddle east toward Head Harbor

---

[25] Spiking the Guns – An iron spike would be driven into the firing hole of the cannon, rendering it incapable of being used by the enemy until the spike was drilled out.

Head Harbor

For the early settlers on Isle au Haut, Head Harbor at the southern tip of Isle au Haut was the closest land to the best fishing grounds, and a small community grew up around the shoreline of the bay. Abiathar Smith came from Thomaston Maine and settled on the Eastern portion of the harbor around 1800. His grandson son George Smith Jr. eventually inherited his grandfather's lands on Isle au Haut. George was said to have been wounded by cannon fire at Antietam during the Civil War and it was said that he had a silver plate in his head from the wound. His hand was also seriously injured, but his friends said that his pipe fit perfectly in his deformed fist!

The Smiths were joined by the Grant family in the 1840s where they occupied land on the western side of the harbor, but they eventually purchased land on Eastern Head as well. Over the years the Grants were involved in running many enterprises including a sheep farm and a store, which supplied goods to residents and to the merchant ships that would occasionally land in the harbor.

In 1880, the Knickerbocker Ice Company set up facilities on Head Harbor. Teams of men would cut blocks of ice on nearby Long Pond, and drag them down to an ice house on the Harbor. The ice was of particularly fine quality. It was said the ice was so clear that you could cut off a two-inch-thick slab and read a newspaper through it. The company had a fleet of ice ships and barges that would take the ice down the coast. A dirt road connected the wharf to Long Pond. The old ice wharf is still visible along the shoreline.

Land your boats at the Head Harbor Preserve

The western side of the Head Harbor is the home of the Head Harbor Preserve, and the land is protected by Maine Coast Heritage Trust and open to the public for day use. Unless it is high tide you can land on the beach in front of the granite seawall.

Launch your kayaks and paddle east across Head Harbor

From the chart, Head Harbor appears to be completely open to ocean swells coming in from the south, but the inner harbor is protected to a large extent by sandbars and ledges. There are several possible landing areas around Head Harbor, one such indentation is named "Squeaker Cove," I assume because it is so narrow. Squeaker Cove is also part of Acadia.

Paddle around Eastern Head and pass between Eastern Ear and Eastern Head

As you pass Cape Anne ledge and turn North you will see a high cleft in the rock known as "Thunder Gulch." During heavy northerly seas, the waves crashing against the undercut cliffs create a sound much like the famous "Thunder Hole" in Acadia National Park in Bar Harbor.

Kayakers can paddle between Eastern Ear and Eastern Head at all tides

Acadia National Park only owns a little less than a mile of the eastern side of the Eastern Head peninsula, but not the rest of the eastern shore.

The Spoon Islands

To your northeast you will see the remote Spoon Islands. These islands are now protected bird sanctuaries and kayakers should not land on them. During calm conditions the mile and a half paddle from the shore to visit the Spoons is a great side-trip. There are few places on the coast where you can see so many kinds of waterfowl in so small an area. It is amazing to watch harlequin ducks and other seabirds bobbing about with their chicks in the pounding surf, while cormorants stand like statues with their wings outstretched drying their feathers in the wind. Great Spoon Island is owned by the Maine Dept. of Inland Fisheries and Wildlife.

Cormorant drying his wings

The name "cormorant" is derived from two Latin words that mean "sea crow," but the bird is not part of the crow family at all, in fact they occupy a rather unique place in the bird world. Unlike other sea birds, cormorants lack an oily covering on their feathers. Without this oil their feathers get wet. It helps them dive but eventually they need to dry them before they can fly again. Most other birds also have hollow bones that reduce weight and assist in flight, but once again the cormorants have adapted to their watery realm and have solid bones.

Be aware that much of the land from Merchant's Point to the eastern portions of Eastern Head is privately owned, as well as much of the eastern shore of Isle au Haut It is best to check a map of Acadia National Park before intruding.

Continue to follow the shoreline north past Sheep Thief Gulch

It seems as if a whimsical cartographer from Arizona was given free rein to indulge his naming fantasies in this area. I can understand "Halfway Rock" which roughly marks the halfway point along the eastern shore, but where in the world did the name "Sheep Thief Gulch" come from? It sounds like something out of the wild west. I have to laugh at the thought of a gang of sheep rustlers hiding near the southern entrance to Long Pond. White Horse and Black Horse Island lie to the east with Horseman Point, and the "Cow Pen," further to the north?

Land on Battery Island

Battery Island

Tiny Battery Island lies just offshore approximately three nautical miles from the tip of Eastern Head. It is not shown on most charts, but it is the first island you will come to after paddling along the eastern shore from Eastern Ear, and you can also use Pats Brook which flows out from the shore opposite the island as a landmark. The name probably refers to some fortification, but I have found no reference to Battery Island being used for much of anything. Battery Island is owned by the state of Maine and is a good spot to rest, the best landing point is on the north side of the island where there are a small cove and a pocket beach.

Launch your boats and paddle between York Island and the coast of Isle au Haut

The channel between York and Isle au Haut is named the Turnip Yard and is littered with reefs and exposed rocks. It can only be navigated in a small boat such as a kayak.

York Island

York Island was named after Captain Benjamin York who also laid claim to White Island on Eggemoggin Reach. In 1796, York sold the island for $240 to James Cooper, from Vinalhaven. In the late 1800s, York Island was used as a base for Deer Isle Fishermen from Stonington would anchor their sail driven boats in York Island Harbor to fish the waters east of Isle au Haut. Taking advantage of their location, the Conley family built a wooden pier along the west of the harbor with warehouses for bait and other fishing supplies, but with the demise of sail and the introduction of gasoline engines the harbor lost its advantage. Today York Island is privately owned and landing is discouraged.

Continue paddling and land on Doliver Island

Doliver Island

Tiny Doliver Island is located just off the northwestern point of York Island and may not be shown on all charts. Reefs nearly surround the island, but if you pick your way through the ledges there is a rocky beach on the southeast side. I have not found any information on why the island received its name. All of the other small islands surrounding York are privately owned, but Doliver is owned by the State of Maine.

Doliver Island is a rugged island with low shrubs and rough irregular rock. A small cairn on the southeast side marks a possible tent site for a small group of no more than four people. Fires are allowed but only with a state fire permit. From the top of Doliver Island there are beautiful views of Isle au Haut to the west and Marshall Island to the northeast.

Launch your boats and follow the shoreline north past Rich's Point and Old Cove

Both of these small coves were used by fishermen during the late 1800s.

Continue paddling around Rich's Point and turn northwest

You will see Burnt Island ahead of you and might decide to land there to rest and plan your return trip back to Stonington.

In the afternoon, the seas around Isle au Haut often build from the southwest. If conditions are questionable you can take advantage of the protection offered by Merchant Island and paddle back on its easterly side, retracing your route back to the launch point. If sea conditions are favorable you can kayak along the western side of Merchant Island between Merchant Island and Nathan, For this book, we will choose the western path.

Land on the eastern tip of Burnt Island (Pond Point)

Burnt Island

Burnt Island obviously, got its name from the land being burnt-over in some long-ago fire. The burning must have taken place before the Revolutionary War because the island is named Burnt on very early maps of the area.

Anthony Merchant, was the first formal owner of the island, purchasing it around 1800 from the Commonwealth of Massachusetts. Henry and Miriam Barter moved to Burnt shortly thereafter and lived out their lives there. During the mining boom of the 1880s an iron mine was dug south of the westernmost tip of the island. In 1890, Burnt Island was sold to Charles C. Beaman, one of the founders of the Point Lookout colony on Isle au Haut.

Beaman encouraged Captain Cain to move from Isle au Haut to Burnt Island and act as a caretaker. Captain Cain, farmed the land and sold his produce to the summer "rusticators" living at the Point Lookout colony. In the family were two girls and two boys. Like their father, the two boys became master mariners, both dying at sea, the youngest during World War I, and the older during World War II, when his ship was torpedoed off the coast of Florida.

Captain Cain's youngest daughter Alice, married the renowned Arctic explorer, Captain Jack Crowell in 1926. Even after her marriage however, Alice returned to Burnt Island regularly and the couple lived on Burnt Island during the 1930s. In 1947, Alice organized a Golden Wedding Anniversary on the island for her friend Mary Beaman Holmes, who had inherited the island from her father. Hundreds of guests were ferried out to Burnt and entertained by a jazz band brought in by boat just for the celebration!

The Cain's old farmhouse still stands and is used for a summer home by the descendants of the Holmes family. It is said that the bath fixtures in the house were taken from the Boston home of the renowned Supreme Court Justice Oliver Wendel Holmes (often called the Great Dissenter). The fixtures were saved by Mary Homes and taken to the island by relatives of the renowned jurist shortly before the judge's house was demolished in the 1930s.

Burnt Island was used primarily for farming and as a base for fishermen, but during the late 1800s a mining "boom" swept Maine, and an iron mine started up on the northwest tip of the island. Like so many others, it only lasted a short time.

The current owners permit MITA members to camp on Pond Point, the eastern arm of Burnt Island. There are now several private homes on the rest of the island and it is therefore off-limits. The best landing sites by Pond Point are either on the north or south sides of the seawall. Burnt Island is an excellent choice for paddlers planning on camping overnight and circumnavigating Isle au Haut the following day.

Launch your boats and paddle along the Burnt Thorofare passing Point Lookout on the northern shore of Isle au Haut

I have to admit that my introduction to Point Lookout wasn't the most welcoming. I had paddled over from Merchant Island in thick fog, and as I neared the shore I spotted a large dock and several buildings in the distance. As I got closer I saw a man sitting in the stern of a large motor yacht anchored near the dock. I paddled over and called up to him: *"I know where I came from and I know where I want to go… but I'm not sure exactly where I am."*

The man looked down at me disdainfully and then finally replied:

"Well, you dammed well shouldn't be here!"

After my first flush of embarrassment and anger had passed, the lines of an old prayer came into my mind and I began to laugh despite myself.

> *Lord we thank thee for thy Grace*
> *that has brought us to this pleasant place.*
> *And Lord most earnestly we pray*
> *please keep other folks far away.*

This turned out to be my introduction to the exclusive summer community of Point Lookout.

Point Lookout

Point Lookout was established by Ernest Bowditch, an MIT trained landscape architect who was the grandson of Nathaniel Bowditch, who was revered by seamen as the author of the "American Practical Navigator" which he published in 1802. Nathaniel's book became the standard navigational manual used by generations of mariners and Bowditch is credited as the founder of modern marine navigation. Naval officers in the age of sail referred to the book as "the immaculate Bowditch."

Nathaniel went on to translate the works of other seminal scientific thinkers of his time and contribute many mathematical papers of his own. In 1804, Bowditch became the first certified insurance actuary in the United States

In 1879, Ernest Bowditch and his friend Albert Otis were returning from Bar Harbor and visited Isle au Haut. Ernest returned two years later for a longer stay and liked the island even more than the first time he saw it. With several other business partners he formed the Point Lookout Improvement Company which purchased a large tract of land on the on Isle au Haut. Being related to such an illustrious figure undoubtedly helped Ernest in his dealings with the Isle au Haut natives. Bowditch built a dock for his guests and developed plans for a large summer community. As time went on Ernest purchased additional land on the island, and with interested wealthy friends formed an exclusive men's fishing club with the following rules strictly enforced: *"No women, no children, no dogs!"*

Members of the club traveled from Stonington to Isle au Haut on their private steamer which docked at the point. The Point Lookout community consisted of some of the Northeast's most influential government and business leaders. Chief Supreme Court Justice Harlan F. Stone for example, was staying at Point Lookout during the final days of the "Sacco and Vanzetti" case in 1927.

The club had its farm by Moore's Harbor which provided the summer people with fresh fruits and vegetables. Members of the Turner family worked as carpenters to build the cottages, and island women took jobs as maids, cooks, and laundresses. Boys on Isle au Haut were raised by their fathers to be fishermen, girls to be fisherman's wives. To earn extra money however, many island men took side jobs at Point Lookout, building and maintaining the cabins and helping out. The community also ran a farm by Moore's Harbor which provided fresh fruits and vegetables. Island women and their daughters took jobs at the Point as maids, cooks, and laundresses.

Despite the obvious hardships of island life, the residents developed close bonds, helping one another when times were rough and celebrating together when times were good. Weekend dances were frequent. One of the older residents of Isle au Haut recalls:

"We used to go down after the dances, and he [Archie Hutchinson] used to play the squeeze – he'd play any instrument you stuck in his hands, but he was really good at the squeezebox. You squeeze this way and you pour the rum in that way, and you just keep going all night. We'd go down after the dances because we had dances all the time, used to put on musicals and everything. And it was Great!"

During the late 19th and early 20th centuries Bowditch and his partners continued to purchase large tracts of land on the southern and central portions of Isle au Haut for practically nothing. They sold building lots to friends but also set aside much of the land as a buffer zone. This land eventually came to be used for conservation and recreational purposes.

Ernest died in 1919 and in 1943 his relatives donated much of his property to the National Park Service to become part of Acadia National Park. As you can see from our chart nearly two-thirds of Isle au Haut is now owned by Acadia National Park.

Turn northwest and paddle towards Nathan Island as you leave the Burnt Thorofare

Nathan Island

Nathan Island was probably named after the rather disreputable Nathanial Merchant who was living on nearby Merchant island in the late 1700s and whose family owned the island during the 1800s. Merchant itself is less than 4 acres but a beautiful shell beach forms on the east end and extends nearly over to Little Nathan Island. During low tide you can wade across to Little Nathan Island, which is nothing more than a ledge with a tiny piece of grass in its center. Like most state-owned islands camping is permitted on Nathan Island.

Launch your kayaks and paddle along the western side of Merchant Island passing between Hardwood Island and the Northern Tip of Merchant Island

Hardwood, Ewe, and Ram Island

Hardwood, Ewe and Ram Island are clustered around the northern end of Merchant. Although these islands were too small for anyone to live on permanently, as the names suggest they were used by the farmers on Merchant to graze flocks of sheep. Hardwood is owned by the State of Maine. The eagle's nest on Hardwood is said to be the most productive nest in the state and the nest site is part of Maine's Eagle Habitat Protection Program. Kayakers should not land between February and August.

Paddle due north from the westerly tip of Merchant Island

Stonington Harbor from Green Point on a quiet Sunday morning

Stonington Harbor

The due north heading will take you directly into Stonington Harbor.

You will see the gray building that houses the Stonington Opera House Arts building overlooking the shoreline as you get closer. The land for the building was purchased by Dr. Noyes for $1,500. The good doctor, whose home was right down the street transferred it to the newly organized Stonington Opera Company.[26] The building was rebuilt in 1912 and is now on the National Register of Historic Places. It is currently run by a group called Opera House Arts which offers films, live performances, dancing theater and music in a cozy informal setting. If you are staying in the Stonington area it is a great place to go after paddling around the islands.

Relationships between the lobsterman and kayakers have improved from years ago when we were referred to disdainfully as "speed bumps," but the lobstermen are doing their best to make a living and it is best to stay out of their way. The same is true for Billings Marine on Bear Island, the next cove to the South. This is a very active boatyard in the summer and kayakers should stay well clear.

Continue to paddle east along the shore to the Cowell Boat Launch

The Take-out

Return to Stonington Harbor and take-out at the Cowell Boat Launch.

---

[26] *Images of America*, pg. 93.

Paddle 4: Circling Little Deer Isle

Distance: Approximately 10 nm
Launch: Causeway Beach, Lat/Long: 44° 09'15.3" N, 68° 39'38.8" W
Charts & Maps: NOAA #13309, Maptech #75, Waterproof #104, Delorme Maine Atlas Map #15

The Trip

This day trip begins at the Causeway Beach on Deer Isle, circles Little Deer Isle and ends at Scott's Landing beach on Deer Isle. The trip was designed to be a gentle paddle in protected waters, however, the usual cautions for weather/sea conditions of course still apply.

Kayakers will launch their boats from Causeway Beach on the northern tip of Deer Isle. Depending on the tide, paddlers may enter Chickadee Cove on Carney Island. At low tide the hulls of old fishing schooners can still be seen in the sand. Carney Island is where the first settler on Deer Isle lived in peace with their Indian neighbors. Pushing off the kayakers will pass Harbor Farm on the shore of Little Deer Isle. Harbor Farm is one of the oldest farmhouses on Little Deer Isle. It is where the artist Leonard Baskin built a small summer cabin and where a local fisherman's lobster boat returned to its home cove after its owner was lost at sea.

The kayakers will then paddle along the southeastern coastline of Little Deer Isle, passing Bar, Eaton and the Scott Islands. The Scott Islands are wherein Robert McCloskey's book *"A Time of Wonder"* the little girl "Sal" lost her tooth, found an Indian shell heap, and ate clam chowder for lunch.

After landing on Sheep Island, the paddlers will explore Blastow and Swains Cove on the southwestern shore of Little Deer Isle. At one time both of these small coves were the home of thriving fishing communities. Passing Birch Island at the western tip of Little Deer Isle, the kayakers will circle historic Pumpkin Island Lighthouse. The original lightkeeper had lost his leg during the civil war and was given the position in compensation for his injuries.

After landing at Eggemoggin on the northern tip of Little Deer Isle, the trip continues along Eggemoggin Reach. The kayakers will pass Pine Hill, the highest point on Little Deer Isle, and then paddle under the magnificent Deer Isle/ Sedgewick Bridge,

After entering Sally's Cove, kayakers will paddle past Stave Island to the northern end of Deer Isle and beach at the Scott Island Preserve, the site of an ancient Indian village, the town ferry, the first store on the island, and in later years, a thriving farm. It was here, at the turn of the last century, that a young Deer Isle man went from helping his father on the ferryboat to becoming a member of the America's Cup racing crew.

The take-out point is on the public beach at the end of Ferry Landing Road in Deer Isle. From there, a short walk will take paddlers back to Causeway Beach to pick up their vehicles.

The Launch Site at Causeway Beach

Launch your boats from Causeway Beach, (named for its location at the eastern end of the Deer Isle Causeway), the raised roadway constructed in 1927 to connect Little Deer Isle to the larger island

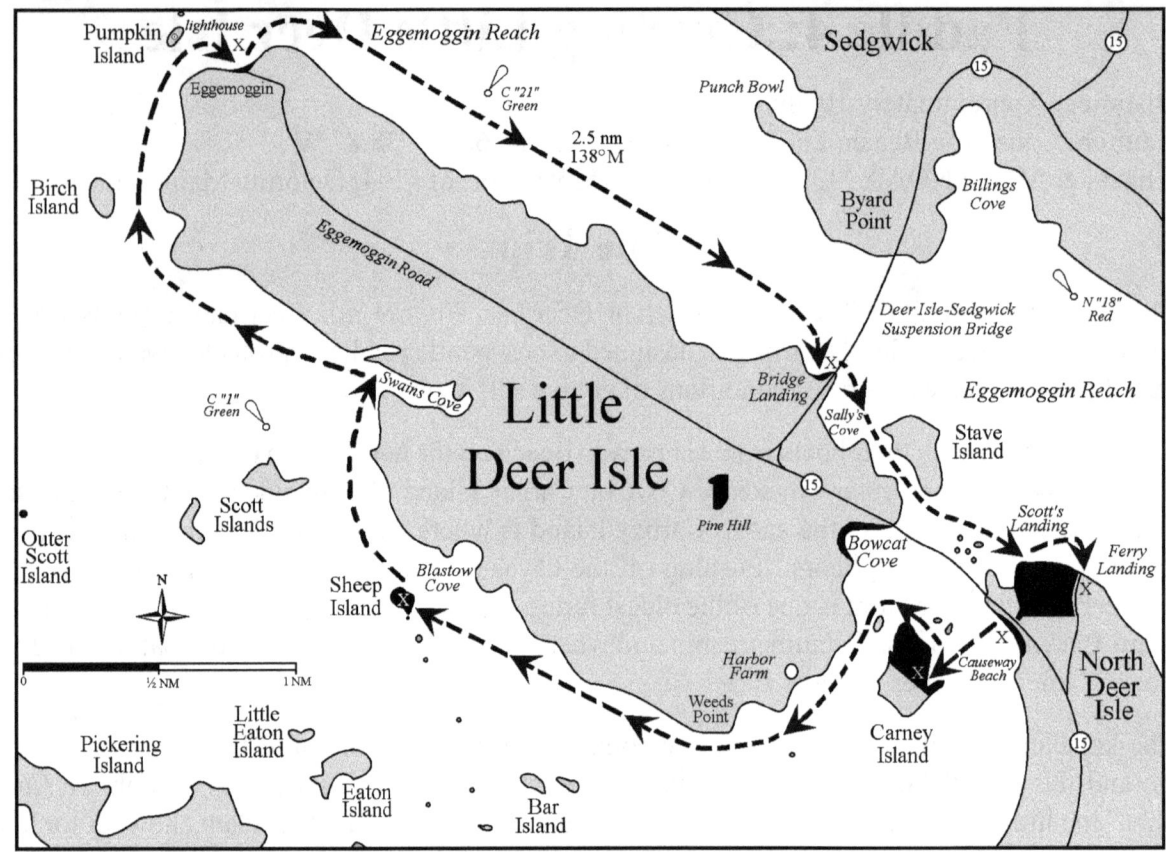

The Circling Little Deer Isle Paddle Chart

Little Deer Isle Camping and Landing Information

ISLAND NAME	GPS COORDINATES	LATITUDE/LONGITUDE
BIRCH (Private), no landing	44.300110, -68.747912	44° 18'00.4" N, 68° 44'52.5" W
BRIDGE LANDING (Town Landing), dock and boat ramp, beach to east	44.290395, -68.692430	44° 17'25.4" N, 68° 41'32.8" W
CARNEY (South end Private, North IHT), eagles nesting site; no landing March-July	44.273507, -68.684285	44° 16'24.6" N, 68° 41'03.4" W
CAUSEWAY BEACH (MCHT), launch, nice sandy beach	44.154253, -68.660786	44° 09'15.3" N, 68° 39'38.8" W
EGGEMOGGIN (Municipal), landing, beach opposite Pumpkin	44.307214, -68.738338	44° 18'26.0" N, 68° 44'18.0" W
FERRY LANDING (Municipal), take-out at beach - walk up road	44.279289, -68.671365	44° 16'45.4" N, 68° 40'16.9" W
SHEEP (IHT), day use	44.278133, -68.724340	44° 16'41.3" N, 68° 43'27.6" W
PUMPKIN (Private), no landing	44.308834, -68.742740	44° 18'31.8" N, 68° 44'33.9" W
SCOTT ISLAND (Outer Scott-IHT), day use	44.282398, -68.741999	44° 16'56.6" N, 68° 44'31.2" W
STAVE (Private), no landing	44.288581, -68.686198	44° 17'18.9" N, 68° 41'10.3" W
SCOTT'S LANDING (IHT)	44.279244, -68.676762	44° 16'45.3" N, 68° 40'36.3" W

of Deer Isle. There is plenty of parking just off the beach, and it is only a short distance to the water. The beach itself is level and the bottom is sandy. Even if you have to wade out a little way during low tide, you won't end up covered in mud. Paddlers can safely drive a car onto the upper part of the beach to park, but unless you have four-wheel drive stay on the firm sand and well away from the water. Causeway Beach is open to the public and maintained by the Island Heritage Trust.

Launch your kayaks from Causeway Beach and paddle southwest into Chickadee Cove on Carney Island

Causeway Beach from Deer Isle at low tide looking towards Bowcat Cove, Little Deer Isle in the background and Carney Island is to the left

Carney Island

Carney Island is named after Michael Carney, one of Deer Isle's earliest known settlers, Michael lived on North Deer Isle around 1762.[1] Local historian Bill Haviland states that the cellar hole to his cabin could still be seen in 2004 about 200 feet from the shore overlooking the island that bears his name. When William Eaton settled in what would become Scott's landing, he purchased Carney's first homestead along with other lands along the west shore of Deer Isle. After a few years however, the Eaton's sold Carney and some additional land to the Lowe family who set up a farm to the east of Scott's Landing.[2]

---
1 Haviland, W. (October 28,2006). *History of Carney Island Explored,* Island Advantages.
2 The Lowes farmhouse still exists as a B & B (The Inn at Ferry Landing).

Having sold his first cabin, Michael Carney moved across the cove to Carney Island. It was a good location for a small homestead. Carney Island had a freshwater spring near the center of the island, and the fishing was excellent. Every year native tribes would construct a huge fish weir between Deer Isla and Little Deer Isle, and spend the summer fishing, hunting and clamming. Michael Carney must have been on friendly terms with them.

Chickadee Cove is a small inlet on Carney facing Causeway Beach. At low tide the entrance to the cove is blocked by a sandbar, but it is possible to land a kayak on the sandy beach and walk across the

*Planking and ribs of old fishing vessels in Chickadee Cove
Deer Isle and Causeway Beach in distance*

raised bar and into the cove.

According to local historian William Haviland, an ancient gravestone or marker was once unearthed on Carney Island by men cutting timber in 1950. The stone was reportedly covered in a strange language which some said resembled Norse runes. A new wave of interest in the marker arose when a Norse coin was discovered a few miles away at Naskeag Point in Brooklin Maine. Haviland wrote[3] that he had searched the island looking for the stone but the spruce trees had grown up since the island had been logged, and he failed to find it. I also spent many hours searching in vain for it.

When the tide goes out most of Chickadee Cove is dry sand. Fishermen used to ground-out their vessels in the cove so that they could be repaired. Looking down into the clear water of the cove you can see old timbers sticking out of the mud. These might be from the *Elia*, a large centerboard sloop that was rebuilt at Chickadee Cove by Eugene Hardy of Little Deer Isle. Hardy must have been a slow

---

3 *The Island Advantage, History of Carney Island Explored,* Haviland, October 27, 2005.

boat builder, by the time that he had completed his repair work, the boat was so mired in the mud that it couldn't be moved!

Another vessel, the *Grace and Alice*, suffered a similar fate. The 52' schooner was sailed into the cove at high tide to be repaired but was eventually abandoned. Burt Leach, a local lobsterman, told me that as a young boy in the early 1960s he and his friends would row over to the island to play on these half-submerged vessels. Today there is nothing left of either of these boats except some planking sunk in the mud.

The northern portion of Carney Island is owned by the Maine Island Heritage Trust and maintained as a bird sanctuary. There is an eagle's nest on the shore slightly to the west of Chickadee Cove and paddlers are asked to avoid this area during the spring breeding season. Birdwatchers often park on Causeway Beach and use high powered telescopes to watch the fledglings and this is the best way to view the chicks. The southern half of the island is privately owned.

Paddle out of Chickadee Cove and turn northwest heading towards Little Deer Isle and Bowcat Cove

Bowcat Cove

The shallow waterway between the Causeway, Carney Island and Little Deer Isle is known as Bowcat (Bo-Cat) Cove. In April 1859, nearly seventy years before the Deer Isle Causeway was constructed, a small converted whaling vessel The *Bowcat* went aground as it tried to cross through the shallow channel separating Deer Isle and Little Deer Isle during a storm. The ship was carrying a load of wooden hoops (used in barrel making), from Northwest Harbor on Deer Isle to a cooper's shop in Brooklin, only a few miles up Eggemoggin Reach. The captain misjudged his position in a storm and the *Bowcat* fetched up on the mudflats just east of Little Deer Isle.

When the storm eased, the *Bowcat* was repaired and attempts were made to re-float her. Two teams of oxen were brought in to pull the ship out of the mud, but the harder they pulled, the more the oxen sunk into the soft sand. Finally, one of the teamsters who had worked on the salt-marshes with his team of oxen took a few boards out of the vessel and tied them to the oxen's feet, creating something like a snowshoe. This worked and the *Bowcat* was finally able to be hauled out of the mud and into deeper water where she could be re-floated at high tide.

The water in the cove is a light green color from the white clamshell bottom. The spring itself is a few feet up from the beach and lined with old cedar boards. For many years an old ornately patterned cast iron plate jutted out of the ground next to the spring, probably all that was left of the old clam stove.

As you paddle along between Little Deer and Carney Island you can see a few small caves cut by ice and water into the northwest side of Carney. These are on a much smaller scale than the caves on Mount Desert Island, but it is interesting to see the same process of creation and destruction at work. About twenty years ago, the ceiling of the largest cave at the end of the point collapsed, leaving a cleft in the rock wall.

Clammers

The mud-flats that held the *Bowcat*, is one of the best clamming grounds in the area. For thousands of years the Wabanaki Indians dug clams and harvested oysters from the tidal mud-flats surrounding Deer Isle. Penobscot legends tell that the Indians were taught clamming from their demi-god/teacher Glooskap and his faithful dog. The story tells that Glooskap and his animal companion were on a long journey and had run out of food. Seeing that his master was hungry, the dog went down to the water and dug in the earth with his two front paws, coming up with a fat clam and laying it at Glooskap's feet.

At the turn of the tide you will often see clammers working the clam flats at Bowcat Cove and Causeway Beach. They look for a small hole in the mud where the clam has buried itself. As they walk along they will sometimes see water out of holes as the sense the footsteps and try to bury themselves deeper into the mud. The squirting gives these types of soft-shelled clams the colorful local name "piss clams."

Most clammers use a stubby rake with anywhere from three to five six-inch tines to dig out the clams, but a few old-timers simply reach down the small hole with their fingers and pull them out! You can buy commercial clam rakes, but the best ones are made out of pitchforks. The clammers saw off the handle leaving a six-inch sub, and then heat the pitchfork tines and bend them over at a 90-degree angle. The rake or clam hoe as it is also called is pressed into the mud a few inches above the hole because you want to avoid the steel tines breaking the clamshell. The handle is pushed down, so the forks lift up. The device acts as a lever, prying up the earth rather than digging at it. The clammers cut a two-inch measuring notch on the handle of the rake so that they can be sure that they are not taking undersized clams.

On the Little Deer Isle side of Bowcat Cove there is a small cove with a unique white clamshell beach a few hundred yards from the western entrance of the causeway. A spring comes out of the cliff a few yards up from the water. Early settlers used to steam open the clams right on the beach, throwing the shells into the water after the clams had been shucked. The clams could then be dried, which is what the Indians did or stored in brine.

<u>Paddle westward toward the Little Deer Isle shoreline</u>

Harbor Farm

As you leave Bowcat Cove heading southwest, you will pass a large white colonial home on the shoreline. This is Harbor Farm, one of the oldest homesteads on Little Deer Isle. (see the Circling Deer Isle Paddle).

Men cleaning mackerel in Harbor Farm cove 1891 (photo courtesy Dick McWilliams)

The property was originally owned by Benjamin Weed, but in 1810 he swapped the land he was farming on Little Deer Isle for property[4] along Fish Creek on Deer Isle, owned by Captain William Hardy. The Hardy family constructed a cape-cod style farmhouse on their new property. They farmed, fished, and built a small schooner on the beach below their farmhouse. After several generations, the Hardys sold their farm to Captain William Blastow, who in turn sold it to Grace Riblet in the early 20th century. Riblet ran a small summer colony on the land for her friends and acquaintances from Boston and New York.

In the 1960s, Harbor Farm was purchased by Leonard Baskin, a prolific artist who worked in a variety of mediums but considered himself primarily a sculptor. Baskin is perhaps best known for his bas-relief for the Franklin Delano Roosevelt Memorial in Washington D.C., and a bronze statue of a seated figure, erected in 1994 for the Holocaust Memorial in Ann Arbor Michigan.

Baskin spent most of his time working and teaching in New England, but he did spend nine years in England, living with his good friend, the poet Ted Hughes. Baskin illustrated Hughes's book of poems, "Crow." Ted Hughes was married to the writer Sylvia Plath, author of "The Bell Jar." In her work, "The Colossus and Other Poems," Plath dedicated the poem Sculptor to Baskin. Baskin worked in a small artist studio a short distance from the main farmhouse, but today the simple cabin has been demolished.

In 1985, Harbor Farm was purchased by the McWilliams family who expanded the old farmhouse. Bruce McWilliams was a former executive of the DeLorean Motor Company, which sold a unique stainless steel-bodied automobile. Their son, Richard McWilliams and his mother "Jimmy" opened the Harbor Farm Store just before the Causeway. The store sold Christmas wreaths, hand-painted tiles,

---

4   Portions of this older structure still exist within the framework of the present home, which has been expanded and renovated.

and a variety of other goods. After the store closed, the McWilliams family hosted weddings at their beautiful shoreline home. The property is now a private home.

Continue paddling along the Little Deer Isle shoreline

Paddling past the farmhouse you will pass Weeds Point Cemetery which sits high on a rocky bluff overlooking the bay on Little Deer Isle. John Weed and several other Revolutionary War soldiers are buried at this beautiful location. It is because of the cemetery, not on account of turbulent waters, that this location is named "Graveyard Point" on some charts.

Weed Point Cemetery looking toward the southern tip of Carney Island

There is a lovely sand beach beyond the graveyard with a memorial marker for Byron Gross, a local lobsterman who was recently lost at sea. It seems like every fear years a lobsterman from the area dies on the water. The old Irish lament: *"Those who do not fear the sea are soon drowned, but we do fear it and are only drowned once in a while."* It seems to tragically hold true far too often.

A bronze plaque marks the point where Byron's empty lobster boat fetched up on the shore less than a half-mile from his house, almost as though it was trying to get back home. Friends and relatives leave shells and small remembrances at the rock where Byron's boat finally beached itself, almost as though it wanted to show Byron the way back home.

Paddle around Weed Point on Little Deer Isle and head toward Bar Island

Bar Island

Bar Island is two islands connected by a sandbar that can be paddled over at high tide. There is a summer cottage on the easternmost island, and both islands are privately owned.

Continue northwest past Eaton Island and land on the eastern shore of Sheep Island

Sheep Island

There are so many Sheep Islands on the Maine coast that it is difficult to keep track of them all. Farmers would take their flock out to the islands on boats, and then leave them to graze throughout the summer. Once on the island the sheep were safe from predators. Unlike other livestock, sheep need little water and will thrive as long as there is enough vegetation for them to eat. In the fall, the farmers would often pay schoolboys to help get their flock off the islands again before winter set in. It must have been quite a sight to see!

Sheep Island is now owned by the Island Heritage Trust and is open for day visits, but landing can be challenging. On the eastern shore there is a pocket beach that is accessible during most tides. A large white boulder just to the north of the beach marks the spot. There is also a landing place on the northeastern side of the island facing Swains Cove.

Land on the eastern beach

There is a path leading up from the beach to the top of the island. Looking eastward you will have a beautiful view of Penobscot Bay.

There is a large birds nest on a ledge of a rock outcrop on the southwest end of Sheep Island. I think it is an osprey's, but osprey's usually build their nests at the very top of the tallest pine trees around, not on a rocky outcrop. It might also be an eagles nest, but once again, eagles don't usually build on rocks either, preferring to nest about midway down high trees. In any case, paddlers should avoid this area until after the middle of August. If left alone, birds of both species will come back year after year to the same nest, raising their young and constantly improving and enlarging their nests.

Set off for Blastow Cove

Blastow Cove

The cove is named for Captain William Blastow, who at one time owned Harbor Farm. He probably kept a small vessel in the protected waters of the cove that is named after him. In the late 1800s, Sylvanus "Vanee" Eaton built a clam factory and fish factory in Blastow Cove. Eaton's factory employed island women who worked canning not only clams but blueberries, string beans and the hearty brown bread baked by Eaton's wife. Business was so good that Eaton installed oil lamps over the packing tables so that the crew could work all night long. When the canning company eventually closed, the building was turned into a restaurant known as Eaton's Lobster Pool. Fishing boats would motor in at high tide to deliver their catch directly onto the old wharf. Diners sat at rough tables, ate succulent boiled lobster dinners, and enjoyed the view across Blastow Cove. Sadly, the restaurant eventually closed, and the old historic building is now vacant.

Paddle out of Blastow Cove and head northwest toward the Scott Islands

The westernmost island, Outer Scott is owned and administered by the Island Heritage Trust and is open for day use. There is a nice beach on the eastern side.

Vance Eaton (center) at his new cannery

<u>**Land on the east side of Outer Scott Island**</u>

The Scott Islands

The three Scott Islands were named after their early owner, Nathaniel Scott, the early Deer Isle settler who purchased them in 1804 for $40, a considerable amount of money at the time. As I mentioned earlier, Scott had previously purchased much of William Eaton's land on North Deer Isle and owned additional property on Little Deer Isle.

The Scott Islands are also known for being the place where the author Robert McCloskey located his beautifully crafted children's stories "A Morning in Maine," and "A Time of Wonder." In the books, the little girl Sal lost her tooth, the sisters find Indian shell heaps under uprooted firs, and the family ate clam chowder on the beach. Condon's Garage, where Sal's father took his outboard to be repaired, is still in operation in nearby Bucks Harbor.

Out on the islands that poke their rocky shoes above the waters of Penobscot Bay you can watch the turn of the world, minute to minute, hour to hour, day to day, season to season.[5]
From "A Time of Wonder"

Several years ago, a salmon farmer applied to the state of Maine for a permit to set up aquaculture pens in the waters between Pickering and the Scott Islands. "Sal," no longer a little girl, and now the attorney Sara McCloskey, heard about the project sued the State of Maine to stop it, successfully arguing that the waters of the bay belonged to all of the people of Maine and that a for-profit fish

---

5   McClusky, R. (1957). *A Time of Wonder.* New York, NY: Viking Press.

factory did not belong in the middle of such a scenic area. Against all odds, her suit was successful and the salmon farmer's application was denied.

Launch your boats and paddle north towards Little Deer Isle and enter Swains Cove

Swains Cove

Swains Cove is the largest cove along the south side of Little Deer Isle. The cove was named for William Swain, one of the first settlers on Little Deer Isle. Captain Swain was a master mariner who emigrated from Scotland in the middle 1700s. In 1779 Swain was living in Castine where he probably witnessed the defeat of the American Penobscot Expedition. Until Pearl Harbor, this was the worst naval defeat in our nation's history.[6]

It was in Castine that William met his wife Miriam. Her father, Samuel Matthews lived in Castine near what is now Morse Cove.[7] Like many residents of Castine, Matthews and Swain were staunch loyalists. When the American's won the Revolutionary War, Swain, like many British sympathizers, was forced to leave Castine, and he resettled his family on little populated Little Deer Isle where his political affiliations were not known.

Swains's Cove eventually became a self-contained community with churches, schools, and even its own post office. Village prosperity was supported by fishing, boat building and a small cannery. During the late 1800s steamships docked at the Swaine's Cove and summer visitors came ashore to enjoy a simple lifestyle. They rented cottages along the shore or stayed with local families.

When the Deer Isle/Sedgwick Bridge opened in 1937, automobiles quickly replaced steamboats and railroads as the preferred method of transportation. The bridge gave Little Deer Isle residents easy access to the mainland. After it was built the residents of Swain's Cove no longer needed to be as self-sufficient, as they once were. Life was certainly easier, but the interdependence that had kept the community vitalized for so many years quickly began to fade. The clamming factory closed and the small boat building shops consolidated and then closed. Instead of renting, many summer visitors purchased land and built summer homes. Others simply decided to vacation elsewhere. The population of the community began to shrink and over the years the community of Swains Cove became a shadow of what it once was.

I have followed the remnants of an old island road leading from the overgrown interior of Little Deer Isle down to the Swains Cove beach. Walking along this road you will pass the old town cemetery and the stone foundations of buildings and stores that existed many years ago, but alas are now no more.

Paddle out of the cove and follow the coastline northwest toward Birch Island

---

6 The area around Castine was then known as Majabigwaduce.
7 It had been named Mathews Cove until the British lost the Revolutionary War.

Birch Island

Birch Island, is located off the western tip of Little Deer Isle. The island was originally known as Head Island because it was at the western head of Eggemoggin Reach. According to McLane the island still bore this name in 1820. Today the birch trees have been replaced by spruce. McLane records note that sometime during the 1800s, the original birch forest was cut down and the trees turned into spindles for the weaving industry at a lumber mill in North Penobscot.

Birch Island is one of the many Penobscot Islands that are known as "unorganized lands by the State of Maine. It is strange to think that in our modern world there are still lands that are not part of any established township or larger community, but there were reasons why many early settlers avoided formally founding a formal town.

The state required that residents wishing to form a town commit to support a school, build a church, hire a pastor and form a local government. On small islands such as Birch, there simply weren't enough people to support such undertakings, and settlers on the unorganized lands enjoyed freedom from irksome taxes and town imposed rules. Despite their unorganized status, the early residents on these islands often worked together for their mutual benefit. They assisted one another during harvests, traded their fish for produce, and of course, often intermarried. It was only natural that island men should choose for their brides women who were used to an isolated island lifestyle and who had been trained from childhood to be self-sufficient and frugal.

As Blue Hill Reverend Jonathan Fisher wrote about his wife Dolly: *"Thank God she is an economist!"* Coming from someone who dried cat's bones and made buttons out of them, this was a real compliment.

They had to know everything from how to dry fish, sail a boat, and raise a child. During the long periods when their husbands were at sea fishing or sailing around the world, they had to cope with the everyday problems of life on a small island. They may have had the support of their neighbors and families, but it still must have been a challenging life.

The residents of unorganized lands in the Penobscot Bay area seemed to have formerly come together as a group only twice. Once during the Civil War when they banded together to resist Army recruitment, and then shortly after the Civil war ended when they once more joined together in a legal action to demand compensation for the island men who had volunteered to serve in the conflict!

There is a romantic tale about Birch Island that has survived through the years. It goes like this:

"In the early 1700s, a French seaman supposedly fell madly in love with an Indian maiden. The two made plans to meet on Birch Island and run away together. But their plans were discovered and the sailor was locked up on the ship. Filled with despair, the young girl tried to swim to his ship but the current was too strong and she drowned. Unaware of her death, the French sailor managed to escape. He stole a lifeboat and rowed back to Birch Island to meet his beloved, but on the way he found her body floating in the Reach. With nothing to live for, he rowed his boat out into the open ocean. It is said that on moonlit nights the sound of his oars can be heard from Birch Island."[8]

---

[8] From a piece by Rosemary Pool in *Farmstead Magazine,* Winter 1975.

The tides in the Reach fill from the northwest and ebb southeast. When wind and tide run against one another the seas can build in the shallow waters between Birch Island and the western tip of Little Deer. During the summer months this cove provides a moderately protected anchorage for small boats. If you keep close to the shoreline you can take advantage of the calmer seas inside a little cove at the tip of the island. Once around the point you will see the lighthouse on Pumpkin Island.

Paddle around the tip of Little Deer Isle towards Pumpkin Island

Pumpkin Island Lighthouse and the "Wickies"

The rocky coast of Maine is home to more than sixty lighthouses, but few are as picturesque as the Pumpkin Island Lighthouse. They continue to serve seamen as they have for hundreds of years, guiding them to safe harbors and warning them away from dangers. Today, nearly all of the lighthouses are automated, but in years past they were served by dedicated lighthouse keepers and often their families. These men and women were called "Wickies," because part of their job was to trim the wicks on the oil lamp powering the light.

The life of a Wickie and their families was difficult but rewarding. In addition to keeping the light illuminated at night, the keeper had to ring a bell or sound a manually operating fog horn during fog or storms. The men were expected to render all possible assistance to any vessel in distress. The women were charged with keeping the keeper's house and tower spotless and asked to cordially welcome any visitors. Inspectors from the lighthouse service could arrive at any time without notice.

It was often dangerous work. Supplies had to be brought in from the mainland by an open boat. On the offshore lights, giant waves were known to sweep completely over lighthouses during the winter storms. During a week-long northeaster, a lighthouse master from Pond Island Light near Popham Beach wrote: "*I never knew how hard it was to sleep in a life jacket.*"[9] It is doubtful that a life jacket would have done him much good in such conditions. In comparison to many other posts, the Pumpkin Island Light, situated just a few hundred yards offshore in the protected waters of the Reach, must have seemed like a plum assignment.

Judging from the letters the keepers wrote to friends and family, most keepers seemed to like their situation. They were relatively well paid by the standards of the day and could rely on a stable income. They knew the importance of their work and had time to spend with their families. Their wives cultivated beautiful gardens, taught the children and observed nature. The members of the Lighthouse Service seemed to have lived quiet productive lives.

In 1933, the Coast Guard decided to decommission Pumpkin Island Lighthouse and sell the island. If the truth is told, the location of the light was never ideal. The light beam was blocked from the south by the hills on Little Deer Isle and in the colder winters of years past, this portion of the bay would often freeze solid, halting all boat traffic until the spring thaw.

---

9 The life of a 'wickie' was difficult, but rewarding (60 years ago along the Maine Coast), Dora Thompson The Working Waterfront, Nov, 2013 pg. 7.

The Pumpkin Island Lighthouse around 1890
(Photo courtesy Deer Isle Historical Foundation)

Today, the lighthouse station looks nearly the same as when it was first built. The keeper's house, tower, boat shed, and the ramp have all been well-maintained by the current owners. The island remains in private hands however, and landings are discouraged. In 1988, the Pumpkin Island Light Station was listed on the National Register of Historic Places.

Paddle into the beach at Eggemoggin and land your boats

Eggemoggin

The small cove at the northwest tip of Little Deer Isle was originally called Indian Cove. The tribe would travel down the Bagaduce River, to Smith's Cove in Brooksville, paddle or portage their way through Bells Marsh to Orcutt Harbor and cross the Reach to the cove. Well into the 20th century, and the area had been named Eggemoggin, the Indians would visit to sell sweetgrass baskets and other items.

The cove was first developed by an energetic ex-soldier named Charles A. Babson, who had served in the Civil War and lost his leg in one of the battles. As partial compensation for his injury, he was given the position of lighthouse keeper on Pumpkin Island.

Babson believed that Indian Cove, as it was then known, would be the perfect location for a summer colony. He constructed a large two-story inn which he named the "Cookhouse" and began welcoming summer guests. From the inn's large wrap-around porch, Babson's guests enjoyed a simple lifestyle, going for long walks along the shore, taking in the cool sea breezes, watching sailboats cruising down Eggemoggin Reach, and enjoying the view of Babson's Pumpkin Island Lighthouse just offshore.

The Inn was immediately successful, catering to visitors who wished to enjoy Maine summers in a relaxed yet genteel environment. With his inn well established, Babson built many "cottages" around the cove which he then rented out or sold to his summer visitors. At one point so many Philadelphians owned Eggemoggin homes that the area was referred to affectionately as "Philly on the

Rocks." Babson's "Cookhouse" was eventually torn down, but seventeen of his original homes are still clustered around the cove at Eggemoggin.

During Babson's day steamboats ran on regular schedules between Boston and Rockland. From there smaller coastal vessels would travel up and down the coast, dropping off passengers and merchandise as they went. By the early 1900s, nearly every coastal community in Maine had a steamboat landing. Today, a pile of granite rocks marks the site of original steamboat wharf at Eggemoggin.

The Cove at Eggemoggin with some of Babson's summer cottages in the background

Push off from the beach and paddle down the northeastern side of Little Deer Isle

According to McLane there were no significant settlements in this area until some decades after the Revolution. During the early years of the twentieth century however, many large summer homes were built on the high hills overlooking the Reach. During the first World War, the Billings family built five schooners on the northern shoreline of Little Deer Isle. One of these boats, the *Mercantile,* still sails there.

It is only a few nautical miles from the Eggemoggin colony to the Deer Isle Bridge. As you near the bridge you will see Pine Hill, the highest point on Little Deer Isle.

Pine Hill

The bedrock making up the Pine Hill outcrop is largely made up of an uncommon rock type known as serpentinized peridotite. This is a coarse-grained igneous rock found in the earth's mantle. Some geologists believe that Pine Hill was created more than 500 million years ago as part of the Castine Volcanic Chain. Others argue that Pine Hill is a chunk of oceanic crust that was caught up when the early landmass Avalonia, slammed into the newly formed North American continent (Laurentia). This event occurred about 400 million years ago and created the mountains of Maine, and formed the Deer Isle granite deposits. Scientists believe that much of the Maine coastline is part of this ancient Avalonia landmass.

Regardless of its origin, the unique chemistry of the rocks makes the soil on Pine Hill high in uncommon minerals such as chromium and nickel. These elements are usually toxic to most plants, but Pine Hill has more than sixteen species of rare lichens, mosses, ferns and other plants that are not found elsewhere in Maine. One rare species of Woodsia fern growing at Pine Hill is found in only one other place on Earth, the Arctic.

The southern side of Pine Hill was heavily quarried during the 1930s to create fill and border stones for the Deer Isle Causeway. The steep northeastern side is still intact.

In 2006, the owners of the Pine Hill property, Pat and Kur Fairchild donated seven acres, including access to the quarry and the hill itself to the Island Heritage Trust. The site is now protected and open to the public.

Bridge Landing

There is a boat launch named Bridge Landing, a few hundred yards west of the Deer Isle-Sedgwick Bridge. This land is known as Sally's Point and was owned by James Merkle who until recently, ran a motel and the Sisters Restaurant on this land. A large dock with a fishing shack or boathouse at the end used to jut out into the Reach. After the restaurant and motel closed the site stood vacant for many years. Eventually it was purchased by the Maine Coast Heritage Trust. The old dock and boathouse was demolished and a new boat ramp constructed. Boaters now have direct access to Eggemoggin Reach.

<u>Continue paddling east under the Deer Isle Bridge</u>

The Deer Isle – Sedgwick Bridge

For me, all suspension bridges are beautiful, but the bridge linking Little Deer Isle to the town of Sedgwick on the mainland seems particularly graceful, and there is no better way of admiring this bridge than from the water. In 1960, the author John Steinbeck crossed the span to begin a cross country trip in a pickup truck with a camper on the back and his dog Charlie on the seat next to him. In his book, "Travels with Charlie," Steinbeck described the Deer Isle-Sedgwick bridge as "*...high arched as a rainbow.*"

<u>Paddle into Sally's Cove and head toward Stave Island</u>

Stave Island

As spring approached, the Wabanaki Indians would travel in their birch bark canoes from their winter homes in the inland forests to their summer encampments along the coast. The term Wabanaki is translated as "People of the Dawn" refers to the Maliseet, Mi'kmaq, Passamaquoddy, and Penobscot people who for thousands of years have occupied Maine and the Maritime Provinces of Canada. The Indians would travel down the Bagaduce River, portage their canoes over the carry at Walker Pond and launch them into the Punch Bowl, cross Eggemoggin Reach and then stop at Stave Island.

Many Indian artifacts have been recovered from the middens on the northeastern shoreline of Stave Island. In their birch bark canoes, the Indian paddlers, like prudent kayakers, would have wanted to spend as little time as possible on the open waters of Eggemoggin Reach. Stave Island would have been one of the closest points of land as they crossed over from the mainland. The island was next to the great fish weir that the tribe constructed between Deer Island and Little Deer Isle, and the Indian village at Eggemoggin on North Deer Isle was close at hand.

Before the arrival of European settlers, Stave Island, like most of the islands along the Maine coast, was covered in hardwood forests. European settlers named the island "Stave" because the oak trees on the island provided the high-quality hardwood used by coopers when they made their wooden barrels.

Staves are the upright pieces of wood forming the rounded sides of the casks. These watertight barrels were used during the age of sail to store everything from pickled fish to drinking water. It is unlikely that the staves were manufactured on the island itself. The island's oak trees were probably cut into boards which were then taken for final finishing to coopers working in the nearby towns of Castine, and Brooklin. The ship *Bowcat* was stranded near the Causeway Beach trying to deliver staves to the cooper's shop in Brooklin.

In 1770, Eliakim Eaton, who owned Stave Island at that time, was a participant in one of the earliest "shotgun marriages" recorded in America. In October of that year, Captain Owen was passing the Cranberry Islands. Aron Bunker, his maid asked the captain if he could go ashore to pay a surprise visit to his sister Mary, who was teaching at the school on Cranberry. As Captain Owen later wrote, the visit turned out to be quite a surprise:

"Alas, the dire mishap! Aeron popped in very unexpectedly I suppose, and found his maiden sister Mary bundled a-bed with the son of a wealthy settler on Deer Island [Eaton]."

The enraged pilot swore he would cut the gallant's throat if he did not repair the honor of the family by marrying his sister: The trembling swain declared his readiness but protested that there was no minister available to perform the ceremony. Aeron replied that his ship's captain would do just fine! Captain Owen performed the ceremony the very next day. He wrote afterward: *"A good substantial, and plentiful entertainment was provided... and a real and genuine Yankee frolic ensued."*

The marriage proved to be successful, because Eliakim Eaton and Mary raised a family of seven or more children on Little Deer Isle, and the descendants of the original family are still living in the area.

In 1905, Stave Island was sold by the Eaton family to Alanson Reed, who owned an organ manufacturing company in Boston. Reed built a large eleven-room home on the island. After he died in 1935 the island and his home were sold for back taxes.

Paddle between Stave Island and Little Deer Isle

If it is high tide you can paddle around the southwestern side of Stave. At low tide however, you will need to go around on the Reach side.

The rocks on the northwest side of the causeway have an interesting geological history. When the ancient continent of Pangaea split apart about a hundred million years ago, it created what would become the continent of North America. This landmass was pushed westward, as the land that would become Africa/Eurasia pushed eastward. The gap was filled with what would become the Atlantic Ocean. The exposed bedrock on the east side of Little Deer Isle matches that which is found on the western coast of Ireland.

For thousands of years, Native American tribes traveled in the springtime from their winter homes in the interior forests of Maine, to the coast to fish. The northern tip of Deer Isle was particularly well suited to their needs. There was freshwater and an abundance of food. The Indians could harvest shellfish by the bushel, hunt waterfowl in the saltwater marshes and deer in the forests. It was the great fishing however, that made this area particularly valuable to the native tribes.

Before the Deer Isle Causeway was built, water flowed freely between Eggemoggin Reach and East Penobscot Bay. The powerful currents surging back and forth across the shallow sandbar attracted huge schools of fish and the Indian constructed large fish traps, or weirs to capture them. Native American tribes have constructed weirs for thousands of years. Stakes from a large fish trap at Sebasticook Lake in central Maine were carbon dated and found to be nearly six thousand years old.

Weirs are an extremely efficient way of harvesting fish. The Indians would sink long poles into the mud and anchor the poles with stones. They then wove brush between the stakes, creating a barrier that allowed water to pass, but prevented the fish from escaping. Schools of fish would swim into the wide opening at the top of the weir but the stakes gradually narrowed, forcing the fish into a small holding area from which they could not escape. Once the fish were trapped they could easily be speared or scooped up with hand nets.

The Penobscot Indians named this area "*k'chisitimokan'gan,*" which (roughly translated), means, "*place of the great fish weir.*"[10] Over time, the original Penobscot Indian name was changed to suit European pronunciation, and the area became known as Eggemoggin. The following drawing was made shortly before 1600 somewhere in Virginia, but similar fish traps were used by the Indians fishing between Deer Isle and Little Deer Isle. Note the entrance to the weir at the upper left. It seems like the women in the wooden canoe have a fire started, perhaps by laying the wood on a layer of sand or rocks. No wooden canoes have yet been found in Maine, and the but we know from Champlain that the Almouchiquois tribe in southern Maine were still using them. The Penobscots probably would

---

10 Haviland, W. (2009). *At the Place of the Lobsters and Crabs.* Solon, ME: Polar Bear Company.

Indians using a weir to trap fish sometime in the late 1500s

have used their birch bark canoes, or simply waded out into the shallow waters to spear and net the trapped fish.

During the 1930s, Joseph Lauren, known locally as "Indian Joe" would camp on Stave Island and sell the beautiful sweetgrass baskets he made. Joseph was an excellent fiddle player and was often asked to provide the music for dances and other events. The new owners restored the house and used it as a private summer residence and boys camp for several years. In March 1958 however, a spark from a garden fire ignited the wooden roof of the main house and it burnt to the ground. The present owners still summer in a boathouse on the southwestern shore.

Eggemoggin – The Place of the Great Fish Weir

Like the Indian trading village at Naskeag Point, a few miles away, the gap between Little Deer and Deer Island was also a good place for Native American tribes to meet and trade. The waters are well-protected and the gap between the two large islands easily located. The area was well-known to European sailors.

In 1726, a sloop was sent from Boston to "Agemogen" (Eggemoggin) with a boatload of Penobscot Indian prisoners who had been captured during the recent Anglo-Abenaki War (Also known as Father Rale's War, Lovewell's War, Governor Dummer's War, 4th Anglo-Abenaki War, or the Wabanaki-New England War of 1722 to 1725). In return, the Indians agreed to exchange the colonial troops that they had captured during the conflict. By the time the English had sailed up from Boston however, it was winter. Penobscot Bay had frozen over, and the ship of Indian prisoners became trapped in the ice. By the time the crew managed to free themselves, the tribe had left with their colonial prisoners for their winter encampment on Mount Desert Island. According to Haviland the exchange finally did take place that spring.

Paddle along the north side of the Deer Isle Causeway

The Deer Isle Causeway

A hard-packed gravel sandbar called Scott's Bar connected Little Deer Isle with Deer Isle at low tide. The sand was firm enough to allow early settlers to cross the bar on horse-drawn wagons and later Model 'T's. In 1928, work was begun on a raised roadway that would permit cars to drive between the two islands at any tide. When the Depression took hold however, the project was halted due to lack of money. It was not until the Roosevelt administration's New Deal program that work was resumed. The federal government paid $5 a day to anyone willing to work on the roadway. With this incentive, the causeway connecting Little Deer Isle and Deer Isle was finally completed in 1937. Once the two islands were connected by the Causeway residents immediately began lobbying the state to construct a bridge that now could connect both Little Deer Isle and Deer Isle to the mainland.

The original roadway was constructed of fieldstone from the old stone walls that had been constructed by early settlers. In 1947, it became apparent that winter storms and high tides were eroding the original road. Additional fill was added with rocks quarried from the volcanic outcrop known as Pine Hill on Little Deer Isle added to edges of the road in the hope that it would prevent cars from driving off into the water. These rough-hewn white painted boulders were called "dragon's teeth" by local drivers because hitting one, even slightly, would "chew up your car something fierce." In 2016, the dragons teeth were finally replaced with a modern steel railing.

The Deer Isle Causeway lined with the "Dragon's Teeth"
looking toward Deer Isle Eggemoggin Reach
is to the left, Causeway Beach to the right

Paddle along the northern side of the Causeway to Scott's Landing in Deer Isle

Six thousand years before Europeans visited the Deer Isle area, it was home to various Indian tribes. Their sites are more numerous on Deer Isle and the surrounding islands than anywhere between Schoodic Point and Islesboro.

The Etchemin tribe, (the name meant "The Real People" in their Algonquian language), were living on Deer Isle. In 2007, archaeologist Steven Cox and a group of his students conducted a dig at this location and determined that a large Etchemin village had been located near the top of the hill facing southwest.

About 450 years ago the Etchemin's formed an alliance with the Abenakis living to the west of them. This alliance, created the Mawooshen Confederacy (People walking together) which for a time, resulted in increased trade and greater protection for both groups. The Etchemin's lived by hunting, gathering and fishing. The Abenaki's also farmed the land and raised corn and vegetables.

In the years following the arrival of Europeans however, disease and savage wars with English settlers reduced the population of the Confederacy so significantly that the Etchemin tribe ceased to exist as an independent group, and in later years the few remaining survivors were commonly grouped with the Penobscot Nation. In the years before the American Revolution the Penobscots had joined with the Maliseet, Passamaquoddy, Maliseet, and even their former enemies the Mi'kmaq tribe to form the Wabanaki Confederacy. In 1776, the Confederacy signed the Treaty of Watertown and joined the American side during the Revolutionary War.

At the site of the ancient village, Dr. Cox and his team uncovered arrowheads, fish weights, pot fragments and other ancient materials buried more than 2,000 years ago during the Early Archaic and Ceramic Periods of Deer Isle's history.

Scott's Landing

Scott's Landing is located directly across the road from Causeway Beach on the northern tip of Deer Isle.

The results of Dr. Cox's archaeological study indicated that the Etchemin tribe living in their village on north Deer Isle subsisted by fishing, hunting and gathering wild food. They probably traded hides of deer, sea mink and beaver for corn and squash with tribes to their south and west who farmed the land. The archaeologists were surprised to uncover the bones of a huge Atlantic sturgeon, a fish no longer seen in our waters. Sturgeon is one of the earliest species of fish with bony plates instead of scales. Adults can grow to more than fifteen feet in length and eight hundred pounds in weight. The archaeologists also discovered the skeleton of a sea mink, a species hunted to extinction between 1860 and 1870 to satisfy the seemingly insatiable demand of the European fur market for prize pelts.

The land on the northwest tip of Deer Isle was originally owned by Major William Eaton, one of Deer Isle's earliest English settlers. William had been born around 1720 in Salisbury, Massachusetts, one of six brothers and one sister. William married Meribah Wardwell in 1742. Meribah's mother Ruth had been captured by the Abenaki Indians during Dummer's war (1721-1726), and Meribah was born during her mother's captivity.[11] In 1762, William brought his wife and family to Deer Isle, becoming one of the first Europeans to settle on the Island. William built his house a short distance south of where the Inn at Ferry Landing now stands.

At the time, the Wabanaki Indians were still living in their seasonal village at the top of the hill overlooking the Eaton farm. After being repeatedly attacked by Eaton's bull, which they called, "All

---

11 Haviland disagrees, arguing that it probably wasn't Ruth that was captured, but one of her relatives.

One Devil," the Indians finally abandoned the village, a site that their ancestors had occupied for more than 3,000 years and moved away from Eaton's farm and his hated bull.

During the Revolutionary War, William Eaton served as a major in the militia that was commanded by Colonel Jonathan Buck. When his wife Meribah died in 1781, William immediately remarried Olive Lord of York, Maine. In 1786, he sold his home at Deer Isle and his "first settlers rights" consisting of two seventy acre lots to Nathanial Scott. Eventually this property became known as "Scott's Landing." In 1790, at seventy years of age, William Eaton and his second wife moved to Seabrook, New Hampshire, but most of their descendants remained on Deer Isle.

The Scott's Landing Ferry

Before the Deer Isle bridge was completed in 1938 everything that the Deer Isle residents needed from the mainland had to be transported over to the island by boat. Sometime before 1806 John Scott, son of Nathaniel, had started ferrying people across Eggemoggin Reach.

In 1807, the town formally voted to allowed John Scott to run a ferry from the quaintly named Tarethemdown Cove to the mainland. Amateur historian Clayton Gross speculates that the original European name was based on the word 'tar,' and referred to a place where rigging, fishing gear, etc. were soaked in tar before being used. Tarethemdown Cove is known today as Scott Cove - in my mind a poor substitute.

For the next 120 years, until the Deer Isle- Sedgwick bridge was completed, the Scott family ran a ferry service from the western tip of Deer Isle (Scott's Landing) to a dock in Sargentville on the other side of Eggemoggin Reach. The ferry ran daily at half-hour intervals from 6:00 a.m. to 9:00 p.m. Fares were 25 cents for passengers, $1.50 for automobiles and $2 for trucks.[12]

Shortly before the turn of the century, Charlie Scott was traveling back and forth across Eggemoggin Reach on his family's ferry when he was chosen to participate in the greatest adventure of his young life. He was selected to become a crew member on the Herreshoff designed 130-foot yacht *Defender*.

The Scott Ferry before the bridge was built

---

12 *Images of America*, pg. 10.

Ellsworth Shist

If you walk north up the beach from the Richardson's old dock you will come to White Rock Point a few hundred feet to the north. A huge white boulder gives the Point its name. The whitish weathered surface and tightly folded layering of this rock identify it as Ellsworth shist, a type of stone making up most of the bedrock of North Deer Isle.

These rocks were deposited nearly 500 million years ago as muddy sediments on the seabed of an ancient continent known as Avalonia. Buried miles beneath the earth's surface high temperatures and pressures re-crystallized the mud into a type of layered rock known to geologists as a *shist*. Floating on the molten crust of the earth, Avalonia slowly moved northward until it eventually collided with the continent we know today as North America. At some point in time the boulder we paddled past was forced to the surface only to be eroded by the forces of water and wind. The silvery white color that makes this particular rock so visible is due to layers of quartz and feldspar that were embedded in the rock as it formed. From a distance the white rock point boulder looks substantial, but it easily fractures into thin sheets called mica. Nearby rocks have a greenish color caused by a different type of mica known as chlorite.

Ellsworth Shist on Scott's Landing Beach looking up the Reach toward Sedgwick

He and his fellow "Deer Isle Boys" would have their chance to sail for glory in the 1895 America's Cup race!

The America's Cup

In 1851, the Royal Yacht Squadron sponsored a race around the Isle of Wight in England. Against all expectations, the race was won by the schooner *America*. It is said that Queen Victoria, who was watching at the finish line and reported to have asked who was second, the famous answer being: "*Ah, Your Majesty, there is no second.*" The trophy that the American's received for their victory was renamed the "America's Cup," after the winning yacht, and given to the New York Yacht Club. Known affectionately as the "Auld Mug," this supremely ugly trophy has become the most contested prize in yacht racing.

The America's Cup (The Auld Mug)

In 1895, Lord Dunraven from the Royal Yacht Squadron, built a new racing yacht, the *Valkyrie III,* and challenged the New York Yacht Club to another America's Cup race. The New Yorkers chose Nathaniel Herreshoff, America's foremost yacht designer, to build the boat they named *Defender*.

Prior to the 1895 contest, American yachts had been crewed by Scandinavian sailors. These men were professional racers who, could "climb like cats, swim like seals and work like beavers." After seeing local Deer Isle fishermen racing their small boats against one another, however, members of The New York Yacht Club reasoned that if their new yacht could be designed, built and captained by Americans, there was no reason why it couldn't be crewed by Americans as well.

In 1895, Captain Hank Huff, who had been selected to be Captain of the *Defender,* and C. Oliver Iselin, representing the New York Yacht Club, came to the Pilgrim's Inn[13] in Deer Isle village to meet

---

13 The the inn was named "The Arc" at the time.

The Defender shortly before the first race

The "Deer Isle Boys" the Defender's 1895 crew
"Captain Hank" Haff (in the beard) in the middle

with Captain Fred Weed to select a crew for the race. Weed was one of Maine's most experienced seamen. He was one of the few captains in New England licensed, *"to take any kind of vessel anyplace in the world."* No man was better qualified to judge the capabilities of a sailor. He chose Charlie Scott and thirty-two other young sailors from the local Deer Isle Community.

Weed had chosen well. In the 1895 America's Cup race the *Defender*, under the command of Captain Hank Haff, sailed to victory against the *Valkyrie III*. The "Deer Isle Boys" returned home to a hero's welcome.

In 1889, a second Deer Isle crew was selected to race the *Columbia* which had been once again designed by Herreshoff and was financed by J.P. Morgan. The *Columbia* sailed against the *Shamrock,* financed by Sir Thomas Lipton, owner of the Lipton Tea company. The twenty-two Deer Isle men selected for the *Columbia's* crew were once again victorious, and once again a member of the Scott family was a member of the crew, this time William "Billie" Scott. It is said that when one of the ropes jammed during the race, Billie climbed up to the top of the hundred-foot mast and freed it, saving the win for America.

Land on the sand beach by the old stone dock used by Richardson's Store

Richardson's Store

Richardson's Store was established in 1807, shortly after John Scott had established his ferry service. Goods from the mainland were loaded onto a boat in Sedgwick which was then rowed or sailed over to the crude stone wharf built in front of the store.

After beaching your boats you can follow a trail a short distance to the store's old cellar hole. The area is heavily overgrown with alders and other brush, but some ancient apple trees still shade the cellar hole. These trees could be descended from fruit stock planted by the Richardson family hundreds of years ago.

Walk up the beach to White Rock Point

Paddle around White Rock Point along the Sand Beach Shoreline

Sand Beach (on North Deer Isle)[14]

Sand Beach, on North Deer Isle, is part of the Scott Island Preserve. In the 19th century, the Scott family was using what was then a salt marsh above the beach to graze their dairy cows. A small freshwater spring flowed down from the hill and the Scott's built an embankment or dike to protect the field from the ocean. They used the coarser cordgrass (Spartina alterniflora) which grew at the water's edge for bedding, insulation and roofing and fed the salt hay (Spartina patens) and highly nutritious black grass (Juncus gerardii) that grew in the field behind their dike to their livestock.

---
14 Note there is another "Sand Beach" in Stonington.

Salt marshes were an extremely resource for the early settlers. Cattle could be grazed on the salt grass during the summer months. In the fall, the grasses were cut and either brought into the barn by a barge-like boat called a gundalow, or simply stacked in the fields on wooden platforms sunk in the marsh called staddles to be harvested when the marsh froze in winter.

The diking technique used by the Scott family was perfected as early as 1650 by the Acadian settlers who colonized the area surrounding the French colony of Port Royal in Canada. The Acadian farmers reclaimed tidal lowlands from the sea using a method that historian John Faragher called; *"One of the most remarkable developments of seventeenth-century North American colonization."*

They constructed an earthen dike with a wooden clapper that would block water from entering when the tide rose, but open and allow the fields to drain when the tide changed.[15] Every few years, the Acadian farmers would open up their dikes and let silt and nutrients from the rivers and sea rejuvenate their lands. Over the years, as the salt was gradually leached from the land the fields could support other less salt-tolerant and more valuable crops. By reclaiming unused land, the French Acadians avoided conflicts with Native American tribes. The English colonists, all too often, simply took possession of the best Indian farmlands. As the terrible epidemics devastated the local tribes the settlers rejoiced, believing that *"God had prepared the way for them."*

The raised earth and sand dike that the Scott family built can still be seen if you walk along the shoreline, but today the field itself has reverted into a swamp.

The Take-out – Old Ferry Landing

Take-out your boats on the beach at Old Ferry Landing

Pull your kayaks up on the beach at Old Ferry Landing. Directly in front of you will be The Inn at Ferry Landing, a comfortable bed and breakfast.

In 2006, the Island Heritage Trust purchased 24 acres of shoreline west of the road and created the Scott's Landing Preserve.[16] Eaton's original 1762 homestead was located immediately to your east. The old cellar hole was still visible until the 1940s.

Secure your boats on the public beach and walk up Old Ferry Road

You can walk up Hardy Hill along the paved Old Ferry Road, but about halfway up the hill there is a shortcut that leads across a field through Scott Island Preserve and connects with the Preserve's parking lot where you left your cars by Causeway Beach. It is only about half a mile walk either way.

The public path winds through the open fields of Scott Island Preserve to a parking lot overlooking Causeway Beach. The trail is clearly-marked and you will enjoy beautiful views of Eggemoggin Reach and the opposite shore. Birds migrating down the coast make Scott's Landing Preserve one of the best bird-watching areas on the east coast. Every year the Trust sponsors a day of field trips and talks for birdwatchers.

---

15 Faragher, J. (2005). *A Great and Noble Scheme*. New York, NY: W.W. Norton & Co.
16 http://www.islandheritagetrust.org/news-archives/scott's-landing-preserve.html.

Scott Island Preserve

After a short walk you will arrive at the Preserve's parking area. A twenty-five-ton granite sculpture created by Hungarian sculptor Attila Rath Geber for the 2010 Schoodic International Sculpture Symposium stands near the end of the trail. The theme for the symposium was "Wings, Waves and Woods." The massive sculpture that Geber carved frames a view overlooking the Causeway, Carney Island, and Little Deer Isle. The small hill on which the sculpture stands is very near the site of the old Etchemin village and Cox's archaeological dig

Walk down the driveway toward Causeway Beach and your cars. You will pass a small stream bubbling out of a spring on the hillside. The Indians living in their village at the top of the hill probably drew fresh water from this very spring. I often thought of them gathering clams and tending their fish weir in this lovely place. I bet they enjoyed their Maine summers every bit as much as we do today.

Wings Waves and Woods

Paddle 5: Little Deer Isle to Butter Island

Distance: Approximately 9 nm
Launch: Causeway Beach, Deer Isle 9:00 a.m., Lat/Long: 44° 09'15.3" N, 68° 39'38.8" W
Charts & Maps: Maptech #75, Waterproof #104, NOAA #13305 & 13309, Delorme Maine Atlas Map #15

The Trip

Butter is not only one of the largest islands in the area, but it is also one of the most beautiful. Like the previous paddle, the trip to Butter Island begins at the Causeway Beach in North Deer Isle. Both legs of the paddle to and from Butter Island are rather long, but the waters are reasonably protected. Paddling outbound it is possible to land at Bradbury island or (after the nesting season) at Crow Island.

Leaving Causeway Beach, the kayakers will pass Carney, Bar and Eaton Island and head towards Pickering Island where a strange doctor built an ominous iron-barred house and guarded it with a pack of ferocious dogs.

The paddlers will continue to Butter Island, site of the whimsical summer colony of Dirigo, where summer "rusticators" slept in ornate Arabian tents. The island later became the summer home of a distinguished Boston family whose members were instrumental in creating the Maine Island Trail.

Butter Island is privately owned, but from June 28th through September 10th, the owners allow the public to land on Orchard Beach on the east side of the island, and Nubble Beach to the southeast. If you wish to camp overnight on Butter Island you must request advance permission[1] and open fires are not permitted. There are paths from the two beaches that lead to the top of Mount Montserrat. A beautiful view awaits those who make the climb. The nearby Barred Islands, just to the west of Butter are also well worth exploring.

On the return trip kayakers can either retrace their inbound path, or paddle eastward to enter Northwest Harbor and explore the charming village of Deer Isle before heading back to the take out at Causeway Beach.

The Launch Point

Launch from the Causeway Beach just over the Causeway on Deer Isle.

Launch your kayak and paddle west along the eastern shore of Carney Island

You will pass a large boulder known as Mink Rock jutting out into the water. Until the Causeway was completed in 1939, local fishermen would build a herring weir between the boulder and the island shoreline. When the new roadway was built, it blocked the natural flow of water from Eggemoggin Reach, and the huge schools of fish that had once swarmed through the channel disappeared forever.

---

1 Call 207-446-4147 to request permission to camp. Requests usually need to be made well in advance.

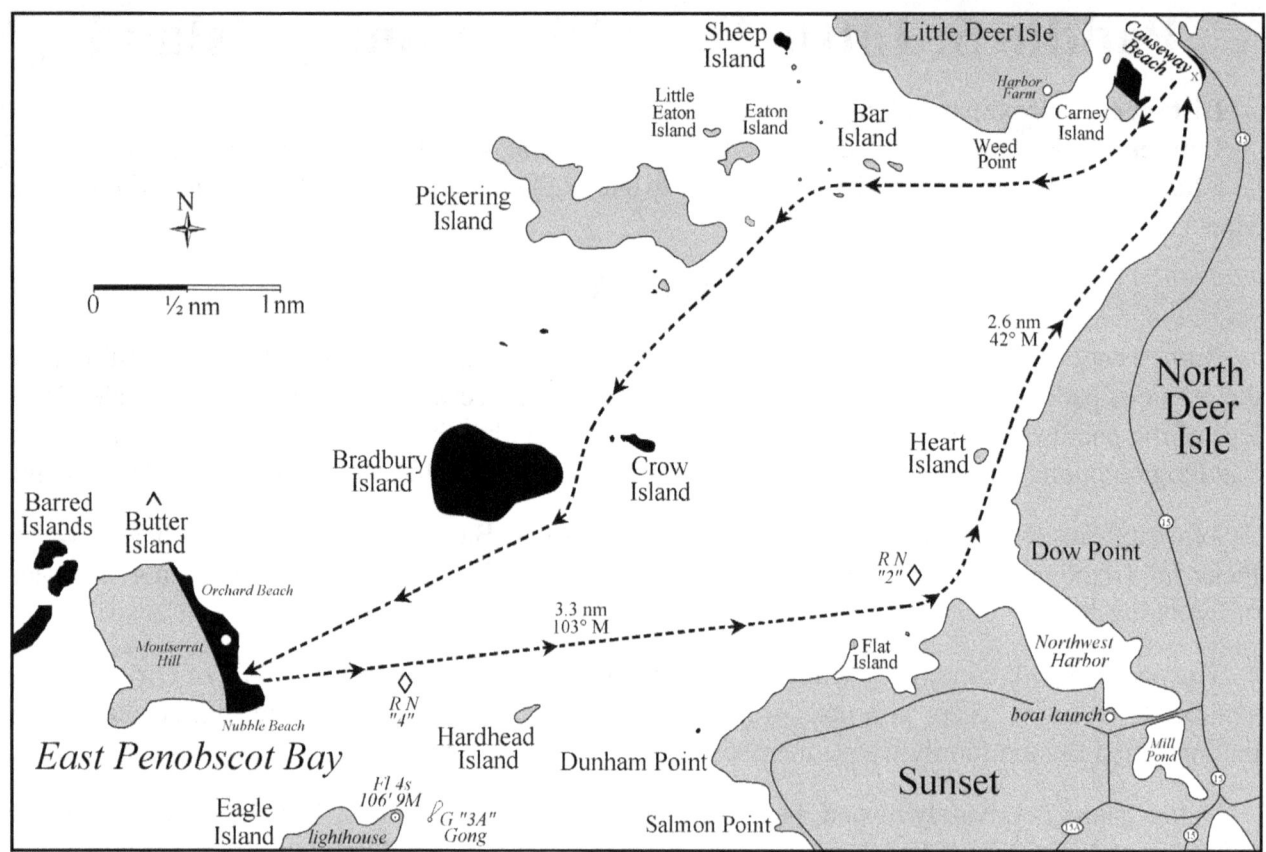

TheLittle Deer Isle to Butter Island Paddle Chart

Butter Island Camping and Landing Information

ISLAND NAME	GPS COORDINATES	LATITUDE/LONGITUDE
BRADBURY ISLAND (Private), difficult landing	44.244711, -68.751789	44° 14'41.0" N, 68° 45'06.4" W
BUTTER ISLAND, restricted camping, 2 sites, 8 campers	44.228515, -68.783822	44° 13'42.6" N, 68° 47'01.8" W
CARNEY, landing north side only, bird sanctuary, no landing February-August	44.272053, -68.685542	44° 16'19.4" N, 68° 41'08.0" W
CAUSEWAY BEACH (launch point)	44.154253, -68.660786	44° 09'15.3" N, 68° 39'38.8" W
CROW ISLAND (Private), bird sanctuary, no landing February-August	44.246680, -68.743006	44° 14'48.0" N, 68° 44'35.3" W
HEART ISLAND (Private), no landing	44.244909, -68.702880	44° 14'41.7" N, 68° 42'10.4" W
NORTHWEST HARBOR, harbor entrance boat landing east end	44.233798, -68.705012	44° 14'01.7" N, 68° 42'18.0" W
PICKERING (Private), no landing	44.264723, -68.741748	44° 15'54.3" N, 68° 44'31.2" W

There are a small cove and pretty sand beach at the southern tip of the island. The rock formations surrounding the southern cove are particularly colorful (I believe they are a form of schist). There is a tent platform a few hundred yards up from the cove, but this part of the island is privately owned.

A few hundred yards off the southern beach is "Half-tide Rock," which, as its name suggests, first appears at mid-tide. To the west along the Little Deer Isle shoreline is a large white house known as Harbor Farm, one of the oldest homesteads on Little Deer Isle (see the Butter Island Paddle).

Kayak southwest towards Pickering Island passing Bar Island, Eaton, Little Eaton and Little Pickering Island

Pickering Island

Pickering Island named after Samuel Pickering, who was awarded a settlers deed of 100 acres in 1775. In 1776, the remainder of the island, (as well as Long Island, Little Deer Isle, Great Spruce Head and Bradbury Island) was sold by the Commonwealth of Massachusetts to John Reed. John quickly resold the islands for the same low price to James Bowdoin, the Governor of Massachusetts. Cynic that I am, I can't help but smile at these "coincidences," was there perhaps a little inside trading going on at the time?

Dr. Collins House on Pickering Island

For nearly a hundred years Pickering Island was farmed by various owners. In the 1860s, a small fish-oil business was set up "Pogy-house Cove," but the menhaden were soon fished out and the enterprise was forced to close. In 1883, the island was sold to the mysterious Dr. Stacy B. Collins for $2,000. Shortly after purchasing the island, Dr. Collins built a strange house on his land. There were no windows on the ground level, and the windows on the second and third floors were heavily barred. An ominous turret with narrow slit-like windows projected out over the second story.

Some say the cottage was built to keep a deranged relative of the doctor locked up inside. Others suggested that Collins conducted strange medical experiments in an attempt to find a cure for mentally ill female patients.[2] Others were less charitable, suggesting that each summer the Doctor brought over a new group of barmaids from Boston to serve his perversions.[3] It was said that to ensure his privacy and guard against unwelcome intruders, the reclusive doctor kept a pack of fierce dogs that roamed the island unchecked and attacked anyone who tried to land.

No one will never know if Dr. Collins was a dedicated medical professional or a deranged maniac. He moved to Deer Isle in 1907 and his ominous building fell into disrepair. Even after he was gone however, the strange events on Pickering seemed to continue. Local deer hunters fled after supposedly hearing the howling of the Doctor's abandoned dogs and a group of picnickers reported the front stairs suddenly burst into flames as they neared it. In 1954, the Doctor's strange old house was finally torn down.

Pickering is currently privately owned and landing should not be done without permission from the owner.

Paddle towards Crow Island

Crow Island

Crow Island received its name from the hundreds of crows that would inexplicably fly to Crow Island every evening. Some say that the birds were attracted to shellfish exposed on the sandbar that at one time encircled Crow Island. When much of the bar eventually washed away, the crows left as well. Appropriately enough however, Crow Island is now protected as a bird nesting site and landing is seasonally restricted.

Paddle along the east side of Bradbury Island

Bradbury Island

Bradbury Island was originally called Bear Island. There is a story of the island being named for an English deserter named Bradbury who fled to the island after the American revolution, but McLane dismisses the story for lack of evidence. The earliest recorded settler was John Vickery, an Englishman who built a farm on Bradbury Island in the 1830s. He sent for his wife and two children to join him, but they perished at sea. John remarried and raised five children.

In 1844, the virgin forest on Bradbury Island was cut to provide lumber to replace the "Old Meeting House" that had been built on Deer Isle in 1773. A meeting house was usually one of the first structures to be completed in any new settlement, followed closely by a church and usually a tavern. The meeting

---

2 Caldwell, B. (1988). *Maine Coast*. Portland, ME: Guy Gannett Publishing Co.
3 *McLane, pg. 228.*

house was used for all public functions, as a schoolhouse, a place of worship, a town office and for public gatherings, and even dances.

The next settlers on Bradbury were several generations of a family named Staples. They lived by fishing and farming and a Samuel Staples fought in the Civil War. There is an old cellar hole near the high ground on the western end of Bradbury that probably marks the location of the Staples farm.

In November 1887, two fishermen nearly perished from exposure on the island after their boat was driven ashore in a storm. They managed to build a fire that was seen by Captain John Scott, the caretaker on Pickering Island. Despite the storm John and his two sons rowed across the bay and rescued the two men who were on the verge of freezing to death.

Bradbury Island is now protected by the Maine Coast Heritage Trust and is open to the public, but it is difficult to find a good landing spot on the island's steep and rocky shoreline.

You will see Butter Island directly ahead of you as you paddle southwest. Eagle Island with its lighthouse lies directly to your South and the hill at Great Spruce Head Island[4] rises to the west.

Paddle southwest to Butter Island and land on Orchard Beach on the northeast side of Butter Island

Butter Island

McLane writes that the island may have received its name from early settlers who sold butter and dairy products to the British at Castine during the Revolutionary war. This is certainly possible as the English soldiers stationed at Fort George relied on island farms for food.

Samuel Waldo and the Great Proprietors

Brigadier-General Samuel Waldo,[5] was a wealthy merchant and land speculator. During King George's War, he captured Fortress Louisbourg in 1745 and planned the attack that resulted in the French surrender of Louisbourg once again in 1758. In 1731, Waldo was appointed the agent for a group of wealthy Massachusetts Bay land speculators known as the Great Proprietors[6] who based their land claims on the feudal grants given by the crown to Sir Ferdinando Gorges. These men planned to buy land in Maine for next to nothing, induce poor immigrants to settle on these lands as tenants, and then collect rent. They would become, if not the nobility of the new world, at least the landed aristocracy. Butter Island was part of General Samuel Waldo's extensive land holdings, and the story of how thousands of acres of land were transferred under sometimes rather dubious circumstances is worth telling.

In 1729, Colonel David Dunbar, the "Surveyor General of His Majesty's Woods" arrived in Boston to announce that the crown had annexed all of the land between the St. Croix and Kennebec Rivers

---

4 Great Sprucehead is owned by the author Eliot K. Porter's family and was the site of his book *Summer Island.*
5 The Maine towns of Waldo, Waldoboro, and Waldo County are named for their early proprietor.
6 Also known as the "Thirty Proprietors."

for a new colony that would be named "Sagadahoc," after the short-lived Popham Colony that George Popham had attempted to land near the mouth of the Kennebec River in 1607.

Colonel David Dunbar whom Jonathan Belcher, the Governor of Massachusetts described as: *"the most malicious, perfidious creature that wears human shape,"* argued that the land had reverted to the Crown after the French and their Indian allies had "conquered it," claiming that when the British eventually defeated the French the land reverted to the crown as a right of conquest. Governor Belcher was getting ready to carry out a military expedition against Dunbar's colony in 1730 but was forbidden to do so. King George II of course, stood to gain if Dunbar's argument was accepted by the English courts.

The Great Proprietors sent Samuel Waldo over to England to plead their case. The historian Thomas Griffiths described Waldo as a worthy adversary to Dunbar: *"In all his undertakings Waldo was aggressive, ruthless, and avaricious, and in his dealings with others utterly without mercy... without a single generous impulse toward benevolence."*[7]

The Great Proprietors had chosen the right man to plead their case because in 1731, the British ruled that Dunbar's claim was invalid. As a result of this ruling, the Great Proprietors (at least in English eyes) would control the entire Maine Coast from the Kennebec River to the St. Croix! In return for his services, the grateful land speculators gave Samuel Waldo thirty-six square miles in Maine.[8] Waldo later purchased the rest of the Proprietor's lands, and this enormous tract became known as the "Waldo Patent." Since islands within one mile of the shore were included in the grant, Waldo now also owned Butter Island.

To clear his forests and farm his new lands Waldo enticed hundreds of Scotch-Irish and German settlers to emigrate to America. He promised to give them 120 acres of land and employment. When they arrived in America however, they found that Waldo had confiscated their goods to pay for their passage. He housed them in unheated sheds "totally unfit for habitation," where many of the immigrants perished from hunger and disease. To make matters worse, in 1744 the French and English were at war again, and the Mi'kmaq and Passamaquoddy tribes sided with the French. Many of the settlers who survived the long sea voyage, and the dreadful conditions that awaited them when they arrived in America, often fell victim to the Indian attacks that raged during this time.

Samuel Waldo died at Fort Point[9] on the Penobscot River in 1759. He had gone not only to view the fort but also to settle some dispute about the boundary line of his patent. After landing, so the story goes; General Waldo stepped back a few paces on the bank, and, looking about him, cried, *"Here are my bounds,"* and instantly fell dead.[10]

Samuel's wife Lucy inherited Butter Island and sold it to General Henry Knox, who was in the process of building up his island empire and who had married Samuel Waldo's grand-daughter. The Knox's built their impressive home Montpelier on Waldo's tract of land in Thomaston, Maine.

---

7 Woodard, C. (2005). *The Lobster Coast.* London, UK: Penguin Books.
8 This enormous tract of land would become known as the Waldo Patent.
9 The actual fort was named Fort Pawnall in honor of the Governor of the Province of Massachusetts Bay Thomas Pawnall.
10 Some say he died inspecting his properties near Bangor, and was only buried at Fort Point (Stockdon Springs)

John Lee of Penobscot eventually bought Butter Island from the Commonwealth of Massachusetts, but there must have been other settlers on the island because he was required by the laws of the time to "quiet" the claims of any original settler by giving them 100 acres of land.

In 1802, John Witherspoon came to Maine to manage General Knox's estates and purchased Butter Island. John Witherspoon was the nephew of the Reverend John Witherspoon, signer of the Declaration of Independence and President of Princeton University. John established a farm on Butter Island and remained there for more than thirty years. Both John and his wife are buried on the island.

Dirigo

In 1905, two brothers, George and Emory Harriman purchased Butter Island to develop a tent and cottage resort. They originally called their enterprise "The New England Tent Club," but later it was known as simply Dirigo.[11] In their advertising brochure the brothers tried to attract "genteel Bostonians" to their resort, which banned dogs, and "intoxicating liquors" and stressed open-air activities such as hiking, tennis, fishing and sailing. The dogs were probably banned because flocks of sheep were grazed on the island. Photographs of Butter Island at the time show that the sheep had cleared out the underbrush so well that nearly half the island was open.

The original idea for an exotic Arabic tent city on the eastern shore of Butter Island never fully materialized. Instead of the nearly 500 tents that the brothers originally envisioned, traditional wooden cottages were built. A two-story building named the Casino was linked by a covered veranda to the old Witherspoon home known as "The Clubhouse." In that soft turn of the century time before World War I, guests returned year after year to enjoy long summer holidays. Most stayed in the central buildings, but a few purchased lands and built their cabins on the island.

The resort was very popular. From 1905-1910 nearly a hundred guests stayed on the island. The ladies would be elegantly attired, the men in white pants, stiff collars and straw hats. Families would go on long walks together and perhaps cross over to the Barred Islands[12] at low tide to search for shells. There were tennis, golf and swimming and a two-day yacht regatta in August. In the evening after dinner guests would sit on the veranda enjoying the cool breezes and talking about the events of the day. As night came on they would retire to the Clubhouse for a leisurely game of cards before walking back to their cabins.

World War I brought about an end to this way of life, as it did to so many things. The abandoned buildings were soon stripped of everything useful by scavengers who in some cases carried entire buildings away to Deer Isle. By the end of the 1920s nothing was left but cellar holes.

Hike the trail to the top of Montserrat Hill

---

11 The State Motto of Maine – "I Lead."
12 Day use is permitted to the Barred Islands, but not to Big Barred, Little Barred, and the string of smaller islands linked by sand bars.

Montserrat Hill and the Cabots

A long looping trail climbs the hill from Orchard Beach up to the top of Montserrat Hill. The owners request that visitors stay on or very near the trail itself. There is a beautiful view from the peak of Montserrat. At the top of the hill is a granite bench bearing the following quote from Tennyson's poem Ulysses: *"Come my friends, tis not too late to see a newer world."* Engraved on the top of the stone is a carving of a lovely ketch named Avalinda and on the side of the bench the names Thomas D and Virginia W. Cabot.

Near the bench is a brass plaque set into a granite boulder. The poem on the plaque reads in part: *"I've found a rest where ospreys nest, and seagulls cry and waves break high."* (Thomas Dudley Cabot 1917-1945).

Bench at the top of Montserrat Hill
"Come My Friends, Tis Not Too Late to Seek a Better World" (Photo Jim Claus)

Ever since I first climbed Montserrat Hill and came upon the granite bench and read the engravings I became interested in knowing more about the family. Thomas Dudley Cabot came from a wealthy and prominent Boston Brahman family whose members could trace their lineage to colonial days. The nature of the Boston Brahmin is hinted at by the doggerel "Boston Toast" by Harvard alumnus John

Collins Bossidy: *"And this is good old Boston, the home of the bean and the cod, where the Lowells talk only to Cabots, and the Cabots talk only to God."*

The Cabot family included ship captains, businessmen, philanthropists, and statesmen such as Henry Cabot Lodge.[13] Thomas himself had a distinguished career in business as President of his family business; the Cabot Corporation, and also United Fruit Company. In 1951 he served as Director of Office of International Security Affairs at the Department of State under President Truman. In this role he supervised the disbursement of 6 billion dollars in foreign economic aid. He also reportedly worked undercover for the CIA on several covert operations to discredit Fidel Castro. I can't help but wonder if these covert operations were carried on from the Caribbean Island of Montserrat and that this is the reason for the name Montserrat Hill - but I am probably letting my imagination run away. Despite his many accomplishments, Thomas loved to say that his neighbors called him "just plain as dirt."

In the 1930s, he purchased Butter Island, and throughout the years continued to acquire many more Maine islands. In 1970, he joined with his close friend Mrs. David Rockefeller to form the Maine Coast Heritage Trust, an organization that has pioneered the use of conservation easements for island protection. The islands that Cobot and Rockefeller donated to the public became the nucleus of the Maine Island Trail.

In 1936, Cabot had a lovely 32-foot sloop *Avelinda* (Spanish for Beautiful Bird) built for him at the Gamage Shipyard in South Bristol, Maine. This is the boat inscribed in the stone on the top of Montserrat Hill. He wrote a book about the cruises that he made on the *Avelinda* with his wife Virginia and their children along the coast of Maine.[14] In his book,[15] he wrote that he hoped that when he died, a simple bench would be set up at the top of the hill overlooking the island that he loved so that others could enjoy the view. When he passed away his family honored his wishes.

Butter is one of the largest islands in the Maine Island Trail system. It is privately owned but the beaches on the northeast side are available for day use by members of MITA. Two campsites are available, one at Orchard Beach and the other at Nubble Beach (off the southeastern point). These campsites that can accommodate up to eight people and are available to MITA members from July 25th to September 10th. Reservations are required and should be made well in advance of your intended visit.[16]

When I recently called to ask about reservations the phone was answered by Thomas Cabot's grandson. He mentioned that the family had recently cut away some of the trees from the top of Montserrat Hill to improve the view and mentioned that they had also created a new trail from the Nubble Beach campsite to the top of Montserrat. I thanked him and his family for all they had done he replied dismissively: *"It's a labor of love."*

---

13 Note: There were two members of the family named Henry Cabot Lodge, the first was a Massachusetts Senator serving in the Roosevelt administration. Another Henry Cabot Lodge, a grandson of the first one, represented Massachusetts in the Senate (1936-53), served as United Nations Ambassador (1953-61) and was the running mate of Richard Nixon in their unsuccessful campaign in 1960.
14 Cabot, T. (1991). *Avelinda, the Legacy of a Yankee Yachtsman.* Rockland, ME: Island Institute.
15 He also wrote an autobiography *Beggar on Horseback.*
16 *Maine Island Trail Guide* 2012, pg 168. The caretaker can be contacted at 207-446-4147.

The Barred Islands

An interesting side trip would be a visit to the Barred Islands. These are a string of lovely small islands located to the northwest of Butter Island. As their name suggests many of these are connected by sandbars at low tide. The Barred Islands are shown on the map for the Dirigo summer resort that the Harriman brothers drew in 1896. According to McLane, the Harriman's were the first, but not the last to name these tiny islands. The Cabots renamed the two islands closest to Butter Island, Escargot (from Sugarloaf) and Bartender (from Peak) and the names of many of the other islands in the string have changed over time. The small islands and low-lying reefs stretching away to the south are often called the Chain Islands.

Until the Outward Bound School on Hurricane Island unfortunately closed, the school's instructors would use uninhabited Barred Islands as convenient places to maroon students who were trying to pass the school's solo survival test. After a day without food or water the students were probably couldn't wait to see the sails of the school's lifeboats coming to rescue them!

Bartender Island (also known as Peak Island) and Escargot Island (Sugarloaf) are located off the northwestern side of Butter and are available for day use. East Barred Island is also public, but West Barred is a bird sanctuary. Many of the other islands are privately owned.

Please respects the owner's privacy and do not land at their private dock on Butter Island. Landings on Butter Island are only allowed on the eastern shore.

Launch your boats and paddle to the W shore of Deer Isle and then turn N

You will cross the entrance to Northwest Harbor. If the tide is high you can paddle into Deer Isle Village. There is a very small boat launch (nearly hidden in the rocks) just to the west of the bridge that connects the scenic Mill Pond to Northwest Harbor. During tide changes the flow of water through this narrow opening is impressive. At low tide however, this entire area is a huge mudflat and that is why I have not included it as a landing point. If the tides are high however, it is a worthwhile trip to paddle into Northwest Harbor. Beach your boats and explore Deer Isle Village.

Deer Isle Village

In 1772, Mark Haskell and his sons built a tide powered saw on gristmill close to where you landed. You can see the power of the water as you walk the short distance to the little town. The red building immediately in front of you was built by his grandson Ignatius Haskell in 1793.

Ignatius used his grandfather's sawmill to construct many sailing vessels. In 1806, he launched the *Bolina*, a large fishing schooner that immediately set sail for Labrador. Ignatius was also active in the coastal trade shipping lumber and other products to the rapidly growing northeastern cities. In the 1800s, Deer Isle Village included a millinery shop, a tannery, two stables, two sail lofts, a blacksmith shop, a cobbler shop, a customs office, and the town's post office.

The Pilgrim's Inn and The Ark

In 1890, Elizabeth Cush Haskell turned her family home into a guest-house, calling it "The Ark." Summer visitors would arrive by steamer from as far away as Boston and usually stay the entire summer season. Five years later The Ark was used as the meeting place to select the crew to sail the *Defender* in the America's Cup race of 1895. The *Defender* was victorious and a few years later the racing yacht *Columbia* was also victorious. This as the first time in the history of the America's Cup that the entire crew came from a single community. (See the Circling Little Deer Isle Paddle).

In the decades between the world wars Deer Isle Village renamed a quiet place for the guests at The Ark to spend the summer. They would swim in the mill pond, sail the protected waters of the bay and explore the island. In the evening they could enjoy an ice cream at the soda fountain, take in a movie at the theater, or play basketball at the court by the mill dam. There were a roller-skating rink and a pool hall. The small town was the commercial and social center for the northern half of the island.

When Elizabeth Haskell passed away in 1944, The Ark was left unoccupied and fell into disrepair, but in 1975 it was purchased by George and Ellie Pavlov, renovated and reopened as The Pilgrim's Inn. In 1978, it was named to the National Register of Historic Places. The Inn is now owned by Nicole Neder and Scott Hall and opened seasonally.

The Chase Emerson Memorial Library

Across the street from the Inn is the truly charming Chase Emerson Memorial Library which grew out of the older Jennings library which was established in 1906 and the Library Sewing Circle, a women's group in Deer Isle that was active in the early 1900s. The library was named after Chase Emerson, a fairly well known Boston artist who did nothing to financially help out the library named in his honor. A few of his paintings however are hung in the building.

If you have made the side-trip into Northwest Harbor launch your kayaks and paddle out of the harbor.

Turn north and pass between Heart Island and the Deer Isle coastline

The Take-out

Continue north and take out at Causeway Beach

Paddle 6: Little Deer Isle to the Punch Bowl

Distance: Approximately 8 nm
Launch: Bridge Landing: Lat/long: 44° 17'25.4" N, 68° 41'32.8" W
Charts & Maps: Maptech #74, Waterproof #104, NOAA #13309, Delorme Maine Atlas Map #15

The Trip

The Punch Bowl paddle is a short trip through the waters of Eggemoggin Reach. It begins at the Bridge Landing, on the Little Deer Isle side of the Deer Isle Sedgwick Bridge.

Launching into Eggemoggin Reach from the small beach at Bridge Landing kayakers will have a wonderful view of the Deer Isle Bridge as they cross the reach to Byard Point in Sedgwick, the site of an old silver mine. They will turn west and continue to the Punch Bowl, a site once sacred to the Penobscot Indians.

Leaving the Punch Bowl, they will paddle past the remnants of a granite dock where in days-gone-by huge sailing ships would fill their holds with wood, granite, and ice. Continuing onward paddlers will pass the Oakland House, one of the first Inns along this portion of the coast, and still active today as a fine restaurant and B & B. A bit further to the west is the ominous-sounding Deadman's Cove, where according to legend, the crew of a small ship broke into the captain's supply of liquor and were soon too drunk to notice that their ship was being driven onto the shore and was sinking.

The kayakers will paddle past the location of the fabled lost city of Norumbega, where according to the reports of some early explorers, Indian children played with diamonds and their parents dressed in gold. It was also in these waters that the historic schooner *Isaac H. Evans* capsized and sank during a late autumn cruise in 1984.

Entering Bucks Harbor, paddlers will pass Harbor Island, where foxes were once raised in a quixotic attempt to make money from their fur. Bucks Harbor itself is the fabled lost city of Norumbega named after Colonel Jonathan Buck, a local Revolutionary War hero, who according to legend, was the recipient of a witch's curse.

Leaving Bucks Harbor, the paddlers will cross Eggemoggin Reach, land on the beach at Eggemoggin, and then head down the northern side of Little Deer Isle. The trip will end with a take-out at Bridge Landing.

Paddle 6: Little Deer Isle to the Punch Bowl – 145

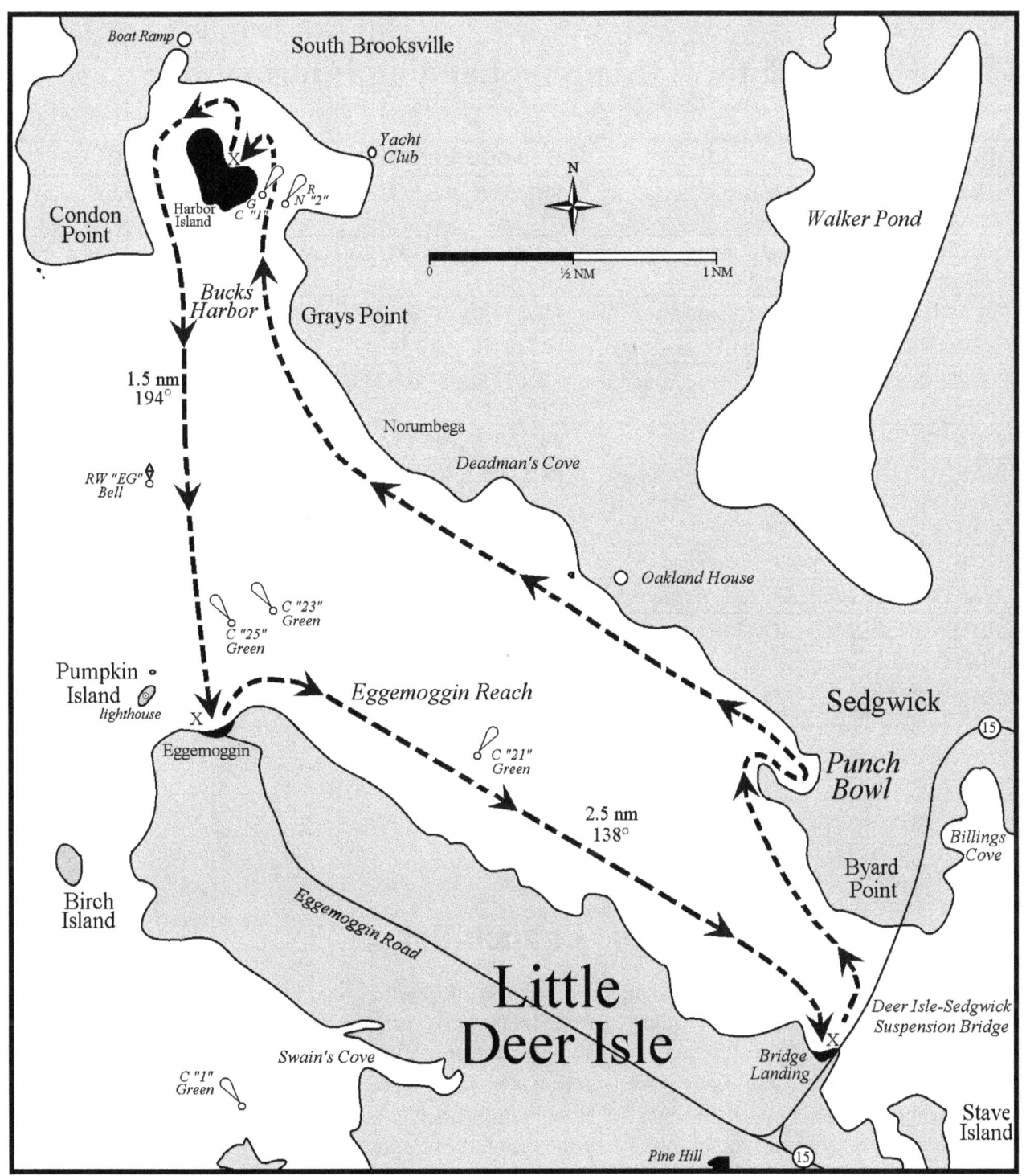

The Little Deer Isle to the Punch Bowl Paddle Chart

Punch Bowl Camping Landing Information

ISLAND NAME	GPS COORDINATES	LATITUDE/LONGITUDE
BRIDGE LANDING (Municipal), launch, dock and boat ramp	44.290395, -68.692430	44° 17'25.4" N, 68° 41'32.8" W
BUCKS HARBOR RAMP (Municipal), boat ramp northwest end near road	44.341895, -68.741767	44° 20'30.8" N, 68° 44'30.4" W
BYARD POINT (Private), no landing	44.296511, -68.685232	44° 17'47.4" N, 68° 41'06.8" W
DEADMAN COVE (Private), no landing	44.320110, -68.719030	44° 19'12.4" N, 68° 43'08.5" W
EGGEMOGGIN (Municipal), landing sandy beach	44.307214, -68.738338	44° 18'26.0" N, 68° 44'18.0" W
GRAYS POINT (Private)	44.327047, -68.73271	44° 19'37.4" N, 68° 43'57.8" W
HARBOR ISLAND (Maine Coast Heritage Trust - MCHT), day-use only, land in the cove on the northeast side	44.335163, -68.73841	44° 20'06.6" N, 68° 44'18.3" W
NORUMBEGA (Private), no landing	44.320558, -68.722873	44° 19'14.0" N, 68° 43'22.3" W
OAKLAND HOUSE (Private), no landing	44.278552, -68.679691	44° 16'42.8" N, 68° 40'46.9" W
PUMPKIN ISLAND LIGHT (Private), no landing	44.308834, -68.742740	44° 18'31.8" N, 68° 44'33.9" W
PUNCH BOWL (Private), no landing	44.305598, -68.693841	44° 18'20.1" N, 68° 41'37.8" W

The Launch Point

Bridge Landing is a public boat launch located at the foot of the Deer Isle Bridge on the Little Deer Isle side of the bridge. For many years, this property was the site of a small motel and Sisters Restaurant. After sitting abandoned for many years, the property was sold to the Maine Island Heritage Trust. Most of the old buildings were torn down as well as the picturesque but dilapidated fishing dock. Working together with the town the Trust built a concrete boat ramp, paved the parking area and established a pretty picnic site at the foot of the bridge. The sandy beach to the east of the boat ramp is a good launching site for kayakers.

Paddle out from the Bridge Landing beach leaving the Deer Isle Sedgwick Bridge to the east

The Deer Isle Sedgwick Bridge

Paddling out onto Eggemoggin Reach from Bridge Landing you will have a wonderful view of the Deer Isle Sedgwick Bridge which was completed in 1939. Before that time the residents of Deer Isle relied on a small ferry barge that ran from Smith's landing on Deer Isle to the mainland. Until the Deer Isle Causeway was constructed a few years earlier, residents of Little Deer Isle had to wait until low tide before they could cross the sandbar to reach the Smith Ferry house on North Deer Isle.

The Deer Isle-Sedgwick Bridge
(looking northeast from Little Deer Isle toward Byard Point in Sedgwick)

The local community repeatedly petitioned the State of Maine to construct a bridge. As one resident wrote in 1932: *"Here we are on this island, the second largest on the Maine coast…its just like bribing your jailer when you want to get out. We want a bridge! We have been imprisoned long enough!"*

It was the middle of the Depression however and the state of Maine didn't have enough money in the state treasury to build anything. The winter of 1934 was brutally cold. Winter weather arrived early and record-breaking cold continued for months. The waters of Eggemoggin Reach and much of Penobscot Bay froze solid and Smith's ferry on North Deer Isle couldn't run. The federal government sent a Coast Guard ice-breaker to open up a pathway so basic food and other supplies could get through, but the powerful ship got stuck in the ice as it tried to enter the Deer Island Thorofare and the rescue attempt had to be abandoned. The islanders stayed isolated for much of the winter and referred to that year as the winter of the "The Ice Embargo."[1]

---

1 *Images of America, Deer Isle and Stonington*, Deer Isle-Stonington Historical Society, 2004, pg. 18

At the end of the year however, federal "New Deal" Depression-era relief funds became available and Maine state legislators approved the bridge. Clayton Gross, in his book "Steel Over Eggemoggin" wrote: *"No other event has brought so many changes in our lives, brought us so many benefits, and created so many new problems."*[2]

The bridge was designed by David Steinman, who at the time was one of the greatest suspension bridge engineers in the United States. To reduce costs and speed construction Steinman used prefabricated elements whenever possible. The huge support coffers were built on Staten Island and barged from New York up to Maine where they were assembled by a crew of only fifty men. These new construction techniques resulted in the bridge being built for less than a million dollars.

Steinman's bridge is 2,505 feet in total length with a main span of 1,088 feet. The support towers are over 185 feet high. At the center of the bridge the roadway is nearly a hundred feet above Eggemoggin Reach. It was rumored that Steinman was persuaded by his friends at the New York Yacht Club to build it that high so that the huge masts on the boats in the club's racing fleet could easily sail under it.

Deer Isle residents often joke that the Deer Isle Bridge is the only one of Steinman's bridges that hasn't collapsed. They point to the Tacoma Narrows Bridge, better known as "Galloping Gertie," which collapsed during a windstorm only a few months after it was opened. The two bridges look very similar, not only did Steinman not design Galloping Gertie, he also warned that the chosen design was "inherently flawed."

The Deer Isle Bridge however, was not without its problems. During construction, workers complained that Steinman's innovative lightweight deck was moving up and down in the wind. Galloping Gertie had shown the same type of movement shortly before it collapsed. To solve this problem, Steinman's company installed additional bracing, but a severe storm in the winter of 1942–1943 damaged some of the supporting stays. More bracing was added and motion sensors showed that movement was significantly reduced.

In 1978, however, James Merkle, who owned the motel at the Little Deer Isle end of the bridge noticed that the structure was once again going through wave-like motions. A state trooper called to the scene stated that he thought *"the bridge was going to sprout wings and fly away."*[3] The bridge was closed temporarily and the supporting stays were re-adjusted. In 1993, the bridge received additional protection from the wind when a special system of fairings was installed to direct wind over the girders. With these final changes in place the stability problems finally seem to have been corrected.

In 2010, state inspectors found that both the Bucksport Bridge and the Deer Isle Bridge were both in a hazardous condition and in danger of failing. The state decided to replace the Bucksport Bridge, but only repair the Deer Isle Bridge. For several years, work progressed without incident, but as workers were taking down the safety nets tragedy struck when one of the workers slipped and fell to his death only a few days before the work was due to be completed.

Paddle north across Eggemoggin Reach to the shoreline of Sedgwick

---

2   Gross, C. H. (1989). *Steel over Eggemoggin.* pg. 25. Stonington, ME: Penobscot Bay Press.
3   Gross, pg. 43.

Eggemoggin Reach

Eggemoggin Reach is the waterway between Deer Isle and the mainland. It connects East Penobscot Bay with Jericho Bay. The Reach is about ten miles long and averages a mile in width. The name "Eggemoggin" is a Penobscot Indian word meaning, "place of the great fish weir" a reference to the fish trap that Native Americans erected in the open channel that existed between Little Deer Isle and Deer Isle before the roadway connecting the two islands was built.

The nautical term "reach," refers to a sailboat traveling approximately perpendicular to the wind. For most modern sailboats "reaching" will enable the vessel to achieve its fastest speed. On Eggemoggin Reach, the prevailing winds during the summer months are from the southwest, enabling boaters to sail in either direction up and down the waterway. As Robert Carter wrote in his 1858 book "Summer Cruises on the Coast of New England" *"There cannot be a finer sheet of water in the world than this Reach, which is bounded on every side by superb views."*

Paddle across Eggemoggin Reach to Byard Point

General Robert Sedgwick

A 1671 map of the area commissioned by the Governor of Acadia Chevalier de Grandfontaine, shows an Indian fort located just over the Bridge on Byard Point in Sedgwick. The town of Sedgwick is named for Major General Robert Sedgwick, an English sea captain who sailed for Oliver Cromwell.

In 1654, Sedgwick raised a force of a few hundred colonial soldiers to attack Dutch forces when he received the news that Britain and Holland had signed a peace treaty. After spending his own money to raise his band of men Sedgwick was determined to find someone to fight and attacked the French trading post at Castine. The small French garrison at Fort Pentagouet could only offer token resistance as Castine Sedgwick and his men took control of the outpost. The French reported that Sedgwick and his men: "beat, mistreated, and misused [the Indians] outrageously." Following his victory Sedgwick sailed north, capturing the French Forts at St. John and Port Royal and (at least for a time) established English control over French Acadia.

The Eggemoggin Silver Mine

In the 1870s the Eggemoggin Silver Mine was established at Byard Point. During this period it seemed that mining fever struck the coast of Maine. Based on glowing reports by so-called "experts" local businessmen were only too willing to invest in schemes they were told would make them rich. Fancy gold embossed certificates were printed to lend legitimacy to the all too often fraudulent nature of the mining business at the time.

The owners of the mine at Byard Point eventually found enough gullible investors to start the operation, but the cost of the mining far exceeded the value of the silver that was extracted, and the mine soon closed down. Today there is little evidence of the mining activity that once took place there. Only "Silver Mine Road" which runs along the coastline west of the Deer Isle Bridge indicates that the mine ever existed.

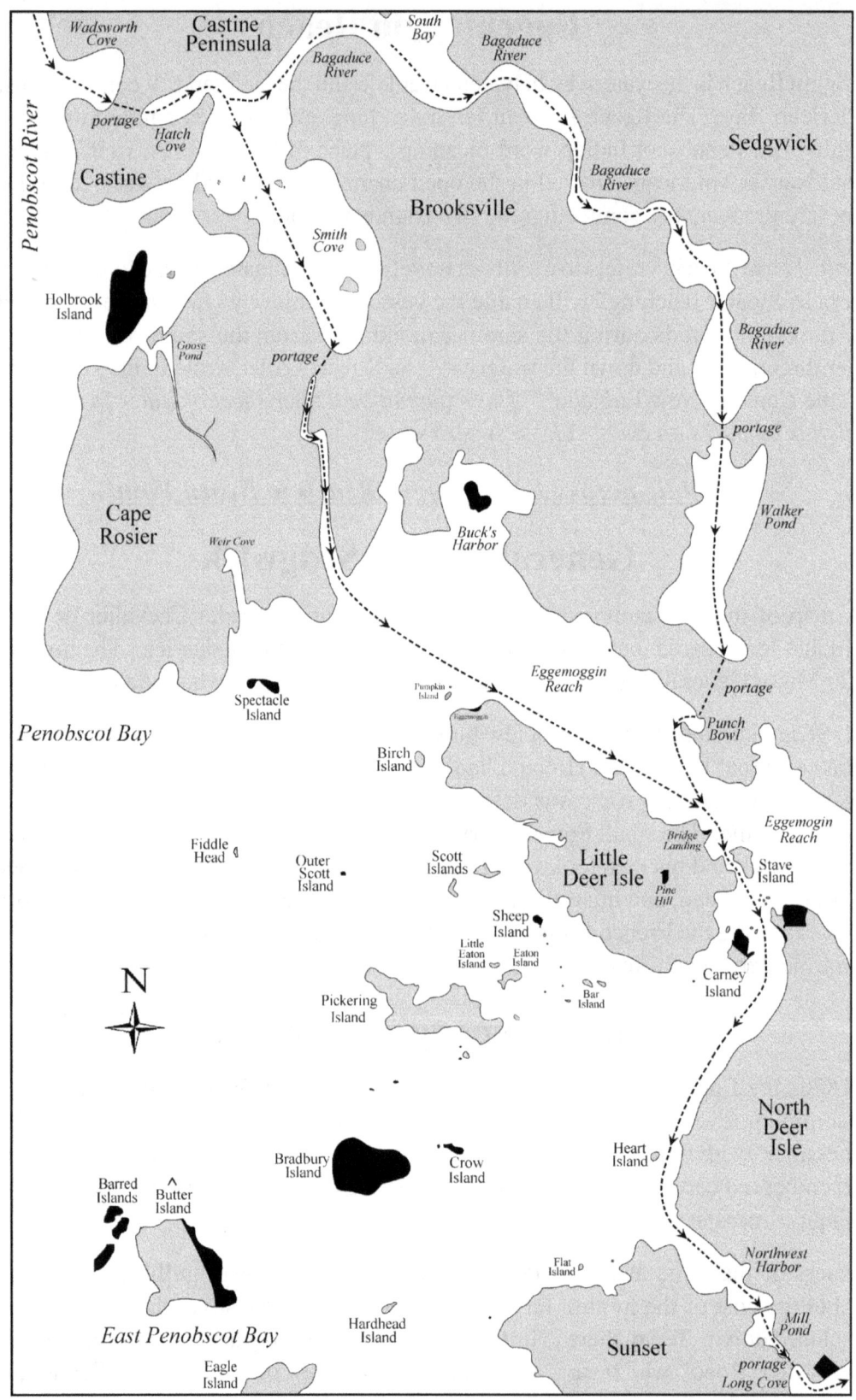

The Meniwokin and Deer Isle Canoe Trails

Paddle northwest along Eggemoggin Reach into the Punch Bowl

The Punch Bowl

The Punch Bowl is a small oval-shaped cove about a mile northwest of the Deer Isle Sedgwick Bridge. This beautiful and protected cove was part of the old Indian canoe trail connecting Castine, Brooksville, and the Penobscot River lands to the north with Deer Isle, Blue Hill, MDI and the islands to the South.

For thousands of years, the Penobscot Indians paddled their large seagoing canoes down what they called "Meniwoken" or "many directions route."[4] Traveling south in the spring from their winter villages in the northern forests, the tribe canoed down the Bagaduce River to Walker Pond (Winnewaug).[5] From the southern end of the Walker Pond they portaged their canoes to the little cove that Europeans later named the Punch Bowl for its rounded shape. This inland route enabled the Indians to avoid the often turbulent waters of Penobscot Bay. It also reduced the danger of being captured by the bands of armed Mi'kmaq raiders who at that time prowled the coast in the small seagoing vessels they had learned to sail from the French.

The Mi'kmaq were one of the first tribes to encounter Europeans, and they were quick to take advantage of the iron tools and weapons that the French traders offered them in return for furs. It wasn't long before they had become important middlemen in the fur trade. When Bartholomew Gosnold sailed from England to Maine in 1602 he wrote that his ship the Archangel was approached by: *"a Biscay shallop with sails and oars"* manned by eight Mi'kmaq's who wore breeches, cloth stockings, and shoes and speaking some English. In later years the Mi'kmaqs joined with the other Wabanaki tribes in resisting the incursions of the English into their lands.

Up until the time of Sedgwick's raid the Penobscot area had been under the control of the French, who established Fort Pentagouet at the mouth of the Bagaduce in 1635. The transient French traders were not considered a threat by Native American's. When they did set up settlements they created strong bonds with the Indians by marrying into the tribes. When Samuel de Champlain explored this area for France in the early 1600s, it is said that he told the Indian leaders; *"Our sons will marry your daughters and we will be a single people."*

The English, on the other hand, considered the Indians to be little more than savages and treated them with contempt.[6] This pattern of English abuse started early. In 1605, George Weymouth, the first English explorer of Penobscot Bay lured five Indian braves onto his ship, taking them back to England as captives. Other early English explorers continued the practice. In 1653, Robert Sedgwick, for whom the lands around the Punch Bowl were eventually named, led an expedition to drive the Dutch out of the New York area, (then known as the New Netherlands). Before he could attack however, a peace treaty was drawn up between Holland and England. Unwilling to disband his forces Sedgwick turned his forces against the French in Acadia, capturing the French fort at Penobscot and going on to

---

4 Haviland pg 5.
5 The outlet to Walker Pond would have been navigable at that time.
6 Any Native American baptized into the Catholic Faith was considered to be a French subject.

take St. John's and Port Royal. Sedgwick's conquests drastically reduced French influence in the area and weakened the tribes which had supported them.

The Penobscot name for the Punch Bowl can be translated as, "where the bird is perched on the rock."[7] According to tribal lore, at one time there was an image of an eagle located near the entrance to the cove. I have been unable to determine whether this was a natural feature, a petroglyph, or an ancient carving created by the Indians themselves. Tribal members say[8] that their sacred image was defaced and later destroyed by early English colonists, either because it was a hazard to navigation, or more likely because it offended their religious beliefs.[9]

In 1660, the Penobscot Tribe had enough. They seized a British fishing vessel in the Punch Bowl, killing the crew and setting fire to the small ship. In retaliation, the English launched a raid on the large Indian village on the northern shore of Walker Pond, killing everyone they could find and setting fire to the village.[10] Perhaps it was during this raid that the Punch Bowl's stone eagle was destroyed.

Paddle out of the Cove toward the northern side of the Punch Bowl

The Billings Homestead

One of the first white men to settle in the Punch Bowl was John Billings, who moved from Little Deer Isle across the Reach to what is now Brooksville in 1767. By that time the Penobscot Indians had rebuilt their village at the end of Walker Pond, and once again were hunting and farming on their ancestral lands, Land agents of King George however, didn't see any problem in selling the land between the Penobscot village and Eggemoggin Reach to John Billings and his wife Hanna. The tribe was probably not even aware of the land deal, because the Billings family which had built a log cabin on the southern end of Walker Pond seemed to have lived at peace with their Indian neighbors. Their children played with the Indian children, and the Billing's family survived, as the Indians did, by farming, hunting, fishing and trading.

During the late 1800s, the state of Maine was in the middle of a huge mining and granite quarrying boom. Northeast cities were expanding and granite was the preferred building material of the time. Although the largest quarries were in the Stonington area, beautiful granite could also be mined from the deposits in Brooksville, and the deep water at the entrance to the Punch Bowl allowed ships to come in close to the shore to be loaded. The Billings leased part of their land to a mining company and soon granite blocks were being shipped to cities all along the east coast. The granite was used to build the towers and anchorages for the Brooklyn Bridge and several federal buildings, including the Bronx Court House in New York City.

In 1805, Frederick Tudor shipped 180 tons of ice from Boston to Martinique. The Boston Gazette reported, *"No joke - a vessel has cleared at the Custom House with a cargo of ice. We hope this will not prove a slippery speculation."*

---

7   "Sep'sis-edal-apskitahan-sit."
8   Conversations with Mr. Soctoma, historian of the Penobscot nation.
9   Perhaps it was obliterated by the same raiding party that in 1660 attacked the large Indian village at the north end of Walker Pond.
10 Haviland noted that the Indian village at Walker Pond continued to exist at that location even after the colonial raid.

The Mountain Ice Company on Eggemoggin Reach on a winter's day

The joke proved to be on the doubters. Tudor built himself an empire as he developed novelties such as ice cream, medical ice packs, and chilled drinks. He rapidly expanded his operation and began delivering ice to cities throughout the world, earning himself the title "The Ice King" of Maine. In the winter of 1846–47, the writer Henry Thoreau watched a crew of Tudor's ice cutters at work on Walden Pond and recorded these remarks in his journal: *"The sweltering inhabitants of Charleston and New Orleans, of Madras and Bombay and Calcutta, drink at my well. The pure Walden water is mingled with the sacred water of the Ganges."*[11]

Due to its frigid climate, Maine could produce as much ice as anywhere in the world. In 1868, it was reported that there was "ice in the bay as far as the eye can see," and residents of Castine were walking over the ice to Brooksville. Maine had another advantage. The deep-water docks and huge ships that worked the granite industry could also be used to transport the ice.

The development of the ubiquitous icebox enabled people to store food for many weeks within their own homes. Neighborhood "icemen" were soon delivering blocks of frozen Maine water regularly to homes and businesses throughout the nation. By 1856, 130,000 tons of Maine ice was being shipped from the state each year.

The Billings property in Sedgwick was especially well situated to take advantage of this demand. Their land abutted the spring-fed waters of Walker Pond and the pond itself was located less than a mile from the deepwater granite docks on Eggemoggin Reach. During the winter months thousands of tons of crystal clear ice could be taken out of the pond without reducing the water level at all! It truly was a renewable resource. The ice cut at Walker Pond was also particularly prized by the dealers because it was clear and had few bubbles. As their business expanded the Billings family leased portions of their land to the Mountain Ice Company, which was in a position to expand the operation.

The Mountain Ice Company operated on Walker Pond throughout the 1800s and into the early 20th century. As soon as the pond was deeply frozen, a horse-drawn rake cut precise rectangular groves in the ice. Men sawed along these grooves until individual blocks were free. An elevated conveyor

---

11 Thoreau, Henry, David, *"Waldon."*

carried the blocks up the hill to huge icehouses on the hill overlooking the shipping docks at the Punch Bowl.

The foundations of the old icehouses on the hill at the top of Walker Pond can still be seen today. The foundations are about fifty feet wide and a few hundred feet long. Big as these buildings must have been, they were small compared to some of the icehouses on the Kennebec River. Some of these buildings were more than six hundred feet long. The icehouses were all built with double pine walls, sawdust was packed between the walls for insulation.

The blocks of ice were trimmed by machines to a uniform 22x44 inches so they could be stacked neatly on top of one another. A two-inch gap filled with sawdust separated each stack. Insulated in this manner, the blocks could be stored without melting for nearly a year. When a ship came into the Punch Bowl dock to be loaded, workers took the frozen blocks from the ice house and slid them down an iron ramp to the dock.

It was a rough life for the ice workers, but it gave the farmers winter work. To save money most men stayed at the bunk-houses that the company had built for them. After working all day, the men ate their dinner, wrapped themselves in their blankets and slept on the floor. In some bunk-houses the men were packed in so tightly that there was barely room enough to move. At the cry of; "Break Joints" the men rolled over in unison.

Paddle past the old granite docks at the entrance to the Punch Bowl and continue northwest along the shoreline to the Oakland House

Oakland House July 4th, 1889 – photo courtesy Sally Littlefield

The Oakland House

On Independence Day July 4, 1889, Emery H. Herrick and his wife Flavilla opened their newly renovated homestead on the shore of Eggemoggin Reach[12] as a hotel and inn. The Oakland House has continued under family control ever since. In the cozy waiting room just outside the dining area you can see the original greeting sign put up by Emery so many years ago to greet guests.

Over the years cozy cottages and cabins were added to the original house. During the summer months Herrick's Landing in front of the Oakland House is used by guests for sunbathing, and swimming.

Opening day at the Oakland House

Continue Paddling into Deadman Cove

Deadman Cove

Deadman Cove is a small indentation on the Brooksville shoreline. The name certainly suggests that at one point in time something ominous happened here, and there are many legends.

The amateur historian Hosea Wardwell of Penobscot relates one of these stories in a journal that he kept:

"During the war, a Tory raiding party sailed down the Reach and spotted a prosperous looking farm overlooking Deadman Cove. The crew went ashore with the intention of stealing goods and cattle, but the captain found the farmer so polite and obliging that he sent his crew back on board their vessel while he remained overnight to enjoy the farmer's hospitality. Freed from their captain's authority, the crew broke open the ship's liquor cabinet and proceeded to get roaring drunk. Later that night a gale of wind came down Eggemoggin Reach and their ship was dashed against the rocks and sank. A single body eventually washed ashore and was buried on the bank of the small cove."

Paddle out of Deadman Cove toward the fabled city of Norumbega

---

12 The beach is now called "Herrick's Landing."

The rugged cliffs between the Punch Bowl and Deadman's Cove

Norumbega

During the 1500s, Spanish conquistadors filled Spain's treasure vaults to the bursting point with Aztec gold. It seemed only logical to early explorers, that the North American continent would also hold vast riches of gold and silver.

When Giovanni da Verrazzano sailed up the coast of New England in 1524 he stayed for several weeks in a beautiful bay which he called "Refugio." After returning to France, he wrote a glowing report to French king Francis I, describing the inhabitants of Refugio as "aristocratic" in bearing and the land as beautiful and fertile. Verrazzano told the king that Refugio would be the perfect location for a French settlement.

Most historians now believe that the idyllic region that Verrazzano described was Narragansett Bay in Rhode Island, but when the map of his voyage appeared in 1529,[13] Refugio was for some reason named "Oranbega" and located far to the north near the Penobscot Bay area of Maine.[14]

---

13 This map was drawn by Veranzano's brother.
14 Many believe that Refugio was located in Narragansett Bay.

Subsequent cartographers changed the wording to "Norumbega" and used it to refer to the entire northeast region. Some linguists believe that the name Norumbega originated in a Malecite Indian word meaning "river that flows backward." If true, this might refer to the strong tidal flows of the Penobscot River. The use of the Malecite word would have also encouraged explorers because it was believed that the fabled Northwest Passage could be identified by waters that flowed inward from the ocean.

In 1525, the Portuguese explorer Estevan Gómez sailed up the Penobscot River searching for the Northwest Passage and treasure. He found the country temperate and the natives friendly, but on his carefully drawn map of the Penobscot River he ruefully wrote, "No Gold Here." Despite his discouraging entry, the legend of the fabulous city of Norumbega gained credibility once again when the Italian writer Giovanni Battista Ramusio[15] wrote a compilation of travel tales in 1555. Ramusio never left Venice, but what he lacked in travel experience he made up for with a vivid imagination. He described Norumbega as a great city with turreted castles and crystal towers whose walls were covered in gold leaf and encrusted with precious gems!

Norumbega was supposedly found once again by the French navigator Jean Alfonse de Saintonge, who sailed on Cartier's voyage to Canada in 1541. In 1556, Alfonse sailed from Newfoundland to explore the coast of Maine. He reported sailing up a great river on whose shore there was a town whose inhabitants dressed in fine furs, worshiped the sun, and spoke a language that sounded to him like Latin.[16]

In 1560, it was the turn of the English to embellish the tale. The sailor David Ingram described how he was shipwrecked with twenty-four others while sailing with the privateer John Hawkins in the Gulf of Mexico. When their ship was wrecked, Ingram said that he was treated as a great medicine man by the Native Americans and passed northward from tribe to tribe. Eleven months later he was picked up by a ship on the coast of Cape Breton.

Ingram described the New World as a land filled with large settlements where the chiefs were carried in *"sumptuous chaires of Silver or Christal, garnished with divers sortes of precious stones."* During his trip he said that he was shown the golden city of Norumbega and that *"Genirallye all men weare about there armes dyvers hoopes of gold and silver which are of good thickness."* Ingram wrote. *"The women of the country gooe aparyled with plates of gold over there body much lyke unto an armor."*[17]

Was it really possible for anyone to walk through the wilderness from the Gulf of Mexico to Canada in eleven months?[18] It is difficult to believe, but if he didn't, how did he end up in Cape Breton?

As the years passed the quest for Norumbega continued, but without further success. The squalid wigwams that the Europeans found were a far cry from the magnificent jeweled cities they had been expecting.

---

15 *Primo Volume delle Nauigationi et Viaggi, Ramusio, Giovanni Battista*, Venetia, 1550.
16 Baker, Emerson W. (1994). *American Beginnings: Exploration, Culture, and Cartography in the Land of Norumbega*. University of Nebraska Press. pg. 87. Retrieved 2015-01-28.
17 http://www.cbc.ca/history/EPCONTENTSE1EP2CH2PA1LE.html.
18 Ingram claimed to have walked 3,000 miles in 11 months, a seemingly impossible task, but in 1999 the British writer Richard Nathan walked from Nova Scotia to Tampico in 9 months.

Captain John Smith

Captain John Smith

Captain John Smith was a little fireplug of a man, only 5'4" tall, with vivid red hair and a full beard and mustache, that to the clean-shaven Indians made him look *"more bear than human."*[1] He was an experienced soldier who had led an adventurous life even before joining the Jamestown expedition. After distinguishing himself in a battle against the Turks, during which he had cut off the heads of three enemy soldiers he was captured.[2] As Smith describes his fate: *"we were all sold for slaves, like beasts in a market."*

Smith was purchased and sent to Constantinople as a gift to his master's Greek mistress who (according to Smith) immediately fell in love with him. When his master found out about what was happening, he sent Smith to Crimea where he escaped and somehow made his way back to England. In 1606, he joined the Virginia Company in their expedition to colonize the new world, but on the trip over he was accused of mutiny and placed in chains. He would have been hanged if not for the fact that when the colonists unsealed orders from the company, it was discovered that he had been appointed one of the leaders of the new colony.

That was probably the best thing that could have happened. The settlers had exhausted their meager supply of food and many were gentlemen searching for gold and unwilling to perform manual labor. Smith was forced to issue the edict that *"Those who do not work, shall not eat."*[3]

Despite his efforts, in the first year nearly half of the settlers had perished from starvation or disease. Under Smith's command however, the colony managed to survive, until supply ships (one of them captained by Samuel Argall[4]) arrived. When the ships finally did arrive the gentlemen spent three months loading the ships for the return voyage with the golden rocks they believed would make them rich. Unfortunately, when the ships reached London the rocks were found to be utterly worthless *"fools gold."*

In 1609, Smith was seriously injured when his powder pouch mysteriously exploded in what many believe was a deliberate attempt to kill him. In 1619, however, he was back in a ship exploring the northern coastline of America.

---

1 Mann, C. (2006). *1491*, Vintage Books.
2 Smith's coat of arms is emblazoned by three Turkish heads.
3 Smith's quote was a New Testament aphorism attributed to Saint Paul, and also used by Lenin during the Russian Revolution.
4 See *Kayaking Coastal Maine Volume 2* The Castine Paddle and *Volume 3* The Somes Sound Paddle.

In 1604, Samuel de Champlain entered Penobscot Bay and sailed up what he called "the great river of Norumbega." Champlain was convinced that this was the river that Allefonsce had described, but instead of a golden city, he found only the tepees and lodges of Native Americans. He became convinced that the city of Norumbega was only a fable and wrote laconically in his journal: *"I am convinced that the greater part of those who mentioned it never saw it."*

A decade later Captain John Smith further debunked the legend. This is the same John Smith of the Jamestown Colony, whose life was spared by the Indian princess Pocahontas, who threw her body over his to protect him. Years after the event he described what happened in a letter to Queen Anne:

The Isaac H. Evans under full sail.

"At the minute of my execution, she hazarded the beating out of her own brains to save mine; and not only that, but so prevailed with her father, that I was safely conducted to Jamestown."

In a map of this area which he drew in 1616, Captain Smith named the entire region he explored New England. At the express request of King Charles, Smith replaced the Indian place names with the names of English cities on the map he submitted to the crown. The settlers of the Plymouth Colony adopted the name that Smith gave to the area and many other place names on Smith's map survive today such as the Charles River and Cape Ann. The native Abanaki Indians called their homeland Wobanakiak or *"dawnland,"* and referred to themselves as *"People of the Dawn."*

After searching fruitlessly for the golden city of Norumbega along the banks of the Penobscot River, and finding only the wigwams of the Wabanaki Indians. Captain John Scott finally gave up his search for gold and focused on promoting the economic possibilities in the area for fishing, farming, boat building, and fur trading: *"Here every man may be master and owner of his owne labour and land...If he have nothing but his hands, he may...by industries quickly grow rich."*

Despite his favorable opinion of the New England area Smith urged his countrymen to settle further south, probably because he still had a vested interest in building up the Jamestown colony.

The legend Norumbega however, did not entirely die away. In the 1800s, Eben Norton Horsford, a Harvard professor who had made a fortune developing a new form of baking powder, became convinced that Norumbega was the word for Norway and that the fabled city was the site of Lief Erickson's lost Viking colony.

Horsford claimed to have uncovered Viking artifacts in Massachusetts and erected a stone building he named the Norumbega Tower to mark the spot where he believed the Viking fort had been located. His work received little support from serious historians during his lifetime, and his theories receive even less support today.

Continue to paddle toward Grays Point, site of the sinking of the Isaac H. Evans

The Sinking of the Isaac H. Evans

The 65' schooner *Isaac H. Evans* was built by George Vannaman in Mauricetown, New Jersey in 1886. The ship spent most of her working life working as a sail-powered oyster dredger on Delaware Bay. In 1970, the aging vessel was sailed to Maine, and two years were spent completely refitting her as a cruise ship. After the renovations were complete the *Isaac H. Evans* began taking passengers on sailing trips along the Maine coast. Beautiful Eggemoggin Reach was a favorite destination.

On September 26, 1984, the *Isaac H. Evans* was on her last voyage of the fall season. September can often bring gusty winds to Eggemoggen Reach, and the steep cliffs lining both sides of the shoreline tend to increase the force of the wind. The *Isaac Evans* had just sailed past Bucks Harbor and was heading east when she was knocked on her side by a sudden gust of wind and sank in sixty feet of water just south of Garys Point. The ship went down so quickly that only a few of the passengers had a chance to put on their life jackets, but somehow they managed to stay afloat in the frigid water by clinging to debris. The ship's cook swam ashore and the rest of the passengers and crew were saved by local rescue groups. Crew and passengers were all taken to the nearby Oakland House to recover from their ordeal.

According to a local eyewitness on the shore; *"... they were on a southwest tack, a northwest wind hit em - the wind keeled em over and they flooded and sank."*

The *Isaac H. Evans* was re-floated after the accident and is now a proud member of the Camden Windjammer fleet and also a National Historica Landmark.

Paddle around Grays Point and into Bucks Harbor

Bucks Harbor

Bucks Harbor has long been known as one of the most protected harbors in Penobscot Bay. As far back as 1806, the American Coast Pilot, recommended Bucks Harbor as an excellent *"Hurricane*

Hole"[19] because the harbor was deep enough for large vessels and the bottom provided secure anchorage. Harbor Island in the center of the cove has always provided protection from the prevailing southwest winds.

Bucks Harbor is named after Colonel Jonathan Buck, an early settler of Bucksport, an officer in the Continental Army, a former Maine Governor and… the apparent recipient of a witch's curse! There are several versions of the "Buck Curse" story,"[20] each more gruesome than the last. One story tells that Colonel Buck was a serving as a judge when a woman was brought before the court accused of witchcraft. Buck found the woman guilty and sentenced her to be hanged. With her final words, she cursed Colonel Buck, promising that *"she would haunt him in life and his tomb would bear her mark for all eternity!"* When Colonel Buck died in 1789, a strange foot shaped image appeared on his gravestone.

Buck Memorial and the eerie "witch's foot"

More than sixty years later Buck's grandchildren replaced the original stone with a larger one, but the same image appeared on that stone as well! Whether you believe the story of the Buck Curse or not, it makes a great camp-fire tale, and if you visit the Bucksport cemetery you can still see the strange mark.

Bucks Harbor has a rich history. During the Revolutionary War several British warships used the harbor as a base from which to disrupt American shipping, and during the War of 1812, a British warship spent the winter in the harbor supporting English troops in Castine. The massive granite docks in the harbor were used throughout the 1800s to load granite and lumber.

President Franklin Delano Roosevelt came ashore here on his way to meet Winston Churchill in Newfoundland as the United States entered World War II. He is reported to have enjoyed an ice cream cone on the dock before leaving for his meeting[21]

More recently, Bucks Harbor was used as a setting by children's author Robert McCloskey's in his popular book, "One Day in Maine." In the story, Sal's father took his broken outboard motor to

---

19 Hurrican Hole – a good spot to anchor and wait out rough weather.
20 https://www.roadsideamerica.com/story/6159.
21 *Doziers Waterway Guide: Northern Coverage,* 2012, pg. 406.

Bucks Harbor boat launch with Harbor Island in the left background

Paddling back from Bucks Harbor to Pumpkin Island on a quiet summer's day

Condon's Garage to be repaired. The garage is still located in the center of the village. In 2000, Robert McCloskey was recognized as a "Living Legend" by the Congress of the United States.

Land on the sand beach on the northeast side of Harbor Island

Harbor Island

If I had my wish I would rename Harbor Island to Heart Island. There is a slew of Harbor Islands in Maine, but only a few with such a beautiful heart shape. I seriously doubt this will happen since the island has kept its name for nearly a hundred and fifty years.

In 1871, Harbor Island was sold to George N. Howard for $225. Howard set up a small homestead of the northwest cove and lived there with his family for thirty years. McLane records note that around the turn of the century Harbor Island was used to raise foxes, a quixotic experiment that not surprisingly soon failed. In 1927, the island was purchased by two summer residents, Franklin Kurt and Charles Gibson, who said they bought it to prevent the island from being cut over for pulpwood.

Harbor Island is now under the protection of The Maine Coast Heritage Trust and is open to the public for day use. The sandy beach facing the town make the island a great place for a refreshing swim after a long paddle.

The initial money for the public purchase of Harbor Island was raised from donations made by members of the Bucks Harbor Yacht Club, the third oldest yacht club in Maine. At one time, the Bucks Harbor Yacht Club welcomed visitors, but I am told that their policies have since changed. Too bad, the classically simple Yacht Club building was built in 1912 and the clubhouse itself is filled with old photographs and memorabilia. On the wall is an old club flag, the tag attached to it reads: *"The first private burgee[22] to be taken through the Panama Canal.'*

Launch your boats into the harbor and paddle over to the boat launch

The Bucks Harbor public boat launch is located at the northwest corner of the cove. The stepped granite seawall at the head of the harbor above the boat launch was built during the Depression as a WPA project. The seawall built to prevent erosion near the roadway cost so much to construct that the locals jokingly called it *"The Golden Stairs."* If you wish, you can land at the boat ramp and walk the short distance into the small tranquil town of Bucks Harbor. Condon's Garage, where Sal's father[23] took his motor to be repaired is still there, and the Bucks Harbor Market offers sandwiches and drinks for the thirsty paddler.

The Take-out

Launch your boats and paddle across Eggemoggin Reach and follow the Little Deer Isle shoreline back to the take-out at Bridge Landing

---

22 burgee – the small flag of a recreational boating association, usually flown from the main masthead of a sailing vessel.
23 McCloseky, Robert, *One Morning in Maine*.

Appendix A: Float Plan

Give one copy to a responsible person/agency and put the other by the windshield of your car where it can be seen from the outside.

If we do not return by TIME: _____ AM/PM on DATE: _____

Contact: NAME: _____ TELEPHONE # _____

If you cannot reach anyone, call the police (911) or the Coast Guard at (800-440-9549) Report me/us as overdue/missing and provide them with the following information:

TOTAL NUMBER OF PADDLERS IN GROUP: _____
Name: Age: Phone: Kayak color: PFD color: Skill level: Medical information
_____
_____
_____
_____
_____

TELEPHONE NUMBER OF CELL PHONE CARRIED: _____

OTHER SAFETY/COMMUNICATIONS EQUIPMENT CARRIED _____
_____

NUMBER OF TENTS: _____ COLORS: _____

VEHICLE TYPE & COLOR: _____

LICENSE PLATE: _____ PARKED AT: _____

LAUNCH DATE/TIME AND LOCATION: _____

TAKE OUT DATE/TIME AND LOCATION: _____

PROPOSED ROUTE & DATES FOR: CAMPSITES, LANDINGS, ALTERNATIVES ETC. (Continue on back if necessary.):
_____
_____
_____
_____

Appendix B: Contact Information

Conservation Organizations

Acadia National Park, P.O. Box 177, Bar Harbor, ME 04609-0177
Phone: 207-228-3338
https://www.nps.giv/acad
Duck Harbor Reservations: https://www.nps.gov/acad/planyourvisit/camping.htm

Island Heritage Trust
420 Sunset Road, Deer Isle, ME
Mail: P.O. Box 42 / Deer Isle, ME 04627
Phone: 207-348-2455; Fax: 207-348-2455
iht@islandheritagetrust.org
http://islandheritagetrust.org

Maine Coast Heritage Trust (MCHT)
1 Bowdoin Mill Island, Suite 201, Topsham, ME 04086
Phone: 207-729-7366; Fax: 207-729-6863
http://mcht.org

Maine Island Trail Association, 100 Kensington Street, 2nd Floor, Portland, ME 04103
Phone: 207-761-8225
info@mita.org
http://mita.org

The Nature Conservancy, 14 Maine Street, Suite 401, Brunswick, ME 04011
Phone: 207-729-5181; Fax: 207 729-4118
naturemaine@tnc.org

Private Campgrounds

Old Quarry Ocean Adventures, 130 Settlement Road, Stonington, ME 04081
Phone: 207-367-8977
info@oldquarry.com
http://oldquarry.com

Reach Knolls Oceanfront Camping, 670 Reach Road, Brooklin, ME 04616
Phone: 207-359-5555
oceanfrontcamping@reachknolls.com
http://reachknolls.com

Appendix C: Suggested Reading

General Kayaking

Brown, G. (2006). *Sea Kayak: A Manual for Intermediate and Advanced Sea Kayakers*. UK: Pesda Press.

Burch, D. (1999). *Kayak Navigation*. Guilford, CT: Globe Pequot Press.

Cooper, D. (2012). *Rough Water Handling*. UK: Pesda Press.

Dowd, J. (2004). *Sea Kayaking: A Manual for Long Distance Touring*, Vancouver, CA: Greystone Books.

Hosmer, G. L. (1905). *An Historical Sketch of the Town of Deer Isle Maine*. Fort Hill Press

Hutchinson, D. (2004). *The Complete Book of Sea Kayaking*. Guilford, CT: Falcon Guides.

Hutchinson, D. (2007). *Expedition Kayaking*. Guilford, CT: Falcon Guides.

Johnson, S. (2011). *The Complete Sea Kayakers Handbook*. Plano, TX: International Marine/ Ragged Mountain Press.

Robinson, J. (2003). *Sea Kayaking Illustrated, A Visual Guide to Better Paddling*. Plano, TX: International Marine/Ragged Mountain Press.

Tejada-Flores, L. (1978). *Wildwater The Sierra Club Guide to Kayaking and Whitewater Boating*. Oakland, CA: Sierra Club Books.

The Deer Isle Historical Society. (2004). *Images of America (Deer Island and Stonington)*. Deer Isle, ME: The Deer Isle Historical Society.

Guidebooks

Daugherty, M. (2016). *AMC's Best Sea Kayaking in New England*. Boston, MA: Appalachian Mountain Club Books.

Johnson, S. (2001). *Smith Vaughan Guide to Sea Kayaking in Maine*. Guilford, CT: The Globe Pequot Press.

Miller, D. (2000). *Kayaking the Maine Coast, Backcountry Guides*. New York, NY: W. W. Norton & Company.

Venn, T. (2004). *Sea Kayaking Along the New England Coast*. Boston, MA: Appalachian Mountain Club Books.

History

Abbott, J. (2012). *The History of Maine from the Earliest Discovery of the Region by the Northmen Until the Present Time*. Andesite Press.

Appollonio, S. (Ed.). (2011). *I loved This Work...I Have Been Delightfully Busy*. Searsport, ME: Penobscot Books.

Baker, E. (Ed.). (1994). *American Beginnings, Exploration, Culture, and Cartography in the Land of Norumbega*. Lincoln, NE: University of Nebraska Press.

Bourque, B. (2012). *The Swordfish Hunters*. Bunker Hill Publishing.

Bourque, B. (2001). *The Western Abenakis of Vermont, 1600–1800: War, Migration, and the Survival of an Indian People*. Lincoln, NE: University of Nebraska Press.

Calloway, C. (1994). *The Western Abenakis of Vermont, 1600–1800: War, Migration, and the Survival of an Indian People.* New York, NY: Chelsea House Publishers.

Duncan, R. (1990). *A Cruising Guide to the New England Coast.* New York, NY: W. W. Norton Company.

Duncan, R. (1992). *Coastal Maine, A Maritime History.* New York, NY: W. W. Norton Company.

Fischer, D. (2008). *Champlain's Dream.* New York, NY: Simon & Schuster.

Haviland, W. A. (2009). *At The Place of the Lobsters and Crabs.* Solon, ME: Polar Bear & Co.

Hornsby S. & Judd, R. (Eds.). (2015). *Historical Atlas of Maine.* Orono, ME: University of Maine Press.

Hosmer, G. L. (1905). *An Historical Sketch of the Town of Deer Isle Maine,* Fort Hill Press.

MacDougall, P. M. (2015). *Fannie Hardy Eckstorm and Her Quest for Local Knowledge 1865-1946,* New York: Lexington Books.

McLane C. B. (1982). *Islands of the Mid-Maine Coast: Blue Hill and Penobscot Bays,* Woolwich, ME: Kennebec River Press.

Morison, S. E. (1971). *The European Discovery of America.* Oxford, UK: Oxford University Press.

Nicola, J, (2007). *The Life and Traditions of the Red Man*, Durham, NC: Duke University Press.

Philbrick, N. (2006). *Mayflower.* London, UK: Penguin Books.

Severin, T. (1978). The Brendan Voyage, New York, NY: McGraw Hill Book Company.

Smith, J. (2007). *Captain John Smith, Writings with Other Narratives of Roanoke, Jamestown, and the First English Settlement of America.* New York, NY: The Library of America.

Spofford-Watts, E.(1996). *Deer Isle Maine From Pre-history to the Present.* Searsport, ME: Penobscot Press.

The Deer Isle Historical Society. (2004). *Images of America (Deer Island and Stonington).* Deer Isle, ME: The Deer Isle Historical Society.

Van Doren, H. (2012). *An Island Sense of Home.* Searsport, ME: Penobscot Books.

Wheeler, G. A. (2017). *History of Castine, Penobscot, and Brooksville, Maine: Including the Ancient Settlement of Pentagöet.* London, UK: Forgotten Books. (Original work published 1923)

Wilmerding, J. (1971), *Fitz Henry Lane.* Westport, CT: Praeger Publishers.

Young, George F. W. (2014). *The British Capture & Occupation of Downeast Maine.* Searsport, ME: Penobscot Books.

Appendix D: Prehistoric Timeline

Time Periods	Years BP*	12	11	10	9	8	7	6	5	4	3	2	1
PALEO													
Early Paleo	13,000 - 10,500	X	X	X									
Late Paleo	12,500 - 10,500	X	X	X									
	10,500 - 10,000		X										
ARCHAIC													
Early Archaic	10,000 - 3,000		X	X	X	X	X	X	X	X			
Middle Archaic	10,000 - 8,000			X	X	X							
Late Archaic	8,000 - 6,000					X	X	X					
Laurentian Tradition	6,000 - 3,000						X	X	X	X			
Marine Archaic Tradition	5,500 - 4,500								X	X			
Vergennes Phase	5,000 - 3,800								X	X	X		
Small Stemmed Pt. Tradition	5,000 - 4,000								X				
Moorehead Tradition	5,000 - 4,500								X	X			
Susquahanna Tradition	5,000 - 4,500								X	X			
	3,700 - 2,600										X	X	
CERAMIC	2,700 - 500										X	X	X

* Note: BP - "Before Present"

Index

A

Abbe Museum 25, 26
Abenakis 125
Abenaki 27
Acadia National Park 8, 69, 72, 76, 92, 94, 96–98, 102, 165
Adams, George Washington 70, 71
adze 15, 19
Algonquin 23, 25
Allen, Samuel 61
Almouchiccogin 27
American Practical Navigator 101
America's Cup 105, 128, 130, 143
Anderson, Anders 72
Andrea Gail 91
Andrews Island 35, 37, 38, 41, 42
Appert, Nicolas 59
Archaic Period 15–17, 20
    Early Archaic Period 15, 16
    Late Archaic Period 16
    Middle Archaic Period 16
arctic 11, 83, 84
Arundell, Thomas 33
Ash Island. See Saddleback Island
atlatl 15, 21
Avalinda 140
Avalonia 120, 127
Aziscohos Lake 14

B

Babson, Charles A. 118
Baffin Island 83
Bagaduce River 118, 121, 151
Baker, Captain Bill 63
Barberry Pirates 86, 94, 95
Bare Island 74
Bar Island 112, 135
Barred Islands 133, 139, 142
Bartender Island 142
Barter, Henry 100
Barter, Miriam 100
Barter, Peletiah 85
Barter, Ralph 60
Barter, William 81
Bartholomew Gosnold 32, 151
Baskin, Leonard 105
Bassabez, Chief (Sagamore) 33
Battery Island 98, 99
Battle of Dunbar 38
Battle of Hampden 96
bayonets 18, 96
Beaman, Charles C. 100
Bellenger, Étienne 32
Billings Diesel and Marine Company 61, 62
Billings Family 61
Billings, John 152
Billings, Pearl 62
Bills Island 81
Birch Island 105, 115, 116, 117
Black Dinah Chocolatiers 90
Black Horse Island 98
Black Horse Ledge 74
Blastow, Captain William 111
Blastow Cove 113
Bogodomovitch, Lazaro 87
Bold Island 49, 67, 68
Bonaventure 37
Bouque, Bruce 16
Bowcat Cove 8, 107, 109–111
Bowditch, Ernest 101
Bowditch, Nathaniel 101
Bowdoin, James 135
Bowdoin (schooner) 83
Bradbury Island 135, 136
Bridge Landing 120, 144, 146, 147, 163
Brimstone Island 39
British Navigation Act 86
Brooklin 108, 109, 121, 165
Brooksville 73, 93, 118, 151–153, 155, 167
Buck, Colonel Jonathan 126
Bucks Harbor 114, 144, 160–163
Bucks Harbor Yacht Club 163
Bureau of Public Lands (state of Maine) 8
Burke, Jeffrey 92
Burnt Cove 37
Burnt Island 81, 83, 99–101
Butter Island 133–135, 137–139, 142
Byard Point 144, 147, 149

C

Cabot, John 59
Cabot, Thomas Dudley 140
Cain, Captain 100
Camp Island 35, 48, 49, 51, 52, 63, 74, 75
Cannabis Tribe 27
Captain Benjamin York 99

Captain Bill Baker 63
Captain Cain 100
Captain Charles Morris 94
Captain Fred Weed 130
Captain Hank Huff 130
Captain Jack Crowell 83–85, 100
Captain Jim Sharp 84
Captain John Smith 32–34, 85, 158, 159, 167
Captain John T. Crowell 83
Captain Norton 70
Captain William Blastow 111, 113
Captain William Hardy 111
Carney Island 105, 107–109, 112, 132, 133
Carney, Michael 107
Carta Universal 29
Castine 37, 39, 53, 74, 87, 88, 93, 95, 96, 115, 121, 137, 149, 151, 153, 161, 162, 167
Castine Volcanic Chain 120
Causeway Beach 8, 105, 107–110, 121, 124, 125, 131–133, 143
Ceramic Period 21, 22
Champlain, Samuel de 33
Chapman, Dr. Marshall 92
Charrière, Henri 49
Chase Emerson Memorial Library 143
chert 14, 15
Chewonki Foundation 48
Chickadee Cove 105
Chief (Sagamore) Bassabez 33
Church of the Messiah 70
City of Key West 41
City of Richmond 41
Clam City 49, 52
Clam Cove 35
Clammers 110
Cliff Trail 96
Clovis spear point 14
Coast Guard 10, 42, 69, 90–92, 117, 147, 164, 177
Colby, Joseph 74
Collins, Dr. Stacy B. 135
Columbia 130, 143
Colwell ramp 58
Commonwealth of Massachusetts 82, 100, 135
Condon's Garage 114, 163
Conservation Organizations 165
Cooper, James 68, 99
Cormorant 98
Cox, Steven 124
Cromwell, Oliver 149

Crotch Island 35, 40, 42–45, 52–54, 60, 61, 74, 76, 80
Crowell, Alice 84
Crowell, Captain Jack 100
Crowell, Captain John T. 83
Crow Island 136

D

Davenport Expedition 57
Deadman Cove 155
Decatur, Stephen (American naval commander) 95
Deep Cove 93, 96
Deer Island Granite Corporation 44
Deer Island Thorofare 35, 38, 40, 147
Deer Isle 7, 8, 16, 28, 35, 37, 38, 40, 42, 49, 52–54, 56, 57, 60–63, 66–68, 71, 77, 85, 88, 90, 99, 105–112, 114–130, 132, 133, 135, 136, 139, 142–144, 146–151
Deer Isle Boys 128–130
Deer Isle Causeway 107, 109, 120, 122–124, 147
Deer Isle Sedgwick Bridge 144, 146, 147, 151
Deer Isle Thorofare 67, 68
diphtheria 49, 71
Dirigo 133, 139, 142
DNA analysis 12
Doliver Island 99
dragons teeth 124
Dreyfus Affair 49
Duck Harbor 66, 76, 88, 92–94, 165
Duck Harbor Campground 66, 92, 93
Dumpling. See Eastern Mark Island
Dunbar, Battle of 38
Dunbar, Colonel David 138
Dutch East India Company 33

E

Eagle Habitat Protection Program 103
Eastern Ear 97, 99
Eastern Head 77, 97–99
Eastern Mark Island 40, 68
Eaton, Eliakim 121
Eaton, George 71
Eaton, Peter Hardy 70
Eaton, Samuel 70
Eaton's Lobster Pool 113
Eaton, Sylvanus "Vanee" 113
Eaton, William 107
Eben's Head 94
Eggemoggin 123

Eggemoggin Reach 29, 99, 105, 109, 116, 118, 120–122, 124, 126, 131, 133, 144, 147–149, 151–153, 155, 156, 160, 163
Eggemoggin Silver Mine 149
Eltanin 84
Emerson, Chase 143
Escargot Island 142
Etchemin (Indian tribe) 124, 125, 132
Ewe Island 103

F

farming 53, 60, 85, 90, 101, 111, 137, 152, 159
Federalist Party 85
Fish Creek 111
Fishermen's Wharf 59
Fisher, Reverend Jonathan 116
fishing 25, 26, 122, 125, 126
Flake Island 81, 82
Flat Ledge 94–96
Float Plan 164
Forestry Bureau of Parks and Lands 8
Fort Madison 87, 88, 95, 96
Fort Point 138
Fort William Henry 13
French Dreyfus Affair. See Dreyfus Affair
French missionaries 23
Friends of Nature 73
Frobisher Bay 83, 84
Fullers Caravan 38

G

Galloping Gertie. See Tacoma Narrows Bridge
Geber, Attila Rath (sculptor) 132
Gilbert, Sir Humphrey (explorer) 31
Glaciers 11
Glooskap (Indian demigod) 110
Goat Trail 96
Goddard Site 20
Gomez, Esteban (explorer) 28
Gooseberry Island 72
Gordon, Nathaniel 67
Gorges, Sir Ferdinando (explorer) 137
Gosnold, Bartholomew (explorer) 151
GPS 5, 36, 65, 79, 106, 134, 146
Grand Banks 53, 59
granite 10, 42–46, 48, 49, 51–56, 58, 60, 61, 66, 69, 70, 72, 73, 75, 80, 93, 97, 119, 120, 132, 140, 141, 144, 152–154, 161, 163
Graveyard Point 112
Gray, George 37

great blue heron rookery 68
Great Proprietors 137, 138
Great Spoon Island 98
Green Head 37
Green Island 7, 35, 45–47, 76
Greenlaw, Linda 91
Greens Landing 35, 54
Green, Sullivan 45
grog 66
Grog Island 66
Gross and Small company 46
Gross, Byron 112
Gross, Charles 46
Gross, Job 43, 53, 54

H

Half Moon 34
Hamlin, Augustus 18
Harbor Farm 105, 111–113, 135
Harbor Farm Store 112
Harbor Island 6, 76, 81, 144, 161–163
Harbor Island Ledge 80
Harbor View Store 58
Hardwood Island 103
Hardy, Captain William 111
Harriman, Emory 139
Harriman, George 139
Harvey Island 47
Harvey, John 47
Haskell, Elizabeth Cush 143
Haskell, Ignatius 142
Haskell, Mark 142
Hasse, Martin 73
Haviland, Bill 107
Hawkins, John 30
Head Harbor 88, 94, 96, 97
Head Island 116, 137
Hells Half Acre 8, 35, 49, 50, 51, 63, 68
Hero (vessel) 84
Herreshoff, Nathaniel 128
Herrick, Emery H. 155
HMS Rifleman 95
Holmes, Mary Beaman 100
Hook, Josiah 87
Horseman Point 98
Horsford, Eben Norton 160
Hudson, Henry (explorer) 33
Huff, Captain Hank 130
Hughes, Ted (author) 111
Hundley, Margaret 43

I

icehouses 154
Indian Island. See Russ Island
Indian Joe 123
Ingram, David (explorer) 157
Inn at Ferry Landing 108, 125, 131
Iselin, C. Oliver 130
Island Heritage Trust 7–9, 42, 69, 107, 109, 113, 114, 120, 131, 146, 165
Isle au Haut 83, 85–93
Isle au Haut Thorofare 82, 87, 91
Isle au Haut Village 76, 83, 90

J

Jamestown Colony 32, 34, 159
Jefferson, President Thomas 85
Jericho Bay 29, 40, 72, 149
Jones, Paul 37
Juet, Robert 34

K

Keepers House, The 91
Kenduskeag Stream 29, 33
Kennedy, President John F. 44
Kimball Island 66, 76, 82–85
Kimball, Solomon 82
King George's War 82, 137
King Philip's War 27, 38
Knickerbocker Ice Company 97
Knights of Labor 58
Knox, General Henry 139

L

Labrador 24, 29, 84, 142
Laurentian Tradition 17
Laurentide ice sheet 11
Lavinia 70
Lazy Gut Island 16
Leave No Trace 9
Lee, John 139
Leland, Ebeneezer 93
Lewis, Lt. Andrew 96
Lincoln, President Abraham 67
Lindberg, Charles 71
Lindy's Cove 71, 72
Lipton, Sir Thomas 130
Little Camp Island 35, 48, 51, 52, 63, 74, 75
Little Deer Isle 61, 105-112, 114–122, 124, 132, 133, 135, 143, 144, 146–149, 152, 163

Little Isle au Haut. See Isle au Haut
lobstering 89
Long Pond 97, 98
loyalists 115

M

Machias Bay 67
MacMillan, Donald (Arctic explorer) 83
Magellan, Ferdinand (explorer) 29
magnetic north 4
Maine Coast Heritage Trust 7, 37, 44, 46-48, 50, 52, 68, 72, 81, 97, 120, 137, 141, 146, 163, 165
Maine Forest Service 10
Maine Heritage Trust 74
Maine Island Trail 6, 7, 45, 48, 50, 67, 74, 133, 141, 165
Maine Island Trail Association 7, 45, 67, 165
Maine Lobstermen's Association 53
Maliseet Indian tribe 23, 25, 121, 125
Marine Corps Hymn 95
Maritime Archaic Tradition 17-19
Maritime Provinces 23, 24, 121
Mark Island Light 35, 40, 41, 42
Marshall Island 69, 72, 99
Mason, John 33
Mawooshen Confederacy 125
Mayflower II 61
McCarthy III, Jeremiah 46
McCloskey, Robert 105
McGlathery Island 40, 70, 71, 73
McGlathery, William 70
McLane, Charles B. iii
McWilliams, Bruce 112
McWilliams, Richard 112
Mercantile 61, 62, 119
Merchant, Anthony 68
Merchant Island 76, 80, 100, 103
Merchant, Nathaniel 48
Merchant, Robert 49
Merchant Row 46-48, 68, 72
Meribah Wardwell 125
middens 9, 13, 82, 121
Mi'kmaq 12, 23 -25, 27, 121, 125, 138, 151
Mill Cove 35, 42, 44, 45
Millet Island 69
Mill Pond 142
Mink Rock 133
MITA. See Maine Coast Heritage Trust
Mogul 38, 39

Mohammed III 95
Mohawk Indians 23
Molasses Act of 1733 86
Moore Harbor 93
Moorehead Phase 17-19
Moorehead, Warren K. (archaeologist) 18
Moose Island 35, 37, 61, 62
Moose Island causeway 37
Morey, Polly 47
Morey, Steven 48
Mormon. See The Church of Jesus Christ of Latter-Day Saints
Moroccan-American Treaty of Friendship 95
Morris, Captain Charles 94, 95
Morrison, Cressy 69
Morrow, Anne 63
Mountain Ice Company 153, 154
Mount Chamberlain 77
Mount Desert Island 8, 26, 29, 110, 123
murder 55, 87

N

Napoleonic Wars 86
Naskeag Point 108, 123
Nathan Island 76, 102, 103
Nature Conservancy 8, 66, 69, 74
nautical mile 4
Nelson and Shields Granite Company 49
New Brunswick 18, 19, 30, 38, 56, 67
New England 55, 67, 85, 86
New England Stone Industries 44
New England Tent Club 139
New York Yacht Club 148
Norridgewock 27
North Haven 16, 18, 20, 68
North Haven Island 19, 20
Northwest Harbor 109, 133, 142, 143
Northwest Passage 157
Norton, Captain 70
Norumbega 28-31, 144, 155-157, 159, 160, 166
Nova Scotia 20, 30, 34, 53, 88, 157
Noyes, Dr. Benjamin 47

O

Oakland House 144, 154, 155
ocher 18
Old Ferry Landing 131
Old Quarry Ocean Adventures 63, 165
Olmstead House 37
Opera House Arts 104

Orono, Chief Joseph 82
Ottoman slave markets 94
Outward Bound School 142

P

Paleo-Indians 13–15
Palestine 58, 63, 70
Palestine Emigration Association 70
Papillon. See Charrière, Henri
Passamaquoddy Bay 26, 29
Passamaquoddy, The 26
Pavlov, Ellie 143
Pavlov, George 143
Peak Island. See Bartender Island
Peggy Island 35, 60, 61
Peggy (schooner) 87
Penobscot Bay 12, 16, 18, 19, 23, 28–30, 32–34, 37, 38, 40, 41, 44, 49, 57, 68, 82, 84, 86, 93, 94, 113, 114, 116, 122, 123, 147–149, 151, 156, 159, 160
Penobscot East Resource Center 60
Penobscot River 96
Penobscot Tribe 25, 152
People of the Dawn 121, 159
petroglyphs 22
Pickering Island 133, 135
Pilgrims 33, 34, 61
Pilgrim's Inn 130, 143
Pine Hill 105, 119, 120, 124
Plath, Sylvia 111
Plymouth Colony 33, 159
Point Lookout 100–102
Port Royal 131, 149, 152
Potato Island 52, 75
Pring, Martin (explorer) 32
prohibition 55
Public/Private Properties 6
Pumpkin Island Lighthouse 105, 117, 118
Punch Bowl 121, 144, 145, 150–152, 154, 155

Q

quarries 35, 39, 43, 44, 46, 54, 152
Quebec 18, 23, 24
Queen Elizabeth 30, 31

R

Ram Island 103
Ramos, Tony 44
Ramusio, Giovanni Battista 157
Red Paint People 18, 19, 20, 24

Reed, Alanson 122
Republican Party 85
Revenue Agents 87
Ribeiro, Diogo (cartographer) 29
Richardson's Store 130
Rich's Cove 88
Robbins, Clementine 61
Robbins, Hiram 61
Robinson Point Lighthouse 91
Rockefeller, Mrs. David 141
Rock Island 44, 45, 80
Rocky Mountain 77
Roosevelt, President Franklin Delano 161
Rosier, James 33
Round Island 73
Royal Navy 38, 66, 86
Royal Tar 35, 38–41, 44
R. T. Barter Fish Cannery 59
rum 42, 66
Russ Island 35, 47, 48, 52, 61
Russ Stone Quarry 46
Rut, John 29

S

Saddleback Island 63, 68, 69
Salt marshes 131
Sand Beach 130
Sand Island 35, 44
Sawyer Mountain 77
Scott, Captain John 137, 159
Scott, Charlie 130
Scott Island 52, 114
Scott Island Preserve 130–132
Scott Islands 105, 113, 114
Scott, John 126, 130
Scott, Nathaniel 114
Scott's Bar 124
Scott's Landing 8, 108, 125–127
Scott, William "Billie" 130
Seafood Co-Op 52, 53
Seal Trap 92, 93
sea mink 19, 125
Second Island 35, 37
Sedgwick 120
Sedgwick, General Robert 149
Settlement Quarry 8, 66
Shamrock 130
Sharp, Captain Jim 84
Sheep Island 67, 105, 113
Sheepscot 27

Sheep Thief Gulch 98
Shivers Island 51
Sisters Restaurant 120
slavery 29
Small, Eben 44
Small Stemmed Point Tradition 18
Smith, Abiathar 97
Smith, Ben A. 83
Smith, Captain John 32, 34, 158
Souriquois. See Mi'kmaq
Southern Mark Island 40
Spoon Islands 98
Spruce Island 63, 69, 70
Squanto 33
Squeaker Cove 97
Staples, Samuel 137
State of Maine 8
Stave Island 105
Steinbeck, John 120
Steinman, David 148
Stephen Decatur 95
Stonington 152
Stonington Archipelago 4, 35, 76
Stonington Opera House 104
Sugarloaf. See Escargot Island
Sunbeam 41
Susquehanna Tradition 17, 20
Swains Cove 105, 113, 115
Swain, William 115
Swans Island 49
sweet grass 85
swordfish 19, 20

T

Tacoma Narrows Bridge 148
Tarratine Tribe 27
Theband, The Gertrude L. 83
The Bowcat 109
The Church of Jesus Christ of Latter-Day Saints 58
The Fort 7, 8, 35, 37
Thevet, André 30
Thunder Gulch 97
Thurlow, Captain David 40
Treaty of Watertown 125
Tripoli 95
true north 4
Tudor, Frederick 153
Turner Farm 18–20
Turnip Yard 99
Two Bush Island 35, 60

U

unorganized lands 116
USS Adams 94
USS Philadelphia 95

V

Vergennes Phase 17, 18, 168
Verrazzano, Giovanni da 28, 29, 156
VHF 10
Vinal Haven 16

W

Wabanaki, The 23
Waldo, General Samuel 137
Walker, John 31
Walker Pond 121, 151–154
Wardwell, Hosea 155
Wardwell, Meribah 125
Warren K. Moorehead 18
Wass, S. L. 70
Wawenock 27, 63, 72, 73
Webb Cove 7, 63–66, 75, 79, 82
Webb, Seth 66
Weed, Benjamin 111
Weed, Captain Fred 130
weir 37, 83, 92, 93, 108, 121–123, 132, 133, 149
Western Ear Island 94
Western Head 77, 92, 94, 95
West Indies 30, 42, 67, 88
wet smacks 90
Weymouth, George 151
Whaleback Shell Midden 13
Wheat Island 81
White Island 99
White Rock Point 127, 130
Whiz-Bang 89
Wickies 117
Winterport 96
Witherspoon, John 139
W. K. Lewis Bros. Fish Factory 89
Worthy's Island 45
Wreck Island 61, 71, 74

Y

Yankee Gale 53
York, Captain Benjamin 99
York Island 99

About the Author

Author Dick Fleming

Richard (Dick) Fleming is a registered Maine Sea Kayaking Guide. He also holds a Maine Recreational Guide license and is an ACA certified sea kayaking instructor. Dick has worked for many outfitters over the years, most recently as a kayaking instructor for LL Bean. Dick was an officer and pilot in the Civil Air Patrol and participated in many search and rescue activities with the U.S. Coast Guard. He also served as a Force Recon Marine during the Vietnam War and is the author of *Chasing Charlie – A Recon Scout in Vietnam*. He currently lives in Freeport, Maine.

www.ingramcontent.com/pod-product-compliance
Lightning Source LLC
Chambersburg PA
CBHW080919170426
43201CB00016B/2196